Communication
Theory and
Social Work
Practice

Communication Theory and Social Work Practice

Judith C. Nelsen

The University of
Chicago Press
Chicago and London

The University of Chicago Press, Chicago 60637
The University of Chicago Press, Ltd., London

Judith C. Nelsen is associate professor at the
Jane Addams College of Social Work at the University of Illinois—Chicago Circle.

Library of Congress Cataloging in Publication Data

Nelsen, Judith C
  Communication theory and social work practice

  Bibliography: p.
  Includes index.
  1. Social service—United States.   2. Communication—
Philosophy.   3. Communication in social work—United
States—Case studies.   I. Title.
HV91.N43   361.3′2   79-20361
ISBN 0-226-57151-3

To the memory of my
parents, Victor and
Rosamond Du Jardin

Contents

Preface ix

One   Communication as Information Exchange: Basic Concepts 1

Two   Communication as Patterned Interaction: More Basic Concepts 21

Three   Initial Interviews 43

Four   Assessment 66

Five   Interventions with Individual Clients 89

Six   Worker-Client Communication Blocks 113

Seven   Interventions with Families and Groups 134

Eight   Worker-Client Communication Blocks in Small System Practice 157

Nine   Interprofessional Practice 177

Conclusion 194

Notes 197

Bibliography 201

Index 204

Preface

Social workers borrow theory from the social and behavioral sciences mainly to enhance their practice skills. When new theory more clearly explains aspects of human functioning or of intervention, it can be useful for teaching and research as well. Freudian and neo-Freudian personality theories, ego psychology, small group theories, and, more recently, general systems theory and behaviorism have influenced social work practice and education. Communication theory too should have an impact.

The first two chapters of this volume set forth selected communications concepts and consider their relevance for social work. Subsequent chapters pursue the material in greater depth, developing a communications framework for practice with individuals, families, and groups, and for interprofessional practice. Such a framework can integrate and supplement what social workers already know. The practitioner needs theory linking assessment to the range of interventions he must be able to use. While Freudian theory and ego psychology richly conceive clients' personality functioning, their implications for many aspects of intervention are not clear. Systems and small group theories offer other perspectives on assessment and imply intervention goals, but say little about means. For many social workers, behaviorist approaches to assessment and intervention are more balanced but have limited applicability. The communications literature as it stands suggests still different practice insights. But communication theory can also serve as a generic language for assessment and intervention, a metatheory into which other practice theories and models can be translated. I will begin this process in the following pages.

My work relies most heavily on theory about how people are influenced by information, as individuals and in interaction with others. Sources include Jurgen Ruesch and Gregory Bateson, Ray Birdwhistell, Albert Scheflen, and theorists originally associated with the Palo Alto Mental Research Institute such as Don D. Jackson, Jay Haley, and Paul Watzlawick. Some works to be cited offer basic theory. Some offer guidelines for assessment and intervention based on communication theory. All together, the material suggests a unified theory of human functioning and change.

This book grew from my experience using communication theory in my own practice, in graduate classes taught at two schools of social work, in a research study, and in research and practice consultation offered to experienced social workers. Responsible for originally stimulating and nurturing my interest in the theory were doctoral faculty then at the Columbia University School of Social Work, especially Carol Meyer, Florénce Hollis, and Ben Avis Orcutt. Dean Harold Lewis of the Hunter College School of Social Work encouraged me to explore uses of communication theory in teaching practice courses. At the University of Chicago School of Social Service Administration, Professors Bernece Simon and John Schuerman supported both the teaching of practice and research courses based on communication theory and the writing of this book. Colleagues who read the book in first draft, Helen Perlman and Joshua Cohen of the University of Chicago, contributed significantly to improving the final version. I gratefully acknowledge the help and support of all these individuals.

Two other groups must be recognized. Students in my own courses have shared their enthusiasm about communication theory and have helped test the ideas presented here. My family and close friends have provided continued encouragement and emotional support as the book was written.

One	Communication as Information Exchange

Basic Concepts

Any person behaves in response to information about himself and his environment. When people exchange information, they influence each other. Communication theory examines these processes. Its insights can be helpful to social workers in a number of ways. The experienced practitioner can use the theory to gain new perspectives on assessment and intervention strategies. The beginner can use it to grasp generic elements of social work practice. The teacher and researcher can use it to identify what such generic elements may be.

Communication theory exists not as a single entity but as a series of interrelated areas of study. The reader may be familiar with theory about family communication, or with work done on double-binding in schizophrenia. Most social workers have some acquaintance with the literature on nonverbal communication. Most know that they and their clients can experience communication problems based on inadequate awareness of each other's cultures or social class backgrounds. Social workers have heard of such fields as linguistics, semantics, and cybernetics. Communication theory may have reference to any of these areas of study, or to others.

As early as the 1950s, Jurgen Ruesch, Gregory Bateson, Karl Deutsch, and others were developing theory about information and its effects on human functioning. Much of their writing in one sense seems descriptive rather than explanatory. Information, as they see it, is all that a human being can perceive and that can thus influence him. Included are his thoughts, feelings, bodily sensations, memories, and impressions of his current environment. As people process information by perceiving and evaluating it, they continue to function. Sometimes they reject new information and behave as before. Sometimes they accept action implications of new information and change their behavior. In either case, their actions will convey information to others who observe them. On these notions, Ruesch and others build further theory about consciousness, nonverbal communication, people's interaction in groups, and change processes in clinical practice.

The ideas just cited do not explain how people's characteristic patterns began. They do, however, offer explanations of what may be perpetuating particular behavior, and in this way point to options for intervention. Consider the situation in which a parent continues to abuse a child. Communication theory offers no explanation of how or why this behavior may have got started. It does propose that the client is acting on the basis of some information which perpetuates his behavior and which is consistent with it. He may have learned from his own parents that child beating is an appropriate form of discipline. His current family or friends may support this view. What he knows at the time he abuses may be that his anger is uncontrollable. He may wish to stop but cannot until he learns to perceive and evaluate his anger differently. In each of these instances, the implications for intervention are clear. A social worker may question the appropriateness of beating children as a means of discipline. He may help the client perceive his anger in time to evaluate it and to handle it less destructively. And so on. We note that theory about information and its effect on behavior does not negate the importance of a person's past, but identifies as salient that past information which an individual still carries with him to influence him. It suggests that information about his present inner experiences and surroundings, or even speculations about the future, influence him as well. A person's problems may also be due to the way he processes or perceives and evaluates information available to him

Authors who developed their thinking during the 1960s and 1970s at the Palo Alto Mental Research Institute, most notably Don D. Jackson, Jay Haley, and Paul Watzlawick, elaborated the theory of Ruesch, Bateson, et al. These later theorists are especially concerned with what happens when human beings interact. People together, they contend, exchange information not only about themselves and their environment but, implicitly, about how they propose to relate. They decide, among other things, who can do what and who has control over what within their relationship. A marital pair works out that one carries more responsibility for housekeeping or that both share it. They also negotiate the relative power of each in making decisions about such matters. People who interact regularly develop patterns in their communication. From these patterns one can infer their implicit agreements about how to interact, or their operating rules. Such rules tend to sustain family or group functioning. For example, if employees never disagree with their employer openly, it may be because of operating rules within the work group. Further observation could suggest that these employees never express anything, including disagreement, that would define their relations with their boss as egalitarian. The operating rule may thus pertain to power rather than to content, and may sustain the group as one where the employer carries unchallenged authority. Repetitive cycles in any family or group interaction can be analyzed to determine what discussion topics, behaviors, and relative power are allowed or forbidden.

The Palo Alto material, too, may seem descriptive rather than explanatory at first glance. Saying that family or group members regularly put down a scapegoat, for example, does not explain why they do. No one observing an interaction pattern such as scapegoating could claim to know from the observation how the pattern began. However, some factors perpetuating the pattern might be obvious. An individual might typically initiate the scapegoating sequence, and thus tend to perpetuate its occurrence by regularly setting it off. Scapegoats themselves are often observed to have initiated the pattern by doing something to stimulate rejection. Close observation may reveal that the scapegoating occurs only at certain times, perhaps when another family or group member stimulates a rejecting response then directed to the scapegoat. Communication theory conceptualizes something family and group practitioners have long noticed: that people together get into behavior cycles in which one action seems to prompt the next, as if an implicit set of directions were being followed. Directions or operating rules perhaps unknowingly upheld by family or group members may be said to perpetuate the behavior cycle seen. Implications for intervention spring directly from this idea. If a practitioner can interrupt dysfunctional interaction patterns, behavior may change even when its causes are not fully known.

The concepts of individual, family, and group functioning just outlined, and others which build on them, suggest a unitary theory of human functioning and change. Theory about information and its effects on behavior focuses on the single human being. Theory about human interaction, on the other hand, considers what takes place within the dyad, the small group, or the family. The next logical level of observation is the community, and then the society, while the physical environment is a larger context for all. The unifying notion here is that of communication.[1] As individuals, people receive information, act so as to send information in turn, and thus participate in communication. The individual, group, and society are human beings observed at different levels of abstraction, not necessarily different human beings. Change occurring at one level must affect what happens at other levels.

Social work needs a unified theory of human functioning and change to organize as well as to add to existing practice knowledge. It needs a midrange theory connecting abstract concepts of other theories to more concrete principles of what practitioners can do to help clients. The brief introduction to communication theory given above will be elaborated in this and the following chapter, and its implications for social work assessment and intervention previewed. First, let us address the issue of how communication theory relates to other theories and models used in social work practice.

General systems theory is widely used as an organizing framework for social work practice knowledge. A core theoretical concept here is that of the system—any dynamic organization, greater than the sum of its parts, which maintains some sort of internal balance and interacts with its environment. An individual can be considered a system, since he maintains equilibrium both physically and psychologically as he copes with his surroundings. Small social systems, which also tend to maintain an internal organization while dealing with their environments, include the family, the peer group, the work group, and a social worker meeting regularly with a client or clients. Larger social systems include institutions and communities. Change in one part of a system can affect the balance and thus lead to change somewhere else. For example, a mother helped to feel better about herself may more benignly parent her child. An individual is likely to be involved in,

and thus influenced by, a number of social systems. A convenient way to
assess interpersonal reasons for anyone's behavior is to look at the demands
and opportunities for coping inherent in his family, peer group, and work and
community groups.

Communication theory builds on the conceptual foundation just elaborated. The individual as a system maintains equilibrium by perceiving and
evaluating information from within himself and from his environment. The
man who feels hungry, finds food, and eats has put together information
from internal and external sources and has acted to restore his own balance.
In a system such as a family, members receive information from their environment and behave so as to give outsiders information in turn. They also
maintain equilibrium within the system by exchanging information among
themselves. Their communication ultimately reflects system operating rules.
If a child brings home a poor report card, his parents must respond to it.
They may discuss the matter with other family members, or may nonverbally show distress, with which others must deal. The response chosen
depends on this family's rule for handling disappointing actions by members.
The child's behavior as he returns to school provides information to outsiders, reflecting family functioning.

Ego psychology, a personality theory often used by social workers, addresses individual functioning at the emotional, cognitive, and behavioral
levels. The theory assumes that people are strongly influenced by their past
experiences, including past conflicts between their own wishes and their
environment which have been pushed out of consciousness. Ego psychology
also recognizes that people deal with current reality, that is, with their continuing inner needs and with their surroundings. The ego, or mediator between inner needs and the environment, is defined by its functions such as
memory, intelligence, affectivity, and maintenance of human relationships.
A rich literature uses ego psychological theory to explain both normal and
abnormal human functioning, and to suggest options for treatment. Treatment has to deal, above all, with resistance, a client's inevitable difficulties
achieving change; and with transference, his bringing of feelings or thoughts
from the past into his relationship with the practitioner.

To a degree, communication theory reconceptualizes content from ego
psychology. In considering how a person perceives his inner and outer

reality, thinks about these matters, and reacts, one may speak almost synonymously of his ego functioning or of the way he processes information. Some ego psychological concepts seem clearer when translated into communications terms. For example, one may relate the concepts of resistance and transference to the idea of clients' problems in processing information. Resistance usually connotes a client's unwillingness to process specific information a practitioner offers him. A social worker suggests that a client think differently about something, but the client fails to do so. Transference represents distortions in what a client perceives or thinks about a helping professional, and suggests his inability to process some type of interpersonal information in accord with reality. A worker is not criticizing a client, but the client believes he is. Communication theory supplements ego psychology by placing more emphasis on the present environment. It looks at individuals as influenced by information, with the relative influence of information from the individual's past and from his present dependent on what is happening to him at a particular time. Communication theory, unlike ego psychology, also conceptualizes people's interaction in families and groups.

To understand human functioning from a different perspective, social workers sometimes turn to *behavioral theories*. Behaviorists see much of human behavior as learned, when its occurrence becomes associated with achieving something desirable or with avoiding pain. A person may continue to try to please others because this is how he gained approval as a child. He may develop a pattern of running away from his problems because this served him well at one time. Behaviorists also see behavior as maintained by its consequences, the experience that certain actions usually lead to desired goals. For example, the child who gets little positive response from others may have temper tantrums because they evoke attention, at least. A growing number of behaviorists are interested in cognition as this may affect people's learning and ability to change. As with ego psychology, the behaviorist literature helps to explain why people function as they do and, if they need it, how they can be treated.

Both behavioral and communication theories consider people's past learning and their interaction with their current environments to understand their functioning. Both may investigate the influence of a client's cognitive processes. Behaviorists concentrate upon the individual and his immediate environment to determine what sets off his behavior and what consequences perpetuate it. Communication theorists may look at the individual but are likely also to address a whole pattern, of which the individual's behavior is one part. A behaviorist might see a child's school phobia as set off when the mother becomes overinvolved with the child before school, and as reinforced when she allows the child to stay home and play. A communication theorist would look further, perhaps at a cycle in which all family members participated. The father's indifference may have led to the mother's overinvolvement with the child and thus to the phobic behavior. The child's phobic behavior may temporarily engage the father in trying to solve the problem, until he becomes indifferent again, the mother becomes overinvolved again, and so the cycle continues.

Social work practice models today are often based on ego psychology and general systems theory. Ego psychology helps one to understand clients' personality functioning, especially as it is influenced by the past. Systems theory is useful in explaining how the current environment may be affecting clients. Workers using such models have sometimes taken concepts from small-group and organizational theories to strengthen their understanding of how small social systems operate. Two major difficulties remain. First, these theories help workers to assess clients' functioning but sometimes lack clear implications for intervention. Ego psychology relies on psychoanalytic theory for its model of planned change, espousing a set of procedures often inapplicable to social work practice. Systems theory, small group theories, and organizational theory help determine what a social worker should try to change but do not suggest how to bring about such change. Social work models therefore tend to rely on practice principles generated from clinical experience. These principles—such as, "Start where the client is"—may be valid in themselves but form no comprehensive set of guidelines; they lack a theoretical framework. Models based on ego psychology have a further problem: practical precepts like the one just cited as well as more theoretical ones, such as the idea of "building ego," are difficult to define precisely enough for research. Yet only research can ascertain the effectiveness of various social work interventions.

Practice models based on behavioral theories are geared toward intervention. If behavior is learned and reinforced by its consequences, then new learning can replace the old, and environmental changes can lead to behavioral change. The link between assessment and intervention is clear. Indeed, behavioral therapies aim to help clients by interrupting their learned response patterns that have become dysfunctional, by teaching them new behaviors, and by helping clients or others to change environmental consequences of their behavior. Clinical research is part of the behaviorist tradition. Still, the resultant practice models have seemed too limited to many social workers. Some are alienated by the behaviorists' relative lack of interest in clients' past experiences, in their thoughts and feelings, and in what may be more complex aspects of their intrapsychic and interpersonal functioning. A behaviorist tenet that treatment always be geared to change specific behaviors does not fit some social work practice situations. Clients may want concrete services, the chance to discuss a specific crisis, time to explore their motivations and fears, or family counseling geared to achieving nonbehavioral goals such as greater closeness.

Insights from communication theory can be helpful to social workers using any practice model. For example, the Palo Alto theorists' ideas about relationship behavior can help practitioners establish working relationships with clients, including those who are passive, overcontrolling, or trapped in dysfunctional family alliances and splits. The theory is especially useful in assessing—and devising remedies for—worker-client interaction that has become problematic. It is most valuable, however, in integrating other theories and practice models. Communication theory offers a unified view of human functioning and change. Assessment suggests intervention possibilities, with the social worker as information giver and participant in small-system interaction. Practice principles based on clinical experience, ego psychology, or behaviorism can be reformulated in communications terms to reveal their differences and similarities. A worker can use the same language for intervention that he does for assessment, and the same language for intervention with individuals as he does for intervention with families, groups, and communities. Communication theory suggests a precise practice language well suited to research. The worker unable to define "ego building" may define his intervention as "teaching the client how to perceive and evaluate information available to him." Let us now take a closer look at some basic communications concepts and their practice relevance.

Information and
Information Processing

Why do people behave as they do? Communication theory begins to answer this question in terms of the following interrelated concepts: information, information processing, feedback, and information processing rules.[2]

A first premise is that people act in response to *information*—all that they perceive from other people; from the nonhuman environment; and from their own thoughts, feelings, bodily sensations, and knowledge stored in memory. The child who begins to cry when he hears his mother's angry words has responded to information from another person. The man who looks away from a strong light may be said to have received information from his physical environment and to have reacted to it. Inner experiences too, such as hunger, sadness, the thought that the alarm clock is about to go off, or the memory of a pleasant day, constitute information that may stimulate action. Information from any source can be influential even when it is in some sense untrue. The adolescent told that he is too dumb to do anything right may respond by dropping out of school.

Communication theorists use the concept of information very broadly. Anything one individual can learn from another human being is information —from world history to the time of day, from some sense of whether one is loved to some idea of how to cook rhubarb. All sense impressions of our nonhuman environment are information, from an awareness that it is raining to the realization that one's poker hand is a straight flush. Bodily sensations of pain, sexual longing, hunger, thirst, or satiation are information, as are feelings ranging from joy to anger and bitterness. Memories of past experiences are information, as are thoughts, which are often the putting together of bits of related information into some meaningful whole. People deal with considerable information from their external environments and from within themselves at the same time. To test this assertion, we need only close our eyes and list mentally the human words and actions, the attributes of the physical environment, the states of our own body, and so on that we registered in the past moment.

The idea that people act in response to information is important for social workers, who must assess clients' functioning. The child mistreated by his parents receives the information that other people inflict pain, that the world is dangerous, and, perhaps, that he is unlovable. The adult living on too low an income learns from his environment that his financial needs will not be met. Physical pain and difficult thoughts, emotions, and memories are realities with which many people must deal. Sometimes a client suffers from what could be called an information deficit. Past experience may not tell him how to cope with a current difficulty. All social work interventions give clients information about themselves, about the reality with which they must deal, or about the worker who is offering service. Even interventions within a client's environment may be intended to change information available to him there, such as information about whether he will receive needed resources.

Information from the environment or the body may affect behavior directly. A man collides with a tree and finds himself limping. More often, one's responses to information are mediated through one's perception and evaluation of knowledge received, or one's *information processing*. Information processing includes dealing with one's bodily sensations and emotions as well as with other matters. At any given moment, a human being scans countless potential sense impressions to receive information about his internal states and his surroundings through perception. He next evaluates these data against information held in memory and decides whether to reject, store, or immediately use them. That is, he thinks. Finally, he takes action by changing his behavior or by continuing as before. A man notices his wife's troubled expression and wants to help. He refers to past information that she may need reassurance, and that certain ways of giving reassurance are comfortable for him. Then he touches her arm. All of these operations probably took place in an instant. Had the man decided not to respond directly to his wife's behavior, he would still, by rejecting the information she gave him or perhaps by storing it for future reference, have been reacting to it. He also continues to receive and evaluate new information while making the decision about his wife.

As an individual processes information, he translates some of this into *feedback*, a conception of how his behavior has affected his internal states and surroundings. Feedback allows people to plan further actions more effectively. Its receipt involves complex mental operations. First, one has to perceive relevant information. One may do so by routine scanning or by focusing attention. The woman aware of a friend's sensitivity may watch him more closely after offering criticism. One translates relevant perceptions into feedback by evaluating apparent cause and effect. This cognitive process involves noting the proximity and time sequence with which events occurred, bringing in knowledge stored in memory about similar associations between events, sometimes seeking further information through behavior geared toward this end, and continuing to take into account what is perceived subsequently. The woman who criticized her friend may infer she offended him when he immediately looked away, especially if this is how he usually reacts when hurt. She may then test this inference by asking him. Human beings continuously perceive what follows their actions and continuously, although not always accurately, evaluate their perceptions as feedback. From the individual perspective, positive feedback is that which tends to encourage behavior already shown. A friend's welcoming of constructive criticism can lead to an individual's giving more. Negative feedback is that which tends to discourage existing behavior.

In general, people selectively take in information through perception. One needs criteria for deciding what to look for and what to ignore. One must also know what relevant knowledge already held to evaluate with incoming information to decide upon action. Any person's stored information presumably includes a set of implicit *rules for information processing,* rules by which information potentially available within himself and his environment is perceived and evaluated. One woman concerned about neatness will notice any dirt in her house. This is the rule that guides her perception. Another woman's rule is that only certain levels of dirt should register, or that dirt should be noticed only when guests are due. People may have rules governing what information will be evaluated together to arrive at particular conclusions. The woman who thinks of dirt when she is thinking of guests perhaps also recalls memories of her mother's admonitions about cleanliness. People's rules for information processing may govern their awareness of their own cognition. Some perceptions and evaluations are conscious. Most, probably, are not. People are fully conscious of what they are thinking mainly when the resultant actions will be important or innovative, requiring concentrated attention. Much routine information processing can be pulled into consciousness if need be. Some cannot, allowing the inference that the individual has an implicit rule forbidding it. Information, especially that based on past experience, may be taken up for use without one's awareness of what is happening. The man who trembles before authority figures may not remember experiences with his father which informed him that such figures were dangerous. Feelings and thoughts can also prompt action without being available to consciousness.

Clients sometimes seem unable to process information that they need in order to solve problems. They may have difficulties because they do not clearly perceive their external reality or their own thoughts, feelings, memories, or even bodily sensations. Some seem to perceive these things but do not effectively evaluate information gathered to arrive at conclusions for action. People are especially handicapped in dealing with their surroundings if they have trouble receiving information as feedback. Their inability to be conscious of some of their cognitive processes may create problems. In any of these instances, social workers may intervene to produce change in the rules governing clients' information processing. Sometimes they teach clients directly how to perceive and evaluate information differently. Members of a community group may be helped to notice the needs of working women and to evaluate what could be done to meet them. Sometimes social workers aim to help clients become conscious of information processing rules or of information used for action. An adolescent may be helped not only to perceive his own rising anger before it explodes, but also to evaluate better how to discharge the anger. One can conceive of clients' service needs as a hierarchy, in which the worker moves to the next level if the first does not suffice. The first option is to help clients by giving them new information, sometimes by intervening within their environment. The second is to help them with information processing. Parallel possibilities for intervention into family and group interaction will be explored in later chapters.

Communication and Context

Communication occurs when at least one person perceives another's words, actions, or the results of these. It may take place indirectly through such means as the mass media, literature, and art, or directly as in face-to-face interaction.[3] Communication through language and through nonverbal, or analogic, forms often goes on simultaneously. In general, an individual interprets what others say and do according to the context in which communication occurs. Social workers must understand the various forms of communication and the influence of context to help clients effectively.

Verbal communication involves people's exchanges of information through language in all its written and spoken forms. Social workers listen to what clients say to gather information for assessment, and most of their interventions involve the use of words. As a client speaks, he may see that information he is using as a basis for action is incomplete or really points to a different conclusion. After a social worker listens, he may comfort the client by what he says. He may give verbal feedback on something the client has done or is planning to do. Sometimes workers discuss with clients the knowledge the clients already possess, to validate what can be useful and to help them discard what is not. They also give new verbal information geared to clients' needs. For example, they tell the parent of an adolescent that some rebellion is normal at that age. They give needed information about such matters as strategies for social action, community resources, how to deal with others, and common bodily and psychological processes.

Another kind of verbal communication used to help clients is *metacommunication,* when people step back from the content of what they are saying to talk about what is happening between them. They communicate about communication. Thus, group members may discuss their differences, or a worker and client may evaluate their progress together. In any human interaction, people's ability to talk about what is going on between them is freeing.[4] Metacommunication helps family and group members, as well as workers and clients, untangle their communication difficulties, sometimes by realizing they have misunderstood something the other said. Metacommunication, like individual consciousness, permits people to disengage from immediate action for observation and evaluation purposes.

Many theorists use the terms *behavior* and *communication* synonymously since, in another's observing presence, "one cannot *not* communicate."[5] The individual who sits quietly with a friend has communicated something to him, perhaps his comfort in the friend's presence, unless the friend does not notice him at all. Assuming that another person is present to perceive what is going on, nonverbal communication includes a person's actions in general, his dress, facial expression, posture, and gestures. The term is also used to connote voice tone, nonlexical sounds such as coughing, and the use of time and interpersonal distance. People employ many of these nonverbal forms, usually without awareness, as an almost conventional language conveying mood and intent. A frown can tell a child that his mother wishes him to stop what he is doing. One person may demean another by keeping him waiting or declining to stand close to him. Nonverbal modifiers help one to interpret speech. A suggestion given with a smile and light voice tone implies that the choice of response resides fully with the listener, while a suggestion given in an authoritarian manner does not.[6]

Communication through nonverbal channels can reveal what was not meant to be made public. A girl with a secret crush wishes to hide her excitement when the boy in question speaks to her, but her downcast eyes, tremulous smile, and blushing give her away. Nonverbal communication is more believable than speech because it is under less conscious control. In listening to another's words, one looks to see whether his demeanor appears consistent with what is said. Nonverbal communication is *analogic*, that is, it conveys information by concretely representing an object, event, or emotion. Gestures indicate the size of something about which one is speaking, and a person's posture in recalling a depressing incident may signify dejection. Analogic communication is more evocative and probably more archaic than the use of language, in which the association between any object and the name given it is arbitrary. Unfortunately, people's behaviors or nonverbal communication alone are highly subject to misinterpretation. Tears of sorrow or of happiness, a smile or a sneer, eyes downcast in modesty or in shame, are often indistinguishable without additional cues. In most human interaction, verbal and nonverbal forms of communication clarify each other.[7]

Social workers notice clients' nonverbal communication, which may show their feelings or other reactions to events never expressed in words. Clients sense a practitioner's attitudes toward them in his facial expressions, posture, and voice tone. Workers also use some interventions which are primarily nonverbal. For example, they may engage in activities with children, adolescents, and some adults to help them learn that they can master their environment or for other purposes. Play with children sometimes is a major form of treatment.

No communication can be fully understood without reference to *context,* the circumstances surrounding human exchanges of information. The context of any communication includes participants' personal appearances, roles, the impinging physical and social environments, and past interactions between or among the same parties. The more immediate context of a specific communication includes what was said or done just before. People use all such data to evaluate new information received. The process occurs in steps. An individual perceives present context, interprets this in terms of information stored in memory, and uses such understanding to clarify what others' words and actions really mean. A woman talking to her minister shortly after her husband's death would consider his role and her circumstances and understand that his taking her hand was not a sexual approach. However, participants in interpersonal communication can disagree on the meaning even of stable contextual factors such as roles, because each will compare his conception of immediate context with all else that he knows. The context of any interaction includes not only the social situation itself but everything that each participant brings to it.[8]

Context is an important influence on any social worker–client encounter. When a school social worker suggests to an adolescent that they talk together, even if she does so with a smile and light voice tone, the adolescent may respond angrily. He may see an older female who will try to run his life as his older female relatives have. Here he views the worker within the context of his own information. He may see her as a school authority person with an office, who will probably rebuke him for failing a course. Here he interprets her role differently from the way the worker intended but in line with the physical setting and his other experiences with school personnel. The teenager will respond to a suggestion very differently after several interviews, if his memory of verbal and nonverbal interaction with the social worker now assures him of her benign intent.

Learning and Change

To function effectively, human beings must face current circumstances that are not unmanageable. They must have stored useful information from the past, and must be able to process new information that may be helpful to them. That is, well-functioning individuals should be able to learn from their experiences and, when appropriate, to change.

The earliest human learning is probably based on *trial and error,* the individual's primitive but highly convincing taking of action and awareness of what follows. The infant cries, and gradually learns that crying brings food and comfort. Thus, trial-and-error learning depends on feedback. A young child also learns analogically. That is, an individual can receive information about the world and how to deal with it by observing others' behavior. A mother may show a child how to play with a new toy, or may show a fear of thunderstorms and unintentionally teach the child this fear. Analogic learning occurs through such means as empathy, imitation, and identification. Once a human being understands language, he will learn from what others tell him and from the written word. Through language an individual can learn about experiences he has never had, things he has never seen, and the world of ideas. All three forms of learning continue throughout life, with trial and error learning still the most compelling and analogic learning probably far more prevalent than has been recognized.[9]

Clients can obviously learn from what a social worker tells them, but can also be helped through trial-and-error and analogic learning during interviews. Trial-and-error learning takes place when a client tries out a new way of relating to the social worker or to other clients present. A man who risks becoming more open about feelings in an individual or group session can learn whether this relieves his own tension and can find out how others react. Practice with individuals geared toward personality change, family counseling, and group treatment often intend that clients learn how to relate differently to the social worker or to others present, partly through trial and error. A sort of trial-and-error learning occurs when clients role-play behaviors that will take place outside of interviews, or when they discuss very concretely what these behaviors could be and allow the worker or others to offer feedback. Clients learn analogically during interviews by observing how the social worker and other clients act in relationships, how they process information to arrive at decisions, and how other clients change. Clients often identify with social workers, making such statements as, "I thought about how you would analyze the problem and tried to solve it the same way." A client in a family or group session may try asserting himself after he has seen someone else begin to do so effectively.

Just what information from all sources will be useful for individuals to learn depends on their inner needs but also on their unique human and nonhuman environments. Everyone learns ways to satisfy hunger and thirst, to remain as free from pain and discomfort as possible, to deal with sexual longings, to achieve some sense of mastery, and to be confirmed in relationships with others. But the Jamaican learns to deal with these needs differently than does the Eskimo because their environments and cultures are different.

A culture conveys information and inherent premises about what information should be perceived and valued through its language, beliefs, customs, and even arrangements of material objects such as buildings and furniture. As a commonplace example, television commercials for deodorants imply that people should perceive and value negatively their minor body odors. People need to learn different things to function in different social classes and sometimes in different ethnic groups. A poor person may know how to deal with street crime but a middle-class person may be more competent in talking to public officials. An Irish Catholic calls on different information about how to deal with death than does a Sephardic Jew. A person who wishes to function well in two subcultures must learn information and rules for information processing relevant to both. The social worker whose clients are from different sociocultural backgrounds than his, needs to appreciate their different perspectives. Within a culture and subculture, most human learning occurs in groups. Families, peers, school and work cohorts in past and present teach individuals a great deal of what they know about the world, how to get along with others, and even about themselves. These social systems have also influenced and will continue significantly to influence people's information processing.[10] A man's ability to be aware of his own feelings and to accept differences in others may depend on how he has learned to perceive and react to the relevant information. Of course, a person's inherent cognitive capacities at a given age also affect how he learns to process information. The little girl punished for asserting herself during her mother's frequent illnesses may infer that she should not consciously perceive her own needs, although her parents never intended such a message.

Every human being must learn how to deal with new information that is either unclear or discordant with the old.[11] Failure to perceive and evaluate potentially useful new information constitutes an *information processing block*.[12] Lack of clarity in communication is mainly a problem when the individual fails to recognize the communication as ambiguous, and brings to bear inappropriate stored knowledge to judge the circumstances. A man whose wife pulled away from his touch might fairly easily clear up what this meant by asking. If he assumed (mistakenly) that his wife's action meant she did not love him, the minor unclarity might have major impact on their relationship. Sometimes people cannot process new information because this conflicts with their information or rules for information processing on hand. The woman who learned as a child not to recognize her own needs might be unable to evaluate a social worker's suggestions about how to meet those needs. Such an idea would conflict with her earlier learning that she should not do so, and with her information processing rule that she should not think consciously about it. When two or more people do not process each other's potentially useful information offered, the result is blocked interpersonal communication. This phenomenon, to be elaborated more fully in later chapters, is of interest to a social worker whether it occurs between himself and clients, within a family, or in some other formed or natural client group.

Human beings apparently learn continuously in the sense that they are always processing information available from within themselves and their environment, are always storing at least some of it, are always behaving in some fashion, and are always receiving feedback on actions taken. They also change continuously in that they are always making at least minor behavioral adjustments to function within their environment. Change is dependent on the receipt of new information. Most change, however, is relatively superficial. A man notices the room is dark and reaches up to turn on the light. More profound change can occur when information available to an individual implies the need. An adolescent experiences sexual longings, and begins to date. But a necessary condition for change is that people be able to process the information in question, to clarify ambiguities, and to resolve any conflicts between old information and new. If the adolescent were not aware of his sexual longings, he might postpone heterosexual relationships indefinitely. This circumstance might come about if the new information, the longings and their implications for social relationships, conflicted with information stored from childhood or received from his current family that relationships with women were dangerous. People's ability to function is impaired when they are not open to new learning in some area, that is, when they cannot process information that implies a need for change. What may be required is modification in their rules for information processing.

When social workers offer useful information to clients who freely receive it, positive change should occur. Some clients accept information about how to process information differently, as when a worker teaches a man how to notice and evaluate his wife's nonverbal communication. Others may struggle with serious information processing blocks. When clients hold conflicting information, such as a wish to move closer to others coupled with fear of where closeness may lead, a social worker can help them weigh alternatives by exposing the conflict to the light of day. But information previously received from family members, peers, other human figures, or their nonhuman environment may conflict with or override new information from a worker. The child treated as unlovable by his family may not accept the worker's information that he is worthwhile. The man with no money to buy food or clothes cannot use a social worker's suggestion that he should have a better appearance if he wants to get a job. A social worker may discuss a client's information processing block with him—that is, he may initiate metacommunication. Other interventions, sometimes into the environment, may also be appropriate.

Summary. People behave in accord with information available to them from their own thoughts, feelings, bodily sensations, memories; from other people; and from the nonhuman environment as they perceive and evaluate this information in a given context. They may change their behavior on the basis of feedback or trial-and-error learning; and they may learn from others analogically as well as from the content of verbal discussion, the written word, and other cultural forms. Communication between two or more persons makes information available to them, sometimes through discussion of their interaction itself. Communication experiences also affect how people perceive, evaluate, and respond to information in general and in instances when messages are unclear or discordant. Clients may have trouble functioning because their information for problem resolution is inadequate, or because they cannot process constructive information potentially available to them. Social workers help by offering different information and by teaching clients to process information differently.

Two

Communication as Patterned Interaction

More Basic Concepts

People influence other people by making information available to them. One man says something; another hears him and learns something new. Yet people influence each other further as they engage in communication. When two or more individuals interact, even briefly, they enter into a relationship. If the relationship continues, those involved begin to function as a small social system, whether as acquaintances, friends, lovers, co-workers, a couple or family, a social worker with one or more clients, or some other group. Communication within any system becomes patterned over time, maintaining balance and predictability within certain limits. To persist, small social systems also change. Change occurs as individuals, small systems, and the larger environment influence each other. Having established that individuals exchange information, let us now look at human interaction itself.

Content and Relationship Communication

We know that people exchange information through their words and actions. Such interpersonal communication conveys obvious content. It also defines the nature of human relationships, including who will be in control. Some people share control in symmetrical or egalitarian fashion; other relationships are more complementary or hierarchical; or one individual is really in control although he does not seem to be.[1]

Communication *content* consists of what is explicitly said and done between people. A young man walks casually over to his boss and suggests that they go fishing. On the content level, the young man has conveyed some information by his nonverbal behavior. His slow walk may suggest calmness or comfort, especially if his facial expression, posture, and voice tone are consistent with this. The man conveys content information by his words even if he asks a question. The exact information offered may be more or less clear. Thus, "How about going fishing?" and "I'd like to go fishing with you" convey roughly the same content: that the young man wants to go fishing with the boss. "Feel like going fishing tomorrow?" is more specific about time but ambiguous as to whom the speaker expects to be involved. "Tomorrow is going to be a beautiful day for fishing" is more ambiguous still. The content is perfectly clear, but the human referents are left up in the air. In all these instances, however, explicit content information is conveyed.

The sender of any content can be seen as also implicitly proposing a definition of his relationship with the receiver. The young man who asks his boss to go fishing suggests that their relationship include fishing as one of its mutual activities. He seems to propose a peerlike relationship because fishing is something two friends might do together. This is especially true if his nonverbal behavior conveys friendliness without being deferential. If he also touches his boss's arm while they talk, the young man will have further proposed that their relationship include touching. The boss may accept all these proposals with a response such as, "Fine, let's go." He may accept some and not others, perhaps agreeing to go fishing but also shrinking from the young man's touch. Or he may reject the entire proposal, including the suggestion that their relationship be peerlike, with a statement such as, "Get back to work."

People who interact in any fashion enter into a relationship and begin determining its nature. One person on an elevator can speak to another about the weather, proposing a rather impersonal association. The other can agree by responding with more talk about the weather, and can even expand the relationship definition proposed by introducing other topics of conversation. If he smiles or looks away instead of speaking, he is not avoiding a relationship, for he is still responding. He has simply proposed that their association include only nonverbal acknowledgments, or that appropriate behavior between them should be feigned indifference. The definition of a relationship will either be resolved or in dispute at any particular time. Those who know each other in a limited way—a storekeeper and a regular customer, for example—quickly arrive at some agreement about how they will act together. In relationships such as close friendship or marriage, people have more decisions to make about what kinds of conversation and what kinds of mutual behaviors will occur between them. In important relationships which persist, some aspects of the relationship definition eventually will change. A couple in their eighties probably does not handle physical intimacy the same way they did forty or even twenty years before. Relationships between more than two people usually change as there are changes in the composition of a family or group. Still, when people agree for long periods about what will happen between them, relationship negotiations recede in importance and interaction simply confirms what has already been settled. If the young man in our example had already asked his boss to go fishing a number of times, and the boss had frequently agreed, another invitation would not propose any new definition of their relationship.

Social workers constantly convey content to their clients through words and actions, as when a worker calmly reassures a client that his symptoms do not mean he is crazy. Less obvious is that all worker communication proposes definitions of the worker-client relationship. If he gives reassurance all the time, a worker proposes the relationship as one where the client may depend heavily on him for reassurance. If the worker asks many questions about a client's background and problems, he may convey that the relationship is to discuss problems and their ultimate causes rather than possible solutions. Some clients get into the habit of reporting each week what has happened to them, because they have gathered that this is what their part of the worker-client interaction should be. Clients also propose relationship definitions with social workers, some of which are constructive and some not. In many family interviews, parents implicitly propose that the worker be their ally in disciplining the children. In early sessions of treatment or community groups, by deferring to the worker, members may propose that he be the leader and decision maker.

People in a relationship further define who is in control of what. A marital pair can argue about whether to see a movie or go bowling and can switch positions during the course of the argument. The underlying issue may not be where they will go but who can make the decision. At some times in a relationship, communication patterns reveal shared control or responsibility for what happens. At other times, they suggest one party's uncontested dominance. Often these positions vary over time, depending on communication content, as when a boss makes decisions about business matters but respects an employee's equal expertise as a fisherman. Apparent distributions of control within relationships do not always reflect who has greater power. Family or group members may defer to someone defined as the leader, but may make important decisions behind this individual's back. An existing distribution of power, even where control is undisputed, may be dysfunctional. When a mother dominates family members afraid to oppose her, everyone in the relationship, including the overburdened mother, may be suffering.

Communication theory explores relationship control especially as it occurs between two people. The basic concepts involved are used as a way of analyzing worker-client interaction, and interaction within families and groups, throughout this book.

Communication between two persons defines their relationship as either egalitarian or hierarchical at a given time. The prototype of an egalitarian or *symmetrical* relationship is that which exists between two friends. These individuals generally behave similarly, or can do the same things within their relationship, whether competing, helping each other, making decisions together or alternately, or engaging in some other mutual or parallel task. The alternative of *complementarity,* with one partner defined as one-up or more powerful than the other, is exemplified by a parent-child or teacher-student relationship. The one-up individual in a complementary relationship carries greater control and responsibility for decision making, and he can do things the one-down partner cannot. Human relationships tend toward either symmetry or complementarity without being pure types. Although the one-up party in a complementary relationship appears to have more power, his partner implicitly exercises some power because he must acquiesce for the relationship definition to continue.

There are also what are called *metacomplementary* relationships, in which one person either lets the other have control or forces him to take it. Thus a social worker, whose role definition tends to place him one-up, relinquishes control by letting a client talk. During this period the client appears to be in command. Less benignly, a passive family or group member who forces

others to take care of him may be metacomplementary to the others, in that
he appears to be one-down but really has considerable control. Ultimate
power within a relationship is often hard to determine. No one can say, for
example, whether a passive husband or his dominant wife really has more
control of their interaction. Both participate in maintaining it, although the
wife appears to be one-up because she takes the initiative.

Either complementary or symmetrical relationships can be functional,
and no one relationship type is intrinsically good or bad. A good parent is
complementary one-up to his children, caring for and guiding them while permitting increased symmetry as they mature. The danger within a complementary relationship is that it can tend toward distance and disengagement. The
marriage between an authoritarian man and a frightened, depressed woman
can be of this sort. Healthy adult relationships are usually characterized by
shifts between egalitarian and hierarchical positions, with each partner flexible enough to be one-up, one-down, or symmetrical with the other at different times and in different circumstances. Such relationships are ultimately
symmetrical since partners are equal or similar in overall relationship
stances. Exemplifying this type are a marriage, peer, or work relationship in
which two people can carry different responsibilities, be capable in given
areas, recognize each other's accomplishments, and also be competitive at
times. Yet symmetrical relationships can be dysfunctional. When two people
behave similarly by trying to be one-up at the same time, the resultant power
struggle or *symmetrical escalation* can lead to breakup of the relationship.
Some competitive friendships between adolescents end with the two becoming enemies, and competitive marital relationships can end in divorce. A
relationship more subtly based on symmetrical escalation is that in which
two parties compete to be one-down. Two members of a treatment group
may try to describe the worse symptoms or to be the more helpless one.

Constructive social worker-client relationships are typified by flexible
stances, with the worker one-up, one-down, symmetrical with, and metacomplementary to the client at different times. The worker is one-up in
being the expert, the giver rather than the receiver of help. He may have
control of needed resources. He comments on the client's problems,
strengths, and options for action, while the client seldom comments on the

worker's situation or attributes. Yet the worker is also one-down at times, as when he asks for the client's help in getting through some mutual communication block. He is symmetrical when he shares with the client responsibility for structuring interviews, and metacomplementary when he encourages the client to set service goals. The worker is more often one-up with a child than with an adult, and he tends to become more symmetrical with any client over time. When a client readily accepts or himself defines a constructive worker-client relationship, the two can proceed about their business with little further concern about who is in control. Sometimes, however, clients act in an overcontrolling, passive, or helpless manner within a relationship with a social worker. Many adolescent clients alternate between wanting to be fully or not at all in control.

Communication as Message and Response

People within a relationship negotiate the content information they will accept from each other. Their words and actions also propose symmetry or complementarity at a given moment, respond to each other's similar proposals, and negotiate relationship definitions over time. Some of these interactions are relatively simple, with one individual putting forth content and relationship information and the other clearly accepting or rejecting it. Some involve more complex messages, even including disconfirmation of another person as a human being. Certain messages or responses, such as the use of paradox, are subtle maneuvers to gain relationship control.

On both the content and relationship levels, negotiations about what will happen between people never cease. One man remarks that children are expensive and another agrees. On the content level, the first individual has brought up information he had on hand and proposed it to the other, who accepts it at that moment. The two may continue by elaborating this topic or by introducing another. At any moment, either can still reject the original information or the idea that they should discuss their children. A given communication can propose one party's symmetrical or complementary relationship position only at a particular time. The other's response indicates agreement or disagreement, thus settling the relationship definition for that moment. If one party gives an order, proposing himself as one-up, the other can accept it, agreeing to define the relationship at the time as complementary with himself one-down. Or he can give a counterorder, proposing himself as one-up and thus beginning a symmetrical escalation. Two people who laugh together have defined their relationship as symmetrical in a more cooperative manner.[2] If one party, called by his first name, calls the other by his last name, he thus makes the last-name party one-up. One party may be one-up in setting more topics of discussion. Symmetry is especially difficult to capture except in interchange. Two people who call each other by first (or last) names, who can initiate topics more or less equally, or who can equally offer new information to each other are symmetrical. If two people can switch in taking one-up stances, as when a client is telling his story and a worker asks questions about it, their interchange is on balance fairly symmetrical. Only after examining people's interaction on a continuing basis can one determine whether their relationship tends to symmetry or to complementarity.

Social workers assess what content and relationship information clients bring to interviews, and try to use their own content and relationship communication constructively. Clients reveal content information on which they may be basing their actions when they tell about themselves and expose their thinking. The worker may accept the content, reject it, or offer new content in response. He is also interested in what information clients may have about how they can behave in relationships. When a mother tells her adult son to stay at an unfulfilling job, she has proposed that she should make decisions for him. The same man may not assert himself with his wife or with a female worker because he has learned to expect dominance by women. Clients demonstrate their readiness to process new relationship information with the social worker. The client who presents himself as one-down because he thinks this is expected, or one-up because of his assumed vulnerability in any other stance, may be able to show greater relationship flexibility when the worker encourages it. To use his own relationship stances with clients constructively, a worker sometimes proposes symmetry and sometimes complementarity to achieve a flexible relationship. For clients' analogic learning, a worker can also demonstrate stances that clients may be afraid to take—being comfortable, for example, in a one-down stance as he loses a game to a bullying child. In offering such new relationship information to clients, the worker not only helps them use service but teaches them a flexibility they may then be able to try out with others.

When one party has conveyed content and his idea about relationship stances, another present must respond to both.[3] Acceptance of another's content and proposed stance may serve as positive feedback, encouraging the original actor in the direction he has taken. The person who takes another's advice has accepted the content information offered, has agreed to be one-down at the time, and has implied his willingness to accept more of the same. To reject another's content is usually to reject his relationship stance as well. The client who refuses to answer a social worker's question has also refused to let him direct their interaction. Rejection most often is intended to discourage continuance of the content and relationship messages proposed. A third option is *selective response:* accepting either another's content or his relationship message, or part of either one.[4] A child agrees to do what his mother has told him, but stipulates that it is because he himself already wanted to do the same thing. He thus accepts her content but rejects her proposed relationship definition. One can, with care, accept a relationship definition while rejecting content of communication. A social worker openly expresses pleasure that a client has volunteered an opinion, thereby taking a more symmetrical stance with the worker, yet openly disagrees with what he says. Selective response has also occurred when one part of content offered is accepted or when a relationship definition is accepted only under delineated circumstances. A social worker may accept a client's feelings while rejecting his intended actions. A worker may claim to know more about theories of behavior, while noting that the client knows more about his own functioning.

Communication can be mixed on the content level. A girl says no to her would-be seducer while moving closer to him. Within a relationship negotiation, a message may suggest symmetry and complementarity at the same time. The statement "Let's do this if it's okay with you" modifies an overt stance of complementarity toward symmetry. The statement "We'll do this if you want," said in a disapproving voice tone, does the opposite.[5] Some communications are not so much mixed as ambiguous, as when the young man in our earlier illustration remarks that the following day will be a good one for fishing. Mixed or ambiguous messages may be negotiating devices when they implicitly offer possible content or relationship options to the other party. The girl who moves closer while saying no suggests that she is open to persuasion. The young man's comment about the future climate for fishing leaves the boss free to pick up the implied invitation and attendant symmetrical relationship definition, or not to do so, as he chooses. Other ambiguous responses to communication may be accurately or inaccurately perceived as connoting acceptance, neutrality, or rejection of another's content and relationship messages; or they may be seen as indecipherable. The most malevolent response to another's words or actions is *disconfirmation*, accomplished largely by ignoring or perpetually misunderstanding what has been put forth. In effect, he who disconfirms another does not even acknowledge the other's existence as a human being.[6] Disconfirmation can include excessive praise given without real note of another's individualized accomplishments. The father who pats his child on the head and says "wonderful," no matter what the child does, disconfirms him as a real person just as he would if he constantly forgot the child's name.

A social worker should be aware of clients' responses to communication and should carefully regulate his own responses. A client may reveal an information processing block by rejecting content or relationship information or by giving an ambiguous response, including disconfirmation. For example, the client who disagrees with something a social worker says may reject it by stating his disagreement openly, or may momentarily disconfirm the worker by ignoring him and changing the subject. Within a family, more frequent acceptance of one another's communication, rather than rejection or disconfirmation of it, can be taken as a sign of health. As one type of intervention, a social worker can accept in more neutral or more enthusiastic ways the content put forth by clients. He can encourage flexibility in the worker-client relationship as he accepts clients' one-up, one-down, and symmetrical stances. A worker may also reject a client's thinking or potential actions. If he does so without rejecting the client's initiative in thinking or talking something out, the worker is employing selective response. By offering mixed or ambiguous communications, a worker lets the client know that a given piece of information or relationship stance is available without forcing it on him. "I wonder if . . ." suggests the worker's uncertainty about the idea stated, and may forestall the client's premature rejection or approval of it.

One party takes control of a relationship without carrying full responsibility for his actions when he proposes some relationship definition with the proviso that circumstances beyond his control make it necessary. A client looks at his watch frequently during an interview, explaining he has another appointment soon after. The explanation suggests that his taking of responsibility for the time the interview will end does not reflect an intent to be one-up with the worker in general. This type of communication can also be used more dysfunctionally. Psychosomatic or psychiatric symptoms, whatever other purposes they may serve, help a person gain control of a relationship without assuming responsibility for doing so. Consider the situation in which an airplane passenger's seatmate tries to start a conversation. The second passenger seems to have the option of accepting the proposed relationship (of conversational interchange) or of rejecting it and so beginning a battle for control. But instead, he can gain control surreptitiously by declining conversation on grounds of some extenuating circumstance such as a headache. To lie about the headache would still leave the second speaker aware of having assumed responsibility for relationship definition—how much more conscience-freeing actually to have one![7] When a wife responds to her husband's efforts to improve her housekeeping by developing a hand-washing compulsion, this symptom prevents most house cleaning. She thus unknowingly maintains some control of their relationship but cannot be held responsible for doing so. Of course, people who have symptoms often suffer greatly, and usually do not maintain this control over others with any conscious intent. Memories of past disappointments with people may have led to such self-defeating attempts to control others.[8]

The social worker can use a related communication to deal with clients who dysfunctionally control interaction. Such clients may be perpetually one-up, as the individual who will not let a social worker get a word in edgewise, or perpetually one-down, as the passive, silent person. Or they may place themselves in control, like the woman with a hand-washing compulsion, by their symptoms. Within a relationship designed to change them, they will be unable to change. Helping professionals can put any such clients in a *paradox*. In this intervention the practitioner assumes a metacomplementary relationship stance by placing the client in charge. He may greet the client's symptoms, overtalkativeness, or passivity with permissive interest rather than demands for change. The worker seeing a client who has anxiety attacks does not ask him to become less anxious, but permits this symptom and encourages the client to observe when it occurs. If the client continues as before, he is doing what the worker allows and so letting him have some control in their relationship. If he stops, he has changed as the worker ultimately wishes. To avoid relationship struggles with clients who tend to place themselves perpetually one-up or one-down, a worker can overtly affirm their right to be in control. Some clinicians with a communications background take the idea of paradox one step further when they prescribe symptoms or actually tell clients to behave as they have been behaving. They may order a client who cannot get up in the morning to stay in bed until a certain time. When symptomatic behavior no longer enables a client to be in control, he will presumably give it up.[9]

Summary. People exchange information not only by the obvious content of their verbal and nonverbal behavior, but also as such communication serves to define their relationship. Control of a relationship can be shared, with participants able to be one-up, one-down, and symmetrical with each other at different times. Relationships of unequal power can benignly include the one-up partner's caring for the one-down and allowing him some control. More problematic are relationships characterized by continuous power struggles or symmetrical escalations, by complementarity which tends toward distance and disengagement, or by one party's surreptitious control through symptoms. Responses to content and relationship information offered by others include acceptance, rejection, selective acceptance, and various mixed or ambiguous responses. Among these last, disconfirmation of another's communication, which negates his human essence, is particularly malevolent.

Operating Rules in Small Social Systems

Human beings influence and are influenced by small social systems as they bring information to others and receive information from others there. Over time, system members' communication becomes patterned; their exchanges of content and relationship information become predictable. Communication patterning, or the observable regularity of system members' behavior, reflects implicit *operating rules,* not only about how participants can interact, but also ultimately about how they can process information. Threats of system upset may be countered by *homeostatic mechanisms,* behavior serving to enforce the rules. To understand small system operating rules, one may examine what members can talk about and do, their symmetry and complementarity, and—when more than two people are present—their coalitions and pecking orders. These concepts are important to social workers who assess family and group functioning, and who form small social systems with any clients seen.

Participants in any new social system bring with them different information which they can potentially share, and they may also differ in their information processing. They must work out, to a degree, at least, how they will act together, what they will perceive about themselves and their environment, and how they will evaluate their perceptions. A member of a new community group may suggest tackling the issue of property taxes, or he may just complain about his taxes, hoping that others will join in. In the first instance he has also implicitly proposed himself as a group leader. Others may discard his proposals, ignore them, or begin to follow him. The group may share a good deal of information about property taxes, but then decide not to do anything about them. The individual who first raised the issue may emerge as a leader in discussing some other content, or he may not. Those group members whose children are in schools supported by property taxes may not even agree with his evaluation that property taxes are high. Within any new social system, context heavily influences what members will agree to do together and how they will agree to process information. That is, societal values, language, group purpose and the resulting role prescriptions, and the physical and social setting affect the functioning of those involved. When a system persists, members' exchanges of content information become limited, relationship definitions stabilize, and some rules for information processing are accepted by all.[10] For a time at least, the ways in which individual needs are met and system functioning maintained become habitual.

A social worker—as he does premarital and early marital counseling, meets with newly formed groups, and begins interviewing individual clients and families who may or may not want to interact as the worker does—observes people trying to form a new system through accommodation. Most workers have seen young couples struggle to reconcile ways of relating learned in their parental families, or couples entering second marriages struggle to adjust, along with their children and stepchildren. Especially in early interviews, the worker attempts to establish what he believes will be helpful agreements with clients about how to interact—in other words, he tries to influence the operating rules. In a particular case, the worker might suggest that the client be more active in attempting to solve his problems rather than relying solely on the worker. The worker may notice and evaluate certain elements in a client's functioning, and thus encourage the client to notice them. If, for instance, a client hints that he is sexually attracted to a worker—perhaps only by nonverbal behavior such as blushing—and a worker fails to perceive this message, he implicitly encourages the client not to perceive his sexual feelings during interviews. But if the worker both notices and discusses things happening between himself and the client, he helps establish a rule whereby he, at least, can refer to their interaction.

The operating rules of any small system are the members' apparently preferred ways of behaving together and of dealing with information. These rules govern exchanges of content information, as when system members implicitly agree that they may show concern for each other but may not acknowledge anger. There are rules governing who may take particular relationship stances at particular times. One member of a peer group may be expected to lead others in matters of derring-do. When a system includes more than two people, coalitions or alliances tend to occur in some patterned fashion, reflecting implicit operating rules about who may align with whom under what circumstances. Operating rules may even influence people's information processing. They can affect perception—for example, when family members do not notice that parents are unhappy with each other. They can influence how people think, and whether they can make certain memories conscious. Homeostatic mechanisms are behaviors which serve to enforce operating rules and thereby contribute to the stability of a system. One example of such a mechanism is restlessness among family members when a one-up figure's authority is challenged or when someone begins to speak about forbidden matters.[11]

Rules about content exist that are independent of the relationship stances taken by members of a system. A social worker and members of a client group, whatever their respective relationship positions, may agree never to touch each other in any but the most formal fashion. Members of any family or group tend to develop secrets, or matters that everyone knows but no one discusses—such as a mother's alcoholism. They may, in the face of considerable conflicting evidence, maintain myths, such as the belief that one peer group member is dumber than the rest.[12] Small system members must settle on acceptable or forbidden conversation topics, and decide which behavior will be applauded, tolerated, or condemned. Operating rules regulate such factors as the sexuality, dependence, separateness, and assertiveness of the members of a social system. Group purpose naturally suggests certain rules. A neighborhood action group is unlikely to condone overt sexual behavior among members, but may encourage assertiveness in the context of a particular task. A family or group establishes operating rules about how clear its communication will be, whether members can metacommunicate to clarify ambiguities, and whether responses to others' content will be generally accepting or not.

Relationship communication among members of any small system will evolve into repetitive sequences. A complementary relationship, when closely observed, may be seen to consist of repetitively one-up stances by one party and one-down stances by the other, and the degree to which these behaviors are typical can be specified. A symmetrical relationship may be characterized by escalations, by shared decision making, or by partners' flexibility in taking one-up, one-down, and egalitarian relationship positions. Each participant's tendencies to accept, reject, or disconfirm the other's relationship positions can also be observed, as can the use each makes of mixed messages or control of the relationship through symptoms. With three or more people present, such interchanges will still take place between any two system menbers. A parent can be one-up to a child whether or not someone else is with them. But the presence of more people means there can also be coalitions which include symmetrical or complementary pairs, and pecking orders with coalitions within them. A *coalition* implies that two or more people are engaged with each other in a reasonably positive fashion, or aligned against someone else, at a particular time. Two friends within a peer group may form a coalition by sticking together. It is a complementary coalition if one friend is decidedly dominant and the other submissive. Longer-term coalitions or pecking orders can be determined by observing people's interaction for a longer period.[13]

Operating rules in relationships of more than two people can become complex. Individuals may take particular relationship stances that are tied to the relationship behavior of others. For example, one spouse's one-up message may be followed by a one-up message of the other, until stopped by their child's presenting himself as one-down scapegoat for both. The two parents, each claiming they are right about some matter, become angrier and angrier until the child misbehaves and diverts their attention. The regularity of interaction implies a system operating rule: that the child will place himself one-down to end parental symmetrical escalations. His behavior in fact serves a homeostatic function in checking the escalations. In other circumstances, one parent may form a coalition with a child as the two reject or disconfirm the remaining parent. The latter may then reject or disconfirm them, perhaps by passivity or frequent absences from home. Cross-generational coalitions are often dysfunctional in families and even in groups, as when a group leader favors one member, whom others then ostracize. We note that metacomplementarity in small system interaction is difficult to define clearly. If those who apparently have power give up some of it, as when parents allow an adolescent to make certain decisions, the observer can claim to know who is "really" in control. But what if power not freely given were seized by the apparently weaker party? The passive wife who metacomplementarily forces her husband to take care of her cannot do so unless the husband cooperates. Since all participants in system functioning play a part in communication patterns, the "real" relative power of any one is ultimately impossible to ascertain.[14]

Observation within a family or group reveals that patterns of relationship communication among system members may be different in different content areas. For example, a husband's power over finances may be balanced by the wife's tendency to regulate their sexual behavior. Or marital partners may attempt a benign sort of symmetry in most areas of endeavor with complementarity in only a few. Children of such a couple might be allowed a deciding vote in certain other activities of family life. Within a peer group, coalition patterns and pecking order can depend on whether the group is engaged in recreation or in trying to accomplish a cognitively oriented task. When an employer is one-up with an employee except during the office Christmas party, the operating rule is clear.[15]

The social worker who understands the concept of operating rules can infer what content or relationship information, and rules for information processing, an individual client may have received or may be receiving from his natural social systems. He does so by observing the operating rules the client proposes with him. The young woman who cannot talk about sex may have learned from her family and religious cohorts not to discuss the matter or even to perceive the feelings involved. The man who constantly thinks the worker is putting him down may have learned from past experiences that this is what happens to him in relationships. When a worker is aware that he and his clients must establish operating rules, he is more likely to see any dysfunctional mutual communication patterns they have built up. In the case just cited, the worker can notice that any demands he makes set off the man's fear of being criticized, and that the man then provokes the worker to take over the complementary one-up role of criticizer. The worker's awareness may give him more insight into how the client gets into unhappy interactions with others, and may help him decide how to deal with the man more helpfully. Social workers able to assess family or group operating rules that have become dysfunctional can also intervene to change these rules. The family in which only the mother notices the children's needs may have dysfunctional operating rules in that mother feels overwhelmed, father isolated, and the children deprived. Yet to change this system, the worker may not be able simply to teach father greater perceptiveness. He may have to interfere with the operating rule in which the children automatically go to their mother to have their needs met, and mother automatically tries to meet them.

We have shown how individuals influence social systems by bringing to the systems their information and rules for information processing, and have suggested that members of a new system accommodate to each other's ideas of how they should interact. Over time, communication within social systems becomes patterned as members develop operating rules governing their information processing and content and relationship information exchanged.

But individuals, social systems, and the larger environment continue to influence each other, especially as systems change.

Human Functioning and
System Change

Our discussion of communications concepts has now come full circle. In chapter 1 we saw how individuals are influenced by information, and how other people are a source of information and of potential rules for information processing. In the present chapter we have suggested that communication within small social systems becomes patterned, reflecting implicit operating rules. Let us now examine more closely the reciprocal influence between the individual, the social system, and the larger environment. We shall then consider how small social systems show second-order change, or change in their operating rules.

Not only when families or groups are established, but also over time, people bring to these small systems their information stored in memory, new information that they receive from any sources, and their rules for information processing. The larger environment influences them as individuals and as system members by the new information it continuously provides. For example, a family member receives information during his forays into the world as a student, employee, friend, church member, and citizen. People's information from within themselves is also continuously changing as their bodily sensations and feelings vary, as they have an increasing fund of stored information, and as they experience different thoughts. Within a small system itself, people exchange information they have on hand or glean from such sources. When they develop communication patterns reflecting system operating rules, the system as such begins to influence its members. For one thing, communication patterning probably reduces the amount of energy people use to sustain their interaction, just as the formation of relatively stable personality patterns is thought to free psychic energy for work. Then, such patterns influence people's behavior within the system and their information processing. The behavior, perception, and thinking that members are encouraged to exhibit is probably learned by trial and error and analogic means as they interact. At some point it may be said to exist as stored information within each individual's memory. A man in some way "knows" to strike up an argument when his wife says something that always sets him off. People may not see, hear, or feel what they learn to be either valueless or dangerous in interacting with given others. Individuals themselves and the small social system as a collectivity will influence the larger environment. If members of a family carry out a decision to survive by means of crime, for example, their impact on their environment is clear.

It should now be apparent that influence between individuals, small social systems, and the larger environment is reciprocal. In understanding human functioning, one cannot easily delineate how much events seen are affected by an individual's information on hand and information processing, by small system operating rules, and by such larger environmental factors as the physical world, community events, or cultural values. Every individual is influenced by his past as well as his present. Within a social system, each person's behavior is simultaneously stimulus to what follows and response to what went before. The couple who seesaw between the husband's withdrawal and the wife's nagging are caught in an oscillating cycle in which neither partner carries greater responsibility, no matter how each may understand their interaction ("I withdraw because you nag," "I nag because you withdraw").[16] Neither such clients nor the social worker involved with them can immediately know how much their behavior fulfills individual needs, how much it merely conforms to an unintended and perhaps unwanted system operating rule, and how it may be affected by the larger environment. Members of a nag-withdraw couple can have some need not to be close, or they may simply be responding to each other's behavior in a vicious cycle neither knows how to break. They can also be responding to in-laws, or to a society which values achievements the husband does not aspire to.

Social workers try to understand the reciprocity of influence between individuals, social systems, and the environment when they assess clients' functioning and decide where to intervene. At one time, most intervention was done with individuals. More recently, the profession has become aware that small social system operating rules may be a compelling influence on individual functioning, and that change efforts sometimes should be directed to those rules. In carrying out such intervention, two concepts have been salient. One is that system members all participate in communication patterning and thus in maintaining operating rules—a worker normally cannot expect only one member of a family or group to carry responsibility for change. Another is that people may learn operating rules analogically. The worker responsible for trying to change these may do well to use nonverbal means, such as altering people's seating arrangements. Social workers know that sometimes the environment itself must be dealt with to give clients the help they need. Dysfunctional behavior may be largely the result of societal devaluation, poverty, poor housing, and the like.

Change within social systems, whether natural or induced by professional intervention, can occur at two levels. In one sense, any small system is constantly in flux as members pursue their business, interact around the necessities of their life together, deal with impinging events, and so on. But such activity usually constitutes what is called first-order change. This term connotes fluctuations in the behavior of system members while the system itself remains unchanged. That is, as long as the operating rules which govern system functioning persist, no real changes within the system will take place. If mother is the housekeeper and father the breadwinner, then mother's and father's activities as they go about their housekeeping and breadwinning do not constitute system change. If members of a community group have tacitly agreed on what topics they will and will not discuss, their varying discussion within the accepted strictures is not system change. System change, or *second-order change,* occurs by definition when there is change in the system operating rules,[17] in the agreed-on ways in which members interact and process information. A father's taking over the housekeeping or group members' deciding to impose membership requirements, if these behaviors modified existing operating rules, would constitute second-order change.

For such second-order modifications to occur, there must be some stimulus from the environment or from individuals who make up the system. When a wife begins to work outside the home, for example, the husband may take over some of the housekeeping. Any system has to deal constantly with incoming information. That information which stimulates second-order change conflicts in its implications with the system's basic operating rules.[18]

A wife's working would seem to suggest some change in rules governing the distribution of responsibilities in the home. A child's growth into adolesence suggests modification of the family rule that his parents make all major decisions concerning him. System change may take place naturally as members can notice, accept, and respond appropriately to new information implying such a need. The parents of an adolescent may decide to allow him more freedom or may simply begin to do so. Members of a group which has received community sanction may move to clarify its membership requirements.

For a system to be open to change, its members must be able to change their behavior and sometimes their information processing. An adolescent asking for greater freedom within the family must behave so as to indicate that he can assume more responsibility for himself. His parents must be able to notice and evaluate his new functioning. When needed system change fails to occur, it may be that system members do not know how to change their behavior, or that some number of individuals' information processing has blocked. Just as individuals learn in some fashion how to deal with new information which conflicts with the old, so system members presumably develop agreements about coping with the new. Each may be unable to change because of the combined inertia of all. Contextual forces also affect operating rules within any small system for better or for worse, as when a school labels an adolescent a poor learner and thus implicitly one-down to adults there and elsewhere. Consistent with theory is the practical observation that individuals and the larger environment can influence social systems toward second-order change. But changes within systems and the larger environment also affect individuals' behavior and rules for information processing.

When members of a social system cannot adjust operating rules to cope with individuals' needs or with external circumstances, they may need an outsider's help. A married couple's nag-withdraw cycle may leave both feeling unloved. A work group's continued inattention to its members' heavy drinking may reduce its efficiency. One person's symptoms may become incorporated in family or group homeostasis so as to support existing operating rules, while these rules accommodate the symptoms in turn.[19]

When a father's periodic attempts at suicide limit a mother's and son's incestuous coalition, they clearly serve a homeostatic system function. His symptoms place the father in unknowing control of interaction, with other family members in compliance. Such a pattern may also encourage the son to stay with parents who seem to need him long after society and his own maturity suggest he should leave. Marital partners' collusion in neurosis,[20] family members' and co-workers' support of alcoholism,[21] and cooperative double-binding in schizophrenia[22] all seem to prevent second-order individual and system change.

A social worker's ability to differentiate first- and second-order change in small system functioning is crucial. A worker may try to extricate a family or group member from the scapegoat role by praising him, aligning with him, or even seeing him for treatment appointments alone. He may later find that system operating rules requiring scapegoating have not changed, but that members' negative comments are now directed to a different individual. The worker who helps a schizophrenic young adult to separate from his parents may find that a younger sibling then shows disabling symptoms, as family operating rules require another child to be sick to prevent the family's breaking apart. A worker in a community group may persuade members not to hide their disagreements behind humor, only to find that they are now hiding them by missing meetings. That is, the operating rule forbidding disagreement remains. A worker can sometimes move to produce second-order system change by demonstrating something different himself. In the example just cited, a worker might break the rule by disagreeing with someone. Workers and clients in small system practice can discuss rules or the way incoming information seems to conflict with them. In the community group, the worker might note that members seem to have reached an accord that disagreements are dangerous. Sometimes a worker seeks to modify system operating rules by the use of paradox. He may tell an argumentative family that they are showing him how they interact, thus metacomplementarily permitting arguing which had effectively controlled treatment sessions. Or a worker may try to change operating rules within a system by intervening to change part of the environment, such as a school, which he thinks is adversely affecting those rules.

Summary. After an accommodation process when they first meet, members of any small social system begin to show observable patterns in their behavior together. From these, one may infer operating rules, or system members' tacit agreements about what to perceive, how to think, and how to act in each other's presence, including allowable discussion content and mutual relationship stances. Homeostatic mechanisms, such as censure, tend to enforce these rules. Change in a system may be mere fluctuation of members' behavior around operating rules (first-order change), or may be a modification of the rules themselves (second-order change). When families or groups cannot change in response to individual need or new demands from their environment, social workers may help. They must know how to assess any system's operating rules, and must seek to establish constructive ones between clients and themselves.

Three   Initial Interviews

Communication theory probably helps social workers most by clarifying the ways in which their own words and actions influence clients. At no time is a worker's influence more significant than when he and an individual, family, or group first meet. The context of an initial interview, including its physical setting, is at least partially within his control. His earliest interventions can be the deciding factor in whether and how clients use help. Worker communication in initial interviews gives clients information about their problems, about services available, and about relationship stances the worker proposes to take. It suggests operating rules for the small social system formed by the worker and any clients involved. A worker must be aware of how context and his own interventions can affect clients, both to offer constructive help and to assess their behavior in response.

Clients, of course, will also put forth content for discussion and will behave in some fashion, thus demonstrating how they propose to relate. Members of an existing small system such as a family bring with them their established operating rules. A worker will assess clients' functioning throughout any service period, and will influence interview process largely in response to what clients convey. This chapter discusses worker behavior as it may influence clients before and during initial interviews. After clarifying context, and a worker's possible effect on it, we offer excerpts from initial sessions with an individual, a small group, and a family, commenting in each instance on the use of worker interventions in such beginning interviews. A framework and guidelines for assessment will be discussed in chapter 4.

Context of Initial Interviews

Context of initial interviews broadly includes each participant's information bearing on the situation. Clients' relevant information may consist of prior knowledge of the worker and setting, their conceptions of why they are seeking help, their experiences with any other clients related to the case, their eventual perceptions of the worker's and any other clients' personal characteristics, and their awareness of worker-client interaction immediately before a first interview begins. Each client will compare such data to other content and relationship information that he possesses as he decides whether to come to an initial interview and forms an idea of what to expect there. Because context at this very early time can be a powerful influence on client behavior, social workers must seek to understand and, often, to regulate it.

Clients may receive content information about the worker or setting before meeting the worker face to face. Sometimes the worker's name, sex, and (for women) marital status have been indicated when an appointment was set up. Any client evaluates known characteristics of the worker, such as the worker's sex and apparent ethnic identity, against what he conceives as his need for service, to predict whether this helping person is likely to be helpful to him. A woman with a marital problem may wonder whether a male worker will take her husband's side. A client notices the promptness with which appointments are arranged, and how his need for help is labeled in any papers he may have received concerning the appointment. Is he noted as having a problem, a condition, or only a desire to be seen? From brief telephone conversations with the worker or a receptionist, a client looks for indications of the worker's benign competence. He can also react to the name of a setting or its building in view of past information which seems relevant. Thus he may expect the worker at an agency with a sectarian-sounding name to lecture him for not attending religious services. The client who has dealt with other professionals within a setting has received information about it firsthand. When a client actually arrives to see a social worker, he will respond directly to the building, waiting room and office furnishings, receptionist, and the promptness or tardiness with which he is seen.

Clients can also infer relationship messages from such prior knowledge about the social worker or the setting. These contextual data may place clients one-down. The prestige of an agency or institution, the sumptuousness of its building and furniture, and the act of keeping a client waiting for an appointment can indicate a social worker's higher status, unless a client's status in the community, wealth (as perhaps indicated by dress), or time behavior are comparable. People asking for help have initiated the suggestion that a worker-client relationship exist; but, in needing something the worker has to give, they propose willingness to be one-down. Clients' sense of subordination likely varies along a number of additional dimensions. These include whether they will be paying for service, how vulnerable they feel to being refused, how much the need for service seems to indicate personal inadequacy, how many areas of their life they will expose to scrutiny, and how much freedom of choice they have about doing so. The client in a community organizing situation may see himself as fairly symmetrical with the worker. He will not expose himself extensively, and his need for service scarcely reflects inadequacy. Adoption applicants may plan to pay for service and may not see themselves as inadequate. Yet their self-exposure and vulnerability to refusal of service are great. Subjectively most subordinate, perhaps, are people with personal problems who need uncompensated help, and clients who see social workers involuntarily.

Who is to be seen is also part of the context of initial interviews. By arranging an individual appointment with someone who has family problems, the worker seems to imply that only this family member must change. When an appointment is made with a couple, a family, or some other natural group, outside relationships among these clients will influence their coming or not coming in. Individual members are likely to exchange any content-level impressions of the agency or worker beforehand. They may negotiate for one-upmanship regarding this new experience. When a worker tells family or group members that they will be seen with others, this content suggests his view that several people must solve presenting problems together. On the relationship level, the worker cannot avoid being in temporary coalition with those individuals who wanted to solve problems in this fashion. With them he is also by definition temporarily one-up to those who hoped not to be seen together. Clients may wholly misunderstand what such worker communication implies, perhaps believing that the worker will form coalitions along the same lines when initial sessions begin.

At the first meeting, each client will evaluate the general appearance, age, sex, race, ethnicity, and marital status of the worker and any other client he does not already know against his stored ideas about people with these characteristics. For example, the working-class man whose social worker is a long-haired male may expect him to show hippie attitudes. Each individual's personal characteristics again imply relationship definitions. In our American culture, one-up positions have usually been accorded to greater age (at least until late adulthood), to maleness, whiteness, being native-born, showing middle- or upper-class dress and speech patterns, and being married. A client may feel uncomfortable in a formed group when other members' personal characteristics appear likely to place them one-up to him, or devalued in a group where everyone else seems of lower status. Also, any client may initially prefer as a helping person someone like himself, who is fairly symmetrical with him at least in personal status characteristics, or someone of higher status, who presumably will be benignly complementary one-up. Rarely do clients request social workers with less culturally favored characteristics than their own, although they may ultimately relate to such persons and find them helpful. Attributes of the worker or setting which lower the worker's status culturally, such as being young, unmarried, and female in a shabbily furnished office, are often of initial concern to clients because they are putting themselves one-down to someone already one-down to many others.

Before he begins interacting with clients face to face, what can a worker do about the varied, often misleading content and relationship information that clients may glean from context? He can try to ensure that appointments are given promptly and that clients are not kept waiting when they arrive on time. He is clearly responsible for the wording of appointment letters he writes and telephone conversations he has with clients. He may wish to explain briefly by telephone or by letter why he has scheduled an individual, family, or group session in preference to seeing clients some other way. Attention to such matters makes coming in easier for anyone and encourages certain clients—whose prior assumptions about a worker, setting, or type of interview might have turned them away—to show up at the interview. Furthermore, a social worker may well have some choice about the appearance of a waiting room or at least of his own office. He can help train a receptionist to deal with clients constructively and can foster this person's continued good functioning. As for the many contextual factors beyond his control, the worker can try to forestall misconceptions by encouraging clients to raise questions and voice any concerns before the initial interview. Even the male client who wonders whether an unmarried young woman will be sufficiently one-up to help him can be reassured if she is strong enough to ask whether he has any questions about coming in.

Worker communication with clients immediately before first interviews can offer important messages. A worker may meet any clients outside his office, in their home, or elsewhere, and introduce himself. The content of his remarks and his accompanying nonverbal behavior communicate his beginning relationship intentions. He has usually taken a one-up stance in indicating when the interview will begin. Let us assume that he meets clients in a waiting room, leans over with a friendly expression, and says something like, "Hello, Mrs. Smith (or Mr. and Mrs. Smith, or whatever). I am Mr. Porter, the social worker who is going to see you. Will you come this way, please?" The worker's coming to the waiting room himself rather than sending for clients, greeting them, using the same form of address toward them that he uses in introducing himself, and asking them to come with a "please" rather than telling them to do so, all suggest a symmetrical relationship definition. The nonverbal communications of leaning and friendly facial expression are benign, but could accompany either symmetry or complementarity.

Mr. Porter's identifying himself as "the social worker who is going to see you" also connotes interesting relationship messages. First, such a statement symmetrically accepts clients' prior communication if they have asked to see a social worker, but could be rather one-up in forcefulness if not. In the latter circumstance, a worker might instead say something like "... a social worker who would like to talk with you." Then, Mr. Porter's clarifying his professional affiliation is a conscious attempt to convey content information useful to clients. He who can give needed information is more knowledgeable and therefore one-up to another. However, in giving information and thus enhancing what clients know, the worker suggests his intent that their knowledge eventually be more equal with his. In this way a worker's giving of content information is a move, although an incremental one, to make relationships with clients more symmetrical. One should note that the repeated giving of information that another already posses es is by contrast a highly one-up maneuver, almost a disconfirmation, for it negates the other's knowledge.

Not showing up for a first appointment is a client's ultimate disconfirmation of the worker, unless the nonappearance is accompanied by an acceptable explanation. When two or more potential clients are expected for an initial session, any one may simply not appear. This behavior disconfirms not only the worker but also other family or group members, unless these others have colluded with the absent member or even caused his absence. In initial interviews with families, parents may bring only the child identified as having problems, leaving any siblings at home. Or a father may excuse himself from an initial session with or without the mother's tacit approval. In either a family or a group initial interview, the worker's reactions to any absences may be fully perceptible to members. If an absence is unlikely to have been caused by others present, as would be the case with newly formed groups, the worker by simply noting and accepting it implies that there are probably extenuating circumstances and that he is not perplexed by the absence. If family or group members appear to have colluded in anyone's absence, the worker can at some point explore possible concerns of those present about coming with the absent member or members. After an individual or group interview, and sometimes after a family session, a worker may telephone any absent clients to talk neutrally about what happened. The worker who ignores a client's absence, or who shows anger in response to it, communicates to all aware of his response that he will deal with being disconfirmed or rejected by disconfirming or rejecting in retur

As social workers and clients interact during interviews, they move toward becoming a new social system, but one still influenced by contextual factors. These continue to include each participant's perception of all that has gone before; of fluctuations in everyone's personal characteristics, including different ways of dressing or changes in marital status; and of intra-agency factors such as a receptionist's friendliness. In continuing work, different parties' presences and absences form part of context as well. As we have noted, social workers cannot control some contextual influences on their early and continuing interaction with clients. They may not be able to change an agency's misleading name or their own personal characteristics, but they can be prepared to discuss clients' concerns with these. They do not know what prior impressions of themselves or a setting clients may have received but can, for example, ask about past experience with helping professionals in the same agency. Such matters as a worker's continuing promptness in keeping appointments and his continuing conversations with clients before and after interviews and on the telephone are within his control. For example, a worker who hopes to see a client's family may call to explain that he thinks this will be helpful, rather than disconfirming the family by remarking only that joint sessions are required by agency policy.

Initial Interventions with Individual Clients

Worker activities in initial interviews with individuals—and with families and groups, as we shall see later—have certain generic features designed to help clients decide how to proceed. Social workers usually try to elicit information, to provide enlightening content about how they see problems and possible solutions, and to negotiate constructive worker-client relationship definitions. Their communication will influence operating rules about what may be said and done together, and who may take what relationship stances. For example, if the worker asks about the past or mentions any other content which clients have not already raised, he proposes both that this content be allowable and that he can sometimes be one-up by initiating new discussion topics. When clients implicitly suggest operating rules about relationship stances and, by what they include and exclude, about content, the worker can influence the rules by his response to the clients' suggestions. Both his words and his nonverbal communication convey his acceptance of client communication or, when he shows discomfort or impatience, his rejection of it. A worker's handling of content influences relationship operating rules in that clients are more willing to be one-down, as they must at times, to a worker who seems both competent and kind when one-up.

We shall now analyze excerpts from the process recording of a social worker's first interview with an individual client. The accompanying discussion should show how worker interventions in early interviews convey both content and relationship information to clients.

Our sample interview takes place in a large metropolitan hospital, where Mr. Ferlugi, sixty-four years old, is being treated for congestive heart failure.[1] Context of the setting and his physical condition tend to define the client as one-down, although the worker is a young woman. Before the interview begins, the worker introduces herself as from the social service department, tells Mr. Ferlugi that she understands he has some things he wishes to talk over, and asks if he prefers to talk in his room or the sun room. Her initiating interaction at this time is a one-up move. However, she conveys symmetry by sharing what she knows with Mr. Ferlugi, by giving him the choice of meeting place, and—not incidentally—by addressing him by his last name. Her relationship messages so far, then, suggest some flexibility.

> After we were both seated, I further explained to Mr. Ferlugi that my job was to assist him with any problems and to help make his stay as smooth and pleasant as possible. He said that he would try not to take up too much of my time. I explained that my time was for use by patients and that my schedule was flexible enough to allow me to spend as much time with him as necessary. I then said that the nurse had told me he had some questions concerning his health insurance and that I thought I might be able to help. Could he tell me about this?

Many social workers begin first interviews, as this one did, by explaining their function briefly if a client is not likely to have this information. The content operating rule implied is that such a worker is willing to talk about his role, and probably that the client may feel free to ask questions about it. Sometimes a worker defines his role fairly symmetrically, as by saying that he and a client will address problems together. Sometimes he conveys willingness to be benignly one-up, as when the worker in our case example thought she "might be able to help." If a client responds to descriptions of worker role with immediate misunderstandings, a worker can correct these on the content and perhaps on the relationship levels. Making it clear that social workers can offer more than concrete services, for example, is a necessity in some settings. Mr. Ferlugi, by volunteering to take little of the worker's time, conveys his expectation of being in a one-down relationship position. The worker responds with what amounts to a rejection of this stance.

In a typical early move, the worker next opens up interaction by telling Mr. Ferlugi what she knows about his difficulties and by asking for further information. Content about the client's need for service is thereby introduced. While the worker's taking of initiative here means being temporarily one-up once more, her sharing what she knows and citing her appearance as in response to the client's request constitute moves toward symmetry. The worker, in metacomplementary fashion, gives up some control of discussion by asking an open-ended question. Such early content and its accompanying relationship stances should seem familiar to workers in almost any setting, as well as being apparently appropriate here. Note that even when a client begins an interview, the worker who decides to permit it rather than feeling helpless in the face of it is technically in a metacomplementary relationship position.

Mr. Ferlugi stated that he had worked for many years as a tailor. Last year he had to quit because of ill health. He had been feeling better until he got sick two weeks ago and was rushed to the hospital. He found the experience to be terribly frightening because he did not know what was happening at first. I observed that I could imagine how frightening it was for him and he said it was painful too. He added that he is now worried about his hospital bills. I asked questions and clarified that he is still a union member, but is not sure of his insurance coverage since he is retired.

In any first interview, as the client relates his perception of his need for service and as worker-client interaction proceeds, the worker's questions, comments, and nonverbal behavior continue to give the client content and relationship information. To elicit information from the client, the worker can ask open-ended questions, follow leads that the client has suggested, or bring up new areas for discussion. In following the client's leads, he is agreeing to client-initiated rules about content, whereas in opening new areas, he proposes his own. Mr. Ferlugi responds to the worker's opening question by giving data not only about his background and eventually his financial concerns, but also about feelings when he "found the experience to be terribly frightening." He thereby proposes the content-level operating rule that feelings are a fit subject for discussion here. The worker accepts this content, thus the implicit operating rule, and also Mr. Ferlugi's one-up taking of initiative to propose it. Of course, in many instances a social worker first introduces feelings as appropriate content by asking a client questions about them.

A worker's questions designed to elicit information also give information about the line his thinking has taken. With Mr. Ferlugi, the worker could have suggested that his feelings were more important than his financial concerns by choosing to pursue the former. A worker who asks a mother about the way she handles her child implies that such handling could be affecting the child's behavior. A worker's asking only about problems may suggest that he thinks a client has no strengths. Clients will interpret such data according to their information stored in memory, and can block further communication if what they are picking up conflicts with their ideas of what a benign helping person would put forth. Some mothers know they are having trouble handling their children and hope to be helped. But those who suspect that the worker's questions imply blame may answer evasively or not at all. Whenever possible, social workers should be aware of what they suggest to clients by what they explore: what implications of causality, what priorities in considering content, and so on.

Whether intentionally or not, the social worker in an initial interview may also respond to a client's content information so as to give evaluative feedback about it.[2] A whole range of responses is possible, with enthusiastic agreement at one extreme, followed by acceptance, selective acceptance or neutrality which leave some or all areas of response uncommitted, and finally mild and then more forceful rejection. Mr. Ferlugi's social worker accepts his being frightened but does not imply by enthusiastic agreement that he might have been more frightened still. In beginning interviews, a worker often uses mid-range responses to a client's content to avoid committing himself before he is sure enough of assessment data to take any stand. His doing so also tends to maintain symmetry, while the giving of strong positive or negative feedback places him in the position of evaluator and therefore one-up. However, a worker may give feedback more emphatically where he thinks this will be to a client's benefit. He may note a client's right to have feelings without commenting on his actions, perhaps saying he can see why some situation has the client upset. He may support a client's constructive use of social work help by strongly agreeing that talking about his choices might clarify them. And he may place his weight on one side or another of important immediate decisions, such as that the client in a mental health clinic should not leave without seeing a doctor. In the following excerpt, Mr. Ferlugi's social worker offers only mild rejection of his thinking about union benefits before proceeding with other communication.

> I told Mr. Ferlugi I found it hard to imagine he would lose all of his benefits if he was still a dues-paying union member, but that I would certainly check into the situation. I asked him if he had his union card, and he gave it to me to take with me. He thanked me and then began talking about his apartment, of which he is quite proud. He explained that he pays a low rent and that he never asks the landlord to make repairs since he enjoys working with his hands. He has painted and papered the apartment himself and is proud of the way it looks. I said that I admired people who worked well with their hands and that he must have a great feeling of accomplishment. He said he did. Mr. Ferlugi then continued by discussing some of his fears about what is being planned for him medically. We talked about how he might ask the doctor about the procedures, and about what most people do feel in these situations.

Social workers in initial interviews give new content information which may help clients to see why they are having difficulties, to begin to deal with their problems differently, to feel less overwhelmed in view of resources available, to understand the service being offered, and the like. Besides checking on Mr. Ferlugi's insurance coverage, his worker eventually offers him new options in finding out about medical procedures and in understanding his feelings. Brief intervention models, in particular, encourage workers to give problem-solving information as soon as possible. Any social work practice, however, involves some information-giving during first interviews. Such intervention may include the worker letting the client know that the worker will help him obtain concrete services, or that he is otherwise willing to intervene environmentally on the client's behalf. A worker's giving of new content information, as we have noted earlier, conveys his momentary one-up relationship stance but also his wish for a client to know what he knows and thus to be finally symmetrical with him.

In the initial interview, a client can often be symmetrical with the worker or even one-up. First, a client who begins to carry responsibility for what is discussed moves into a symmetrical give-and-take with the worker, as we have seen with Mr. Ferlugi. The worker's acceptance of content offered by the client is a tacit acceptance of the client's exercising some greater relationship control. If a client remains one-down, the worker may try to reject that stance. For example, if a client hesitates to talk, a worker may elicit his opinions about what would be helpful to him, or may make a stronger one-down move by asserting that the client is the only one who can tell about himself. When a client takes a one-up stance that moves his relationship with the worker toward flexibility, the worker may accept it even though the content offered is not useful in itself. Mr. Ferlugi, by introducing his competence at taking care of his apartment, is saying in effect that he can be one-up in some areas of his life functioning if not in his present circumstances. The worker's willingness to accept this stance may be what allows Mr. Ferlugi to go one-down subsequently in telling how afraid he is of medical procedures.

> Later, after returning to confirm Mr. Ferlugi's insurance coverage, I said I hoped he would speak out again if anything else was bothering him. If it was alright with him, I would like to continue seeing him until his discharge and help him with anything else that might arise. He agreed and thanked me for my help. I told him I would stop in to see him Friday.

While the worker in this situation might have elicited more of Mr. Ferlugi's ideas about continuing interviews, she does symmetrically offer him the choice of continuing or not. Generally speaking, a most important exchange of content and relationship information occurs when client and worker discuss their contract for further work together. The client with some solution to his problem or next steps in mind would presumably like some control over what will be planned with the social worker. But he may not indicate his wishes, hoping the worker will take good care of him in benign one-up fashion. The worker who accepts such a role by not negotiating a contract openly can leave the client with misconceptions and even false hopes. He probably cannot guess exactly what the client wants, and so will not be perceived as benign. He has also encouraged the client's belief that a complementary relationship between them will lead to constructive interchange. If the worker can help a client be symmetrical enough to voice his expectations, he can selectively accept those which are feasible, reject or postpone others with an explanation of why he is doing so, and sometimes suggest alternatives. On the content level, the worker thus attempts to bring to the surface and resolve any differences between his own perception of next steps and that of the client, rather than leaving the client to deal with discordant information alone. By assuming as symmetrical a relationship stance as possible, he conveys both that the client need not fear subjugation and that he will be expected to assume some responsibility for ongoing work.

In a sense, contract negotiation formalizes worker-client agreement on some explicit mutual operating rules. Of course, there are no "right" operating rules about content generally, since what is relevant depends on what a particular client needs help with, wants to talk about or do, and what part of the worker's knowledge may be both helpful and acceptable to him. Mr. Ferlugi and his social worker might not discuss his peer relationships unless he indicated difficulties in this area. A worker will talk about different content with a client who wants to organize a rent strike than with an unwed mother. However, part of a social worker's expertise is to know—when the client does not know—what content rules may be useful, that is, what he and the client should talk about or do to move toward problem resolution. A worker may propose discussing local politics before deciding about the rent strike, feelings or motivation before deciding whether to give up an illegiti-mate baby, and so on. In any practice, the effective worker proposes one content operating rule which also pertains to the relationship: that he and the client can air their differences, or metacommunicate. The type of re-lationship definition a client and worker should negotiate also depends on what a particular client can accept, although flexibility between two adults may be the ideal. Whatever stances workers and clients take in initial inter-views, the circumstances under which they do so will constitute tentative relationship operating rules for the worker-client system-to-be.

The social work principle of starting where the client is can be translated into the communications notions just discussed. It suggests on the content level that most of a worker's evaluative feedback should be accepting, neu-tral, or selective rather than rejecting or disconfirming; and that content information implied in a worker's questions or given by him directly should not differ greatly from what the client already knows. On a relationship level the principle is more complex. Starting where the client is may mean ac-cepting a client's preferred one-up stance at the beginning. For the client who approaches a first appointment feeling and acting one-down, the worker may take more responsibility for guiding discussion, yet also try to encour-age some symmetry—suggesting, for example, that the client be one-up in deciding service goals. Clients used to being on equal terms with authority figures can probably accept relationship flexibility with a social worker fairly easily. However, a worker may too precipitously reject the one-down re-lationship definition suggested by a client who really expects to be told what to do, such as a passive man with psychosomatic complaints. Constructive responses to clients who cannot accept social workers' proposed content information or relationship stances offered will be discussed in chapter 6.

Initial Interventions with
Groups and Families

An initial session with a group or family is often preceded by individual interviews with one or more of the participants. Screening interviews may have been held with individuals before a group is formed. A single family member may have originally sought help for what turned out to be a system problem. By the time an initial multiple client session occurs, the worker will have negotiated some agreements about content and relationship operating rules with individuals already seen, will probably have contracted with each for ensuing group or family forms of service, and should have prepared each for what may occur with others present. Preparation is especially important because the very operating rules upon which the worker and any individual have agreed must be renegotiated at the multiple client session. Without such preparatory discussion, some clients will take the worker's benignness in an individual interview to mean that he will ally with them in others' presence. Some will be frightened about the new form of service as they refer back to stored information about how their families have used outside parties against them, or about what usually happens to them in groups. Individuals who know others to be seen can influence their presence and participation by communicating misconceptions to them. The family member who sabotages others' presence by telling them the worker will make them behave is a familiar example. Indeed, the information clients take from preliminary interviews constitutes a special part of context for ensuing group or family sessions.

At an initial interview with a group or family, exchanges of information occur not only between the social worker and each other participating individual but also among all members of the potential client system. Everyone may perceive and be influenced by the total communication matrix at a given time. The worker will not only ask questions, provide useful content, and try to negotiate constructive relationship definitions with clients, but will also seek to influence clients' own exchanges of content and relationship information. He may fairly readily influence operating rules in newly formed groups, in which all members must accommodate to stabilize interaction in the system-to-be. In natural systems with dysfunctional operating rules, the worker may try, even during a first interview, to foster second-order system change.

Let us turn to some process recordings of beginning interviews with a formed group and a family. The discussion accompanying the excerpts begins by highlighting generic features of worker communication in multiple client interviews, and then diverges to consider how interventions differ with formed groups, with well-functioning natural client systems, and with groups and families in which operating rules have become dysfunctional.

Before our sample initial group session occurs, the worker at a family agency has met individually with four troubled sixth-grade girls to suggest that they meet together. She has proposed some symmetry by promising that each girl will have a say in what the group does. However, as is more appropriate with child than adult clients, context of the group encounter clearly places the worker one-up.

> Mildred, Phyllis, and Paula were sitting in the group room when I ar-
> rived, and Ellen got there shortly after. I suggested that we all introduce
> ourselves and that I was Mrs. Reed. Each girl said her name and then
> waited. I said that each of them had told me something about herself,
> and that each had something she was not happy with or wanted to
> change. We could talk about these things together and perhaps help each
> other. But first it might be important just to get to know each other. I
> asked Mildred to begin, and with some prompting she told her age and
> grade at school. I thanked her, and Paula said that she did not like
> school, that the teachers are out to get you. Phyllis added that her
> teacher is nice. I asked Ellen how she liked school, and she said it was
> okay.

Social workers often begin first interviews with a group or family as they do with individuals, by exchanging names, by clarifying their role if neces-sary, by suggesting why the meeting has been set up, and by asking or reaffirming with clients their reasons for being present. Like Mrs. Reed, they may additionally define the multiple-client session as a valid tool for in-formation gathering or problem resolution. The content operating rule pro-posed is that worker and clients may speak about client problems and about the idea of meeting together. To ensure that clients know they may speak about less threatening content as well, a worker can introduce an additional rule making this point clear. Thus, Mrs. Reed suggests that it may be impor-tant for her and the girls just to get to know each other. Such a comment would clearly be less necessary in a community-action or other task-oriented group.

If he is the one who begins speaking in a session, a worker with multiple

clients as with an individual is in a complementary one-up relationship position. Usually this stance is perceived as benign, since the worker acts in a
welcoming fashion and implies by his comments that he wishes to be helpful.
He can then offer greater symmetry to clients by the way in which he
introduces himself, by telling them what he hopes for the session, but especially by eliciting their varying opinions about what should be done. Wording
can convey subtle differences. "This is what I think might be useful for
everyone in the family" carries a more symmetrical relationship message
than "This is what we should do." Mrs. Reed is one-up in describing group
purpose and in asking questions. But she seeks to introduce symmetry both
between herself and group members and among members by choosing words
such as "help each other," and by making sure each girl gives some opinion
about what is being discussed. Most workers in family or group sessions try
to speak at different times to all clients present, to ask for their reactions,
and eventually to achieve accord about what to do. The message is that
everyone must be involved for the endeavor to succeed.

> Paula continued by saying she only had trouble in school because the
> teacher didn't like her. Mildred asked if they had to come here. I said
> they did not if they found it not helpful but maybe now they were just a
> little scared, not sure what would happen here. Phyllis said that she
> would like to play games. I said this was possible and asked what the
> others would like to talk about or do. After some discussion and sugges-
> tions by me, the girls agreed to have refreshments and then talk for
> a while, with the option of playing games if they could not think of any-
> thing to say.

As a group or family session proceeds, workers again may elicit information, give evaluative feedback, or offer content related to clients' problems
and possible solutions. As they do so, they again suggest operating rules
about permissible content and mutual relationship stances. Mrs. Reed with
her girls' group, while going slow in asking about problems, can elicit related
information such as the girls' experiences at school. By accepting Paula's
negative feelings toward teachers and Mildred's doubts about the group,
Mrs. Reed validates the girls' proposed operating rule that they do not
always have to be nice in sessions. This rule will be important in allowing the

girls to speak freely about any matters causing anger or concern. The worker then introduces the useful information that scared feelings are also acceptable. An advantage of family or group interviews is that information given to one individual is given to all. Members of a potential social action group may learn together about their rights. A worker may even say something to one client with the specific purpose of helping another, who cannot accept the information directly. Ellen, the quietest member of the girls' group, may benefit most from learning it is all right to be afraid. Speaking to many ears, however, requires caution. A worker must refrain from saying something to one client that might unduly upset others. He should particularly avoid strong acceptance of content given by one client if this implies rejection of the content of another, and should sometimes avoid rejection of client content in the reverse circumstance. For example, with spouses each presenting his or her own version of the truth, a worker will usually take care to maintain neutrality rather than accepting or rejecting either's content at first.

Throughout an initial interview, a social worker will try to take varied, though age-appropriate, relationship positions with members of any formed or natural group. He will be benign one-up in making sure no member is disconfirmed by others and in guiding the family or group toward a constructive plan of action, perhaps by selective response to different ideas of members. At other times he will allow, offer, and encourage a more symmetrical relationship between the system members and himself by requesting their ideas about problems and solutions, confessing himself not all-knowing about the family's or group's needs, and accepting consensus arrived at by members even when he does not fully agree with their conclusions. He may accept being one-down to emerging or existing natural leaders if these are benign when one-up and willing to share responsibility with less powerful members of the client system. In other words, like Mrs. Reed, the worker will tend to promote the relationship operating rule of flexibility as appropriate between himself and system members and among members as well.

While we were eating, Mildred volunteered that she was not doing very well in school either. She and Paula agreed that school was a drag, while Phyllis said she had trouble making friends. Ellen nodded shyly. Mildred and Paula spent the rest of the session telling about adventures with their friends. I said we could talk about any of these things or do something else next time. All agreed to return.

Contracting is a more complicated matter with a group or family than with an individual. A contract between social workers and multiple clients, as with individuals, implies some mutual accord about how to proceed and makes explicit some operating rules on which participants may or may not be able to agree. The girls in Mrs. Reed's group seem to agree not to talk about problems at first. After a time they venture into this content, but then move into less threatening material which allows Mildred and Paula to compete for dominance. The worker accepts these proposed rules about content and members' relationship stances, since no member appears to be harmed by them and at least the girls are interacting fairly benignly together. She might have tried harder to achieve an explicit contract for continuing sessions. With several clients present, any agreement requires more compromise. A worker's making sure that everyone expresses his thoughts on the contract can allow the surfacing at least of major disagreements about how to proceed. These can usually be resolved, and by helping to resolve them the worker reaffirms his symmetry with the family or group as a whole. Sometimes, all parties cannot reach agreement and some members decline further involvement in family or group sessions. When all system members participate in contracting, however, such an outcome is less likely to occur and, if it does, more likely to leave clients with alternative options for using help.

We must now consider differences in worker interventions with formed groups, and with natural client systems that may have either functional or dysfunctional operating rules. Indeed, the differences have mainly to do with interventions designed to influence such rules. In formed groups, clients have not known each other before the session and will respond variably to the idea of working together to achieve therapeutic changes, community action, or for other purposes. Even if he wishes to participate, each potential group member will bring his own preconceptions about what system operating rules are safe and desirable. Social workers want these rules to be constructive for all, but recognize that an accommodation must occur if the group is to continue. At the outset, members may take a worker's questions as a stringent guideline to what can be discussed. To validate clients' participation in rule making, a worker can give primarily neutral and accepting feedback to what they say and do. When group members differ in their views, a worker may provide the content information that groups can exist in which members disagree. At the same time, to ensure that accommodation occurs, he may respond to the idea of diversity by acceptance, which closes off further inquiry, rather than by probing, which suggests that differences would be useful to pursue. As with individuals, the exact nature of content and relationship operating rules depend on what all parties think is appropriate to group purpose and what all can accept. For a therapy group, members' relationship flexibility, their subdued behavior, their discussion of personal problems, and their exploration of feelings about being in the group may constitute major beginning relationship and content operating rules. Members of a potential social action group may better form a pecking order behind a natural group leader, with informal behavioral interactions and discussion centered around identifying and dealing with common social concerns.

Any family or other natural group already constitutes a system, with its own operating rules regarding acceptable content and relationship definitions between members. Sometimes the family or group is already functioning in a constructive fashion for its members, as with some community groups, social groups, and families needing help in a crisis or concrete services. In response to the worker's questions about what he may do for them, group or family members then demonstrate ability to address needed content, and their relationship communication does not impede work toward service goals. A neighborhood association has strong leaders who already share responsibility with members for decision making. Members of a poor family in which the mother is temporarily disabled are already giving each other emotional support, and have shared tasks under the father's direction, but need a homemaker. In these cases a social worker may accept or affirm system operating rules and offer useful content information. For example, he may describe the institutional system with which the community association is trying to deal, or identify concrete services available to the family. A worker may form a coalition with existing leaders in deciding how to proceed, and may give positive feedback on their functioning, such as their protecting less powerful members.

Natural client systems, however, have often formed operating rules that are dysfunctional. Such systems may be families, community groups engaged in endless power struggles, ward groups, peer groups, or others. An initial family interview with a middle-aged mother, father, and an eighteen-year-old mildly retarded son illustrates some intervention options in such instances. The worker here is a young male in a sheltered workshop setting. Contextually, worker-client relationship positions are mixed. In wishing service the parents are one-down to the worker, but in age they are one-up. The son, who is defined as causing the family's problems, is one-down to everyone. But he may expect the worker to be his ally since he is near his age.

> After getting everyone's name and establishing that there were no other family members living at home, I began by asking what had brought the family to this setting. Mrs. Brown responded that her son John had graduated from a special education program in June and that he now needed some structure in his life. She has tried to provide things for him to do around the house, but he watches TV instead. Mr. Brown said John is not that slow mentally and should get out and work. I said that our program might be a possibility for John, but I would like to know his opinion about what he wanted too. John mumbled that his father is always telling him what to do.

For any family or group with dysfunctional operating rules, the worker is an outside force both threatening and promising to produce needed second-order system change. In response to a worker's invitation to define their service needs, members may compete among themselves for superior relationship positions and may volunteer some forbidden content, but they will generally demonstrate their usual ways of interacting together. The disagreement between Mr. and Mrs. Brown about what to do with John, and John's inability to influence their positions, is very likely a longstanding communication pattern. The implied operating rule is that John may be left out of decisions which concern him, and possibly that he can be denied other adult prerogatives. To avoid condoning such a rule, the worker must take great care not to ignore John as the parents do. His showing interest in John's opinion about what service he wants challenges the rule and, in the process, tests to see how set this particular family's relationship patterns are. John is willing to be more symmetrical by complaining about his father, but this choice of content only invites his parents to reassert their complementarity.

Mr. Brown said this was typical of John's negative attitude, and Mrs. Brown added, with an imploring look at me, that John was not like other boys. I said that since John has graduated, it is natural for everyone to be wondering about what he should do next. They have probably discussed this among themselves and are not sure. Such an important decision should be made carefully and for me to help, I would like to get from all of them some general information about their situation and also their opinions about what to do.

With families and groups showing dysfunctional communication patterns, social workers may need to attempt more control from the outset than in other small system practice. Many practitioners who work with families find it expedient immediately to propose more constructive operating rules,[3] perhaps suggesting some symmetry among members by asking each one to speak. The simple asking of questions may also draw forth content that system operating rules tend to suppress. In the Brown family, the parents' arguing about John could serve to obscure their concerns about the father's employment. The worker's eliciting of background information about the family may threaten to bring this to the surface.

I went on to ask how long the Browns had lived in this city, whether they had other children, what school John had attended (asked of John), and whether the parents were working. Mr. Brown had just begun a new job after being out of work. I gave everyone credit for the fact that John had finished school and said just as he had done this on his own, with his parents' support, he would need to be the one to actually do the hard work of any further programs, again with their united support. Therefore I thought we had to talk further about where everyone really stood on this. When Mr. and Mrs. Brown began disagreeing, I said they had probably been taking care of John for so long it was hard to recognize he was growing up, but again, he must have an opinion on his future too.

Finally Mrs. Brown asked if I were saying they needed help letting him grow up, and I said maybe, in his own way; what did they think of this? Mr. Brown could not see it but with Mrs. Brown's urging agreed to come back to discuss plans for John further. John said very little throughout this but did smile at me sideways at one point.

In practice with families and groups, a worker must still to some degree start where clients are. The skillful worker makes heavy use of selective response here. His unconditionally accepting responses to system members' communication could affirm a destructive status quo. The worker with the Brown family did not agree that the parents could run John's life. Yet too many rejecting responses can drive a client system into refusing help. This might have happened if the worker had told Mr. and Mrs. Brown they were dominating John, instead of implying it more gently as he did, and if he had failed to recognize their adequate parenting so far and good intentions still. To have a constructive effect, a social worker can selectively offer acceptance of such clients' intentions and some part of their behavior, followed by minor requests for change.[4] He may have to propose just enough system change to let members know he can be of help, but not so much that clients cannot tolerate it. The worker does not ask the Brown family to give up their patterns immediately, but asks them to come in to discuss the possibility. Doing so would be a necessary step toward their implied service goal, that John should be able to use the setting constructively. A worker may also respond selectively to families or groups by giving positive feedback to what he thinks is buried under dysfunctional family interaction patterns: members' desires for some positive change. When rigid operating rules are the major problem with natural client systems, even minor change can be hard to stimulate. The social worker's intervention options are more fully elaborated in chapters 7 and 8.

We now present a framework and guidelines for assessment, including consideration of information on which clients' actions may be based, how they process information and sometimes block in doing so, and the intricacies of their small system operating rules.

Four   Assessment

The first step in the assessment process is the worker's information gathering as he listens to clients, observes them, and sometimes hears about them from other professionals or from collaterals such as employers or landlords. The second is assessment itself, when the worker compares this newly acquired information with practice knowledge he already possesses or seeks out, generating hypotheses about why clients are functioning as they are and what he might do to help. Effective assessment leads to intervention choice. Having begun to intervene, the worker notices clients' responses and thereby gathers further assessment data. Assessment which will lead to treatment planning is a central task of early interviews. All these activities, however, continue as long as clients are seen. They represent the worker's own professionally responsible information processing.

Most social workers use several practice theories in assessment. Communication theory serves to integrate these by conceiving all influences on clients' functioning generically. A communications framework for assessment, allowing the worker to consider reasons for clients' presenting problems and possible steps toward their resolution, is relatively simple to use. It begins with the premise that human beings act in an ultimately understandable way. At the individual level, the worker examines information on which a client might be basing his actions, and his ability to process new information without encountering blocks. A worker can observe the small social system of a family or a peer, work, school, ward, or community group for assessment purposes, to see how clients could be responding to information and operating rules available there. In any situation, a social worker also tries to determine what clients are dealing with from their environments generally. Assessment of all these factors leads to intervention as a worker makes new information available to clients or helps them process available information differently. The reader may wish to use other theories of human functioning, such as ego psychology, to complement the assessment framework to be given here.

**Service Goals, Scope, and
Framework for Assessment**

Clients usually come to initial interviews with presenting problems that they themselves or others have already identified. When problems have been identified by others, such as a spouse, school principal, or court official, potential clients may need help to decide what they want to change if only to get others to stop bothering them. Some clients appear at social work settings with vague worries they have trouble pinning down. Or presenting problems sometimes turn out not to be clients' real main concerns, as when a woman reporting minor difficulties with her children later reveals that her marriage is falling apart. Whenever clients seem uncertain as to what they want service goals to be, a worker can offer an exploratory period to help them determine goals. In some cases a practitioner cannot agree to work toward clients' preferred goals because these could be destructive to the clients or others, because achievement of the goals is not feasible, or because the worker or his setting cannot offer the service needed. An example of a destructive goal would be that a teenager remain docile under authoritarian, punitive parenting. Such a goal would also be infeasible with an already rebellious adolescent. When new goals in a case of this kind indicated the need for family treatment, the worker might refer the case elsewhere if his own setting offered services only to adolescents or if professionals there had no training in family practice.

When a worker and one or more clients agree on final service goals, the worker can begin determining possible incremental goals and means toward these. His decisions about what incremental goals to plan and what means of service to suggest to clients require that he have some ideas of why their designated problems exist. The scope of an initial assessment depends on how much information is needed to determine what may be perpetuating problems. Sometimes data gathered in one interview may appear to explain clients' problems. A worker learns that an elderly woman is too crippled with arthritis to prepare her meals. Her financial resources are limited, and her relatives live far away. If there are no other problems with which the woman wants help, the worker may decide he probably knows enough, may ascertain that the woman would like to receive hot lunches from a "meals on wheels" program, and may make arrangements for this. In other cases, presenting problems are more complicated. A ten-year-old boy is truanting from school. Here the worker may need several interviews to review the boy's history or possible information from past experiences; his thoughts and feelings in the present; his intelligence; and his family, school, and neighborhood situations to determine possible causative factors. Engaging the boy and his family to provide these data for assessment may even be the worker's first incremental goal. Possible later goals, such as increasing the boy's self-esteem, freeing him from the position of family scapegoat, and engendering a teacher's interest in him would be intended eventually to decrease his truanting.

A worker's approach to initial assessment should always be flexible. He finds out as much as he thinks he needs in order to proceed, ascertains whether clients can agree with his recommendations about service means, makes some planned interventions, and observes the results. He then may or may not widen his scope of assessment. The elderly woman with arthritis should be followed up to see how the "meals on wheels" program works out. The woman may turn out to have problematic feelings about using the service which were not apparent earlier, or she may be doing fine. The judgment about how much assessment to do before beginning major intervention efforts is always an important one. Clients can be poorly served by inadequate assessment. They can also become discouraged or can terminate service prematurely when assessment drags on too long without much intervention to help them solve problems. As the worker continues to receive information from clients, of course, and tries to understand their functioning, he engages in assessment throughout any service period.

The major difficulty most workers have in assessment is in organizing their thinking, especially where clients' problems are complex. Social workers know that a person's past, what he thinks and feels in the present, and his ability to deal with reality must affect his functioning. They recognize that family and group members can influence each other's behavior, and that any human being must live within a larger environment. The question is how to put together and use these varied perspectives for assessment. Communication theory makes it possible to conceive of all influences on clients in terms of information and information processing.

First, if people behave in response to what they know of their thoughts, feelings, bodily sensations, memories, other people, and the nonhuman environment, then social workers must consider clients' possible information from these sources to assess their functioning. Clients' behavior must be consistent with some salient information on which they are operating. An unhappy, unfaithful wife may be dealing with conflicting information in the form of thoughts that her husband should be punished for not loving her and that she should be punished because she is angry with him. An apathetic elderly couple may be overwhelmed by the information that they have little money to meet their needs. Some mothers neglect their children because they have never been given sufficient information about how to parent. Members of a tenants' group may make unreasonable demands when they believe, inaccurately, that their landlord's willingness to negotiate is an exploitable weakness. After an assessment process, clients' difficulties can often be traced to the information on which they rely. Conversely, so may their strengths. When any of the above clients voluntarily seek help, a social worker may assume they have information based on past experience that other people can be helpful to them.

However, some clients have trouble at least partly because they cannot process constructive information available to them from a social worker or elsewhere. Some simply may not know how. The neglectful mother told by others how she should respond to her child's needs may first require explanations of how to perceive these needs or a demonstration of someone's sensitivity to her. Some clients encounter a block in processing particular information that conflicts with what they already believe, with their own rules for information processing, or with operating rules within their social groups. If the elderly couple learned in childhood that people should support themselves, and now reinforce each other's belief that this is so, they will tend to see financial assistance as charity. The woman who has extramarital affairs may not accept the social worker's interpretation that she does so out of anger toward her husband, if she has learned earlier not to recognize anger or if such recognition violates a tacit agreement between spouses. Members of a tenants' organization may not readily give up a long-held, perhaps socioculturally reinforced belief that an authority figure who offers to negotiate symmetrically is really willing to be one-down.

We conclude that *human beings are at risk when information on which they must base their functioning is insufficient, inaccurate, conflicting, or overwhelming, or when their capacities to process more constructive information are blocked.* Clients can struggle with problematic information or influences on their information processing at the individual, small-system, or larger environmental levels, as the next few pages will elaborate. In any real case situation, *several such difficulties may be combined and several areas of strengths may also be available.* By implication, given different information or use of information already available to them, clients will be able to function more capably.

Clients' bodily sensations or feelings alone can constitute overwhelming information, as in the case of pain or rage, and their feelings may certainly be conflicting. Sometimes thoughts combined with feelings are overwhelming, as when a client obsessively thinks about a situation in which he feels guilt. Clients' information already held can be insufficient for problem resolution—for instance, when a recently divorced woman does not know how to look for work. It can be inaccurate, internally conflicting, or conflicting with other available information: the divorced woman believes she is too unskilled to support herself, but realizes she must. Sometimes what a client lacks is sufficient awareness of his own strengths. However, clients' difficulties may also be compounded by the way they process particular information. A person's information about his internal states may be insufficient or inaccurate because he cannot consciously perceive his own feelings. Nor may he be able to process certain information available within his environment which could enhance his functioning, such as other people's genuine desire to help. His past learning about how to process information, whether about feelings, potentially one-up figures, or something else, may be at fault. Any person will of course weigh information from within himself against data from the outside world before he takes action, and his information processing may respond to operating rules within his present social systems as well as rules learned in the past. In some situations, clients' own information and information processing represent strengths, while external factors are troublesome.

A social worker should be aware that clients' small social systems may expose them to information that is insufficient, conflicting, inaccurate, overwhelming, or, on the other hand, especially useful. An unhappy husband may not really tell his wife how she can help him feel better, or may give mixed messages about what he wants. A group of teenagers may convince each other that they can behave illegally without being caught, or may put overwhelming pressures on one member to go along with such actions. Within any small system, members can make insufficient relationship information available to at least one member for that member to be able to function capably elsewhere. The continually one-down family or group member may not learn to take responsibility for his own behavior with others generally because he is not used to being symmetrical. The child encouraged to scapegoat a younger sibling may not acquire benign one-up skills to use with less competent peers in social groups outside the family. At times, however, information available to clients within social systems can represent an extremely useful resource, as when family or group members stand by to support each other.

Operating rules within small social systems to which clients belong are a major influence on their behavior in general and on their information processing. Some such rules are constructive, as when they allow family or group members to form relationships elsewhere but still appropriately to notice and meet each other's needs. Similarly, in healthy situations, system members can review new information, perhaps about changes taking place within individuals or the environment, that may conflict with system operating rules and lead to second-order system change. When operating rules do not allow such information processing, or the change that should follow from it, they have rigidified dysfunctionally. System members bound by dysfunctional operating rules may have inadequate information about how to change them, or they may be unable to process such information even if it is made available. Parents and an acting-out child can love each other and yet be unable to avoid destructive behavior cycles. They may or may not change when a social worker suggests other options. A small system such as a peer or work environment can also entrap its members with dysfunctional operating rules.

In coping with his larger environmental circumstances, a client may be helped by resources available. A veteran's pension can allow an emotionally disabled man to live adequately and maintain self-respect. Clients can also be handicapped by information from their environments that is insufficient, inaccurate, conflicting or overwhelming. A single parents' program may be unable to help potential members who badly need it, because it has not been properly publicized. Some books available on library shelves still imply that masturbation can cause insanity. Society presents peer groups of minority adolescents with contradictory information that they should stay in school but that no work is available to high school graduates. The family that has no money and is poorly housed will naturally feel overwhelmed. Institutions such as public education, subcultures, and society as a whole also influence the way people process information. Benignly, societies can help change citizens' perception of racial stereotypes by outlawing discriminatory labor practices. Other larger environmental influences on information processing are more problematic. An example is that men in our society have sometimes been discouraged from experiencing tender feelings.

In any actual case situation, as we have noted, assessment is limited by service goals. Clients often identify their problems within a fairly narrow range. They may have insufficient money, or marital but not financial problems. No worker has to assess the total functioning of clients whose service needs are validly circumscribed. But a worker should evaluate relevant information available to clients from various sources and, to the degree appropriate, clients' information processing as affected by their past learning, social systems, and the larger environment to see why they may be functioning as they are. We now offer guidelines for social work assessment at the individual and small system levels.

Assessing Individuals' Functioning

To assess any client's functioning, a social worker first gathers information about the client's difficulties, what circumstances surround these, and what areas of strength or potential resources exist. He may begin even before an initial interview by considering how an application is made out as well as what it says. He may talk with potential clients by telephone or read other professionals' reports about them. He notices clients' sex, approximate age, race, and general appearance, while they are still in a waiting room. To assess any individual's behavior, whether this client is seen alone or with others, the social worker will observe his interpersonal functioning in interviews. He will listen to a client tell about himself, his problems or need for service, his circumstances, and other information relevant to problem resolution. A client may explain his behavior by volunteering information he has on hand—for example, by commenting that he thought if he hit his daughter she would act better. The worker may also at some point speak to professionals who know the client or to the client's family, friends, or others. The more he learns from all of these sources, the better the worker can understand how this client functions, and in what context. He will also ascertain what resources of the client, of others, or of the worker and community might be brought to bear.

As he gleans data for assessment, the worker continuously tries to determine *information on which a client's functioning might be based,* where this may be contributing to problems and where it represents a strength. He carries out this aspect of assessment in three basic ways, and will check what he learns from each against the other for consistency. First and most simply, the worker asks questions about a client's actions at a given time. Sometimes he asks the client directly why he behaved as he did, hoping the client will expose information on which he was operating. For example, in response to a question a child may reveal that he does not study because his parents tell him studying is not important, or because he gets too hungry to concentrate. When a client cannot give reasons for his behavior, the worker can ask other exploratory questions. He can ask what thoughts went through a client's mind just before he took some action. The woman who shoplifts may have been thinking just before that her mother would really be hurt by her dishonesty. He can ask a client what was happening when certain behavior occurred. The man who gets headaches only when he is with his wife may be operating on some problematic information in terms of her behavior toward him or his feelings in response. A client who cannot answer a worker's questions directly may convey reasons for his behavior analogi-cally. A schizophrenic client, asked why he fears assertiveness, may begin speaking of how bombs kill people when they go off. He thereby suggests his idea that he may go too far if he lets any assertiveness escape.

A second way to try to understand a client's behavior is to determine more generally what information the client has available and to think about how it might be influencing him. The worker can consider each of a client's poten-tial information sources separately. He may assume that people have com-mon human needs for physical and emotional comfort, sexual fulfillment, assertion or mastery, positive connection with others, and self-esteem. These constitute part of the information with which every human being must find some way to cope. For example, a recently separated woman may have unmet needs for sexual fulfillment, positive connection with others, and self-esteem. A worker will evaluate whether she is dealing with these inappropri-ately, perhaps in a seductive relationship with her son, or more appropriately as through flirting at work, having friends, and feeling good about her ability to manage. Other information on which clients operate is stored in memory from their early, later, and recent past experiences. Clients can reveal such data in discussion, or the worker may infer them from hearing about the experiences. The client who has run into frequent job discrimination will most likely carry the expectation of encountering it again. The client who describes having been criticized by his parents may think the worker is criticizing him when he is not. Much information on which an individual acts is gleaned from his current environment, including his family and other social groups. In order to understand the possible ways in which the recently separated woman tries to meet her needs, the worker must evaluate what information representing stresses, supports, opportunities for coping, and so on her environment offers her. He can learn about these data from the client or from firsthand observation—for instance, seeing her at least once with her children.

A third approach to this aspect of assessment involves the use of practice theory, research, and the worker's own experience to infer information on which a client might be basing any questionable behavior. Consider the man who at a given time was more irritable with his child than seemed warranted. By asking questions, the worker might learn that the man had been put down at work earlier that day. Recognizing that the client thereby lost self-esteem and that his assertiveness was stifled, the worker could consider how these basic needs would be met. He might rule out the possibility that the man's past learning made him think the child's behavior more serious than it was, and would note other stresses of his environment. But the worker would also bring in practice theory and experience suggesting that exaggerated affects in one situation have often been carried over from another. Thus he might finally speculate that the client's anger and self-aggrandizement with his child stemmed mainly from what had happened at work. Even if the worker started out hearing only about the exaggerated irritability, he could then have considered whether some other aggravation had been transferred onto it. We note that in this, as in many case situations, the problem with the client's available information was not that he had feelings or basic needs to deal with, but that he did not know how to deal with them more constructively. We will comment later on implications for intervention when information on which clients are operating seems inadequate for problem resolution.

As a final task in assessment generally, a worker will evaluate *any client's ability to process content and relationship information.* When a client describes his problems and circumstances, a worker routinely considers what the client seems to perceive and think as well as the behavior that follows. He may ask questions about the client's perceptions and thoughts. Within interviews, the worker should be aware of a client's ability (or inability) to recognize his own feelings and aspects of reality important to him, to think before acting, and to act appropriately. Above all, the worker will notice what happens when he or others, such as family members, expose the client to new information which should be useful to him. The client may hear what is said or appreciate an environmental modification, and use the new information to enhance his functioning. However, most clients at some time block in processing some new content or relationship information, even if only temporarily. The worker who cannot evaluate such problems cannot help clients with them. He will be unable to deal constructively with blocked communication between himself and a client or between clients in a group or family interview. Further assessment therefore becomes crucial here.

Client blocks in information processing can be widespread, pertaining, for example, to all conscious awareness of feelings. Or they can be specific, as when a client cannot receive one interpretation from a social worker. Either difficulty can stem from a client's inadequate knowledge of how to process information given or from conflicts between this and information or rules for information processing which the client already holds. Some people with poor awareness of their feelings may never have learned how to notice them. For others, the possibility of such awareness conflicts with a belief that those who have certain feelings are bad. One client may not follow a worker's language when he makes an interpretation. For another, the content of the interpretation disagrees with a treasured perception of himself. In any such instance, clients may or may not be aware of what information or rules for processing it are influencing them.

Where information offered by a social worker or others is not conflictual, however, clients who have trouble dealing with it can be helped fairly readily to overcome the difficulty. Some clients do become aware of their feelings when the social worker suggests how to recognize them. Some can notice a spouse's moods when they begin to see the need. Some can learn to think through what will happen if they pursue given actions, or consciously to evaluate information on which they are basing their behavior. Many clients who take a largely one-down or one-up relationship stance with a social worker show ability to process at least some new relationship information when the worker asks them to. For example, a lower-class client may insist on being one-down by calling the worker "sir" and requesting advice on many matters. Yet he may well be capable of giving one piece of advice to the worker: namely, to suggest what seems useful to talk about and what does not, thereby taking a more symmetrical stance. A male client with a female worker may vehemently assert his right to think and do as he pleases, but still allow himself to be one-down in utilizing information given by the worker.

If clients show continued inability to process information offered by a social worker or others, blocks may be due to the conflict-arousing nature of the information offered. The conflicts can range from superficial to intense. A client may reject the implication of a social worker's questions—that discussion of a certain matter will help him solve his problem—because discussing the problem with a friend did not help. He may reject reassurance offered by a worker or another family member because he knows something with which the idea of reassurance conflicts. For example, a man is not easily reassured about having been late to a session if he knows he really did not want to come. The client who draws on experience with grade school teachers to determine what relationship stance to take with a social worker may see the worker as one-up and himself as one-down, at least for a while, no matter what the worker's words or behavior suggest. The client who has learned he must be one-up with others as a cultural prescription for his age and sex role can stubbornly insist on being one-up to his wife, although she is struggling in a fairly benign fashion to achieve symmetry. The client whose symptoms, passivity, or helplessness continue to control the worker by putting him into an unwanted one-up position may fear rejection should he respond to the worker's indications that their relationship could be more flexible.

Most clients show occasional problems in processing both content and relationship information. Discrimination between the two can be difficult, that is, a client's disinclination to process particular communication may be a response either to content information put forth by the worker or others, to a proposed relationship stance, or to both. A worker must evaluate repetitiveness of client behavior to see whether blocking is usually evoked by given content information, no matter what relationship stances are taken in regard to it, or by given relationship stances, no matter what the content of discussion. A client may respond positively to the worker's giving new information, a mainly one-up stance, except when his handling of sexuality is discussed. One may then assume that the worker's ideas that sexual feelings are acceptable and can be discussed conflict with what the client believes about one or both of these matters. Another client may insist on guiding discussion, no matter what the content, ignoring any of the social worker's suggestions and otherwise being one-up to the worker at most times. The worker may then hypothesize that a one-down relationship stance connotes vulnerability, weakness, femininity, or some other state incompatible with the client's preferred vision of himself.

Some of clients' conflicts about processing particular content or relationship information stem from their information or rules for information processing learned at a much earlier time. The individual whose parents and relatives taught him that minority groups wish to take over his neighborhood will not listen to rational arguments to the contrary. A woman may not stop hitting her teenaged daughter, even though she recognizes the destructiveness of the behavior, if information stored from her own experience is that adolescent girls may lose control of their sexuality. Earlier learning that took place analogically or by trial and error may be especially hard to displace, because the knowledge involved cannot readily be put into words. People sometimes have stored in memory not only given information but also proscriptions against revealing or updating it. The experience with some kinds of earlier information may have seemed so dangerous, due to the person's own or others' reaction to it, that receipt of any new information in these areas is prohibited. The social worker whose clients cannot expose conflicts between old and newly offered information sometimes infers these conflicts from his general knowledge of a client, from his awareness of symbolism in the client's communications, or from his understanding of personality dynamics. When an obsessive client cannot talk about his dying parent, the worker infers that the idea of doing so may conflict with a fear that the client will break down and reveal ambivalent feelings. Though the client does not say this directly, he tends to be overcontrolled. He tells how his son talked to a teacher about the matter and began crying in class. And the worker knows as part of his professional theory base that fear of loss of control and ambivalence would be typical in obsessive-compulsive neurosis.

Difficulties in processing information offered by a social worker or others may also reflect conflicts between this information or method of information processing and that which exists within the client's family, peer group, other significant social system such as a hospital ward, or larger environment. The adolescent whose parents make separation from them seem dangerous often cannot hear a social worker's assurance that it is not. Neither may the same client be able to achieve symmetry with the worker if every symmetrical move at home is disconfirmed. The client whose peers beat him up will not believe that anger need not hurt others. The man whose cultural group sustains his being·complementary one-up with women will have difficulty accepting another stance with a female social worker. Clients may be unaware of conflicts that involve system operating rules, since learning within the system has often been analogic or by trial and error. To achieve some understanding of possible external influences, a worker has the options of exploring with the client his difficulties in processing information or of observing relevant social systems or the environment to evaluate their impact on the client firsthand.

Assessing Small System Functioning

Social workers may be said to assess small system functioning whenever they use what they know about an individual to make inferences about his family or other social groups. Other professionals and collaterals may also tell a worker about social systems to which clients belong. Yet the worker will often wish to supplement these data with direct evaluation of a family, set of peers, group led by another professional, school, work or treatment program, or community association. He must also attend to emergent system functioning when he forms groups of clients for therapeutic or social action purposes. In any of these instances, a worker should consider whether information exchanged by system members is useful or problematic for their functioning generally. He should also assess the nature of system operating rules shown in his presence and, if appropriate, the system's openness to needed second-order change. He will keep in mind that any system is influenced by its environment and by members' different needs, information processing, and exposure to influences from outside the system. A worker must be aware of individuals' idiosyncratic problems, with which they may need extra help; and of their constructive information or rules for information processing, which he may ask them to share with others. We consider it essential that the worker who sees a group or family be aware of relevant individual and larger environmental circumstances, and of how his own presence may affect observed system functioning. The following discussion assumes such awareness.

First, a worker can assess *information available to members within any family or group* by taking note of what happens in the system and by asking members what they learn from each other there. For groups which meet only in his presence, such as some community associations and most treatment groups, the worker can himself evaluate members' exchanges of content and relationship information. He may also ask how a given individual has interpreted such exchanges, what has occurred in a waiting room or in other contacts between members away from the group. Members of families and other natural groups exchange much more information away from the worker than with him, and they are not always willing to reveal significant things that happened outside the office. In the worker's presence they will usually put forth information regarding problems for which help was sought. In all such interchanges, the worker should distinguish which of the information available to clients within the family or group is inaccurate, insufficient, or otherwise inadequate for problem resolution, and which of it represents a resource for positive change. When several members of a treatment group suggest that another will easily find a job, the worker must consider whether this information is useful or inaccurate. In a family session, a mother who says her son inherited his nasty disposition from his father reveals inaccurate information on which family members may be operating. Members of a family who allow a child greater symmetry than other adults will, are giving him insufficient information about how to behave in the external world. Schizophrenic patients in a ward group may act especially bizarre when someone mentions discharge planning, suggesting that this prospect is overwhelming or difficult for them to assimilate. But a member of the ward group who can talk about his frightened feelings, thus letting others know that these can be faced, provides positive information.

The worker's second major task is to assess *family or group operating rules*, especially when these may otherwise impede clients' efforts to cope. Throughout contact with any group he has formed, the worker must clearly understand how members' allowable discussion content, behavior generally, and relationship stances will be likely to affect their movement toward service goals. With a family or other natural group, the worker must consider existing operating rules before he decides how to intervene. To assess any social system on behalf of one member, the worker will see how operating rules affect this individual's functioning. He relies heavily on his own observations of communication patterns within a system to infer members' operating rules. He can query members about these. For example, the worker asks a child whether he can tell his mother when his feelings are hurt, but the worker should also notice whether the child behaves in line with what he has said. Since assessment of system operating rules can be highly important for intervention, we will consider guidelines for this process in some detail.

By simply seeing what goes on within a family or group, the worker infers that this discussion content or behavior generally is allowable. If a father notices and criticizes a mother's dress, unless the marriage is breaking up, he apparently is not enjoined from doing so. If group members discuss their feelings about a group leader or laugh together, then system operating rules apparently permit these actions. Less clear are proscribed perceptions, thinking, and behavior. People are sometimes allowed to say only good or bad things about one system member. They may have to see everyone outside the family or group as untrustworthy, may never discuss sexual matters, or may not recognize system members' differing opinions on important matters. The worker wonders whether proscriptions exist when he notices an absence of expectable behaviors in response to individuals, the environment, or the system itself. For example, if a couple in marital counseling never mention their major religious differences, these may be something they cannot discuss together. If members of a children's recreation group do not respond when one of them is reported to be seriously ill, the worker may wonder whether group operating rules do not permit tears or discussion of feelings. Of considerable interest are rules governing family or group members' communication. The worker may notice whether people can be clear with each other, whether they can metacommunicate, and, if so, whether they can do so in some but not all areas of discussion. He will also ascertain whether they can accept or reject each other's words and actions, or can remain neutral, as opposed to giving frequent responses that are either ambiguous or disconfirming.

System operating rules are most apparent when someone tries to break them and members react by invoking homeostatic mechanisms.[1] Undisturbed by unusual outside influences, members' behavior or communication within any system tends to follow repetitive sequences of events. Whenever members of a given family become too close, they start to fight, but after a certain amount of fighting they will again become close, and so on. Homeostasis is maintained by the shift in behavior at the crucial time, with an inferred operating rule that too much closeness and too much fighting are undesirable. The worker trying to discern operating rules may note when shifts occur in system members' behavior. Especially when these shifts bring closure to some immediately preceding behavior, or when they move members away from behavior which seems incomplete, the behavior in question may have neared everyone's capacity for tolerance. Homeostatic mechanisms are frequently nonverbal. A daughter stops talking about negatives in the family when her mother catches her eye, or one client in a therapy group touches a friend's arm when the friend starts to fall asleep. The worker may then infer the presumed operating rule such a mechanism enforces. Finally, he can deduce operating rules from the way system members respond to things he does that would violate the rules. If a couple has not mentioned its religious differences and his questions on this content are met by silence and subject changes, the worker is assured that it is out of bounds.

To determine what operating rules govern system members' relationship stances, the worker looks at what exists, considers what might be expected to exist but does not, and notices whether homeostatic mechanisms are invoked when he or someone else proposes change. He may begin by trying to identify who is one-up, one-down, or symmetrical with whom in what areas; who forms coalitions with whom under what circumstances; and what pecking orders are apparent at different times. Any family or group member can propose himself one-up by being the first to choose a seat in a session, unless he simply has arrived first or has been told by someone else where to sit. He can also be one-up by such maneuvers as taking initiative within given areas of conversation, offering to others his greater knowledge about some content, and the like. More subtly, a one-up family or group member sits back and lets others talk but then regulates interaction by a word or glance. System members define themselves as one-down when they ask for or follow directions, do not initiate particular discussion or action, or agree with those who do. Symmetry is demonstrated mainly in interaction. Two or more parties can laugh together, share tasks, or participate in an escalation in which each proposes himself one-up or one-down such that everyone competes. To exemplify competition to be one-down, two children argue about who needs help with homework more. Coalitions may be fairly obvious in seating arrangements if family or group members choose where to sit, and in who agrees with or supports whom in a given conversation. Or those in coalition may simply cooperate in presenting a point of view, as when the women in a family deftly take turns revealing males' inadequacy. The reader may recall that coalitions can be symmetrical if partners fairly equal in power band together, or complementary if one is protecting or mistreating another who remains allied with him. Pecking orders are often apparent between siblings and in groups of contemporaries, although coalitions within pecking orders can also exist.

As he observes system members' existing relationship communication in different content areas, the worker begins to infer possible relationship operating rules. If the father makes decisions about the family's financial situation but the parents cooperate in disciplining the children, father's one-up stance about money and parents' symmetry with each about discipline are apparently prescribed. The worker may also infer relationship operating rules from the absence of expectable relationship behavior or from members' homeostatic reactions to deviations from a norm. One expects parents to be symmetrical with each other, and one-up to children, in many areas of functioning. One hopes that group leaders will share their power impartially with members lower in the pecking order. That is, the worker ultimately seeks age-appropriate flexibility in family or group members' relationship stances; and parents' ability to form a coalition that will make generational boundaries clear.[2] Also in a well-functioning system, members' proportion of accepting responses to others' relationship communication will be high, with less rejection and certainly less disconfirmation or other ambiguous responses. When such hoped-for or expected behaviors do not occur, the worker may wonder whether system operating rules preclude them. He can again check out the possibility by seeing whether system members invoke homeostatic mechanisms when the behavior in question seems likely to occur. For example, if one group member challenges a leader's autocratic decision-making, others will homeostatically shift in their chairs or join to put down the challenger.

Once a social worker has begun to identify system operating rules, he will assess *how these rules affect members' available information and information processing.* Do existing rules dysfunctionally limit what family or group members know about themselves or their environment, or their abilities to perceive, evaluate, and react adaptively to such information? Sometimes they do not, and the real problem is the adequacy of information available to members. A family needing concrete help or a group organized to accomplish social action may simply need information. Sometimes operating rules within a small system seem constricted when contact with a social worker starts, but show signs of moderating as family or other natural group members get to know the worker better or as formed group members accommodate to the worker-client system-to-be.[3] But operating rules within a family or group can be clearly dysfunctional. If a family operating rule supports continued disconfirmation of one member, this disconfirmed individual may have inaccurate information about how he comes across in relationships. Conversely, the disconfirming members may not learn to perceive and respond to others' needs. If an operating rule within a community group is that no one disagree, members may exchange insufficient information about how to solve problems facing them.

A social worker may infer the dysfunctional nature of system operating rules when members are unhappy with the status quo, show symptoms of emotional distress, or are unable to cope with their environment. Even if not all family or group members are distressed, those who are may be unable to change unless operating rules within the system change to permit their altered functioning. When the symptomatic behavior of one member is incorporated in family or group communication patterning, homeostatic mechanisms can be invoked if he tries to change. The question of whether interaction that is dysfunctional for one must be dysfunctional for all cannot be debated here. Social workers who see families hope to help everyone benefit from any rule changes. Those who see groups usually prefer trying to change group norms rather than, for example, removing individuals who have become scapegoated. The rationale in both instances is that dysfunctional operating rules will sooner or later impede everyone's coping efforts, by restricting their individual growth and individual or collective ability to deal with the environment. In communications terms, people will often find it difficult to change their ways of processing information unless there is second-order change within the small systems to which they belong.

If system operating rules are dysfunctional to members, a social worker must try to ascertain whether the rules are open or impervious to change. One indicator is how the system has so far responded to information from members or the environment. Some system operating rules persist unchanged in response to considerable new information suggesting their modification. A late adolescent impelled toward adulthood by physical and social forces is still one-down in family decisions about how his life should be run. Members of a community group participate in symmetrical escalations about who will make a major political decision, as the time to implement any decision runs out. Behavior which probably once met individual needs as well as serving a useful function in system maintenance may persist beyond its utility. For example, a wife may continue to protect her husband from the noise of the children, although the children are becoming a handful and father and children would like to become closer.

Just as some individuals cannot process constructive new information because they do not know how, some families and groups may have dysfunctional operating rules partly because members simply do not know how to perceive, think, or act differently. The man unaware of how to perceive his own affects, or unable to think through alternatives before acting, often belongs to a small social system whose operating rules condone such information processing. The woman who does not discipline her child may belong to a family in which neither parent knows how to take a clear one-up stance. The family or group unaware of how to change their dysfunctional operating rules can often accord the social worker his flexible and sometimes one-up relationship stance as expert, and can respond to his suggestions for change. A newly married couple who have not known how to metacommunicate about differences may readily learn this skill from a social worker. Where a man's failure to think through actions is condoned by his peer group, the social worker may teach the group to think through things together. Parents may accept the worker's advice to take a firmer one-up stance in disciplining their children. A community group may eagerly learn how to notice and fight for civil rights denied them.

Family or group members' conflicts about changing their operating rules become obvious when a worker tries to offer constructive information about this possibility and meets with inertia or overt opposition. He asks questions about a forbidden content area and explains to family or group members why this is important to consider, but operating rules forbidding such discussion remain. He comments that parents are having difficulty getting along, but the family cannot assimilate this new perception. He proposes greater symmetry within a peer or therapy group, but group leaders do not allow more democratic participation by their followers. System operating rules which resist change in spite of a worker's efforts may reflect individuals' conflicts about processing the content or relationship information in question. Such conflicts, as in practice with individuals, may be more or less intense. But with families and groups, conflicts evoked are often shared by at least a few of the system members. When a worker suggests examining parents' marital problems, all members of the family can object. The individual or individuals who originally believed that the marriage might fall apart under scrutiny, or whatever is the family's specific fear, would probably have conveyed this to others through nonverbal behavior suggesting danger whenever the subject threatened to come up.

This chapter has suggested a communications framework for assessment, along with some specific guidelines for assessing individual and small system functioning. A social worker may begin assessment at the level of an individual client, a small social system, or the larger environment as when he examines community provisions for some population at risk. In many case situations he will end up assessing all three. If the worker proceeds along the guidelines suggested above, his assessment should lead to intervention, an activity which subsequent chapters of this volume will elaborate. But on what system level should a social worker begin to intervene? That is, should he work with an individual, a family, a group, or the larger environment? To begin to clarify assessment-intervention links in a communications framework for practice, let us briefly address this issue here.

Deciding Where to Intervene

When clients suffer from insufficient, inaccurate, conflicting, or overwhelming information, a social worker will first seek to make more constructive information available to them. He may intervene in the larger environment when information available to clients there is inadequate for their physical and emotional well-being, especially when he cannot readily help clients make such changes on their own behalf. He may intervene in clients' small social systems for similar reasons, or when members of a family or group lack information for solving problems between themselves or problems that all share. Ironically, when potential clients suffer from inadequacies of available information rather than difficulty in information processing, it may make little difference whether the worker chooses to give new information on the individual, family, group, or even community level. Multiple client sessions will reach more people, but clients helped individually are also likely to share their new knowledge with others, whether it concerns community resources or the handling of interpersonal conflicts.

Even where the problem has to do with clients' information processing or operating rules, a social worker can readily help an individual, a family, or a group if there is no serious blocking involved. An individual client may share with others his newly acquired skills at perceiving and evaluating information. Both members of an elderly couple can learn from a social worker to face their feelings about aging, but either member given such help may also help the other. The member of a community group enabled to change some of its dysfunctional operating rules may change similar rules in another of his social groups.

It is when clients block in processing needed information because this seriously conflicts with what they already believe, with their rules for information processing or with their small system operating rules, that the worker must most carefully consider where to intervene. Yet he often cannot assess such blocks until the intervention process has already begun—until he has tried some interventions and observed the response. Consider the mother in a one-parent family who behaves seductively toward her son until her two daughters create a diversion, then engages punitively with them while the son drifts toward outside relationships, then reacts to his drift by becoming seductive once more. Each party's behavior responds to and triggers the behavior of others, with no real beginning or ending point. Are all four family members finding some expression of their needs for closeness, sexuality, and perhaps anger in this sequence? Possibly. Is the system influenced by larger environmental information, namely the scarcity of males available for dating in the mother's age range? Quite likely. And so on. Yet the social worker really will not know how much individual, system, and larger societal factors influence the behaviors under observation until he tries to intervene and observes the result. He can see this mother alone, try to talk with her about dating, help her resolve conflicts about discussing dating, and then find that her children create crises preventing her dating at all. On the other hand, if he starts by seeing the whole family and talks there about the mother's possible dating, she may be the only one with an information processing block. A worker can try to assess such factors in an intake interview, but he cannot always do so successfully.

At any point, the individual client who seems unable to perceive, think, or act differently because of operating rules within one of his social systems may need the worker to intervene within the system, unless he can and should be helped to leave it. Similarly, one system member unable to change his ways of information processing, perhaps because of past learning, may prevent second-order change which others need and desire. The worker should consider helping this client individually, whether in other system members' presence or alone. Larger environmental circumstances may also block clients' abilities to process information differently at the individual or small system levels. The worker cannot ignore a client's overwhelming life circumstances—for example, asking a woman to perceive her children's needs while no one perceives and meets hers—without doing harm.

A significant factor in deciding where to intervene must be the accessibility of the individual, small system, or larger environment to change. Social workers cannot always modify clients' environments, families, or social groups. Nor can they always reach individuals who are harming other social system members or even the larger environment, as through crime. However, social workers have sometimes underestimated the accessibility of individuals, families, groups and even the larger environment to change, when what was really lacking was their own knowledge about how to bring about change. We shall now examine possibilities for intervention with individuals, families, groups, and finally with other professionals.

Five   Interventions with Individual Clients

Throughout any service period a social worker and client are exchanging information, thereby influencing each other. The worker seeks to control such influence by continually assessing client functioning and by planning what he does in response. The worker's interventions should gather data for assessment as well as providing useful information to a client over time. They must be attuned to what the client will be able to accept, and yet help him move toward service goals. Interventions should suggest constructive worker-client system operating rules, which may change over time.

The present chapter examines basic social work interventions to see how these offer content and relationship information to clients, and to spell out implicit assessment-intervention links. Content and relationship aspects of intervention have been arbitrarily separated for discussion purposes. The interventions to be described can help a client whose information for problem-solving is inadequate; they can enable clients to process information differently for second-order individual change; and they can affect operating rules which govern worker-client interaction itself. A worker uses variations of these same interventions to deal with potential communication blocks between himself and clients and to affect change with families, groups, and other professionals, as subsequent chapters will elaborate.

Content Level Interventions with Individuals

Social work interventions which offer clients information on the content level are of four major types: eliciting information, giving evaluative feedback, offering new information, and attempting to change information available to clients from their environment or from the context in which worker and client meet.

To *elicit information* from clients, a worker uses questions, restatements of what the client has said, comments indicating that further information would be useful, nonverbal expressions of attentiveness or inquiry, and encouragement for clients who are speaking, such as an "Uh huh" or a smile. As a worker elicits information for assessment purposes, he must give information to the client as well. By his direct questions, the worker suggests what he thinks may follow from a client's prior revelations. His questions also imply that certain things the client is saying about himself or his situation may be related to his need for help. By asking about a woman's marriage when she has been describing her problem child, the worker implies some connection between the two. He also proposes an operating rule allowing such content to be discussed. Whenever he encourages a client to continue talking about given content, the worker validates its importance as a discussion topic.

Some of a worker's questions are designated as much to reveal something to the client as to learn something from or about him. A worker asks a man whether he might be envious of a friend to draw the man's attention to his possible feelings. Or, in asking a series of questions, a worker wants to gather information but also to stimulate the client's review of material which had lain dormant in memory. The student frightened about starting college remembers, while telling his story to a social worker, that he felt the same way before his successful high school career. As a client tries to convey what he knows about himself and his situation in orderly fashion, he may also see interrelationships between facts he had not noticed before. Thoughts put into words have a certain immediacy, perhaps because they now exist apart from the speaker and so can be subjected more easily to his own feedback processes. The mother who describes that her hyperactive son was doing fine until she went to the hospital, begins to realize that the boy had a reason to react as he did.

A social worker's eliciting of information can contribute to changes in a client's information processing. By the way he elicits, a worker suggests that he too needs data as a basis for action and that one may use various verbal and nonverbal means to generate information. By being attentive, thinking, and coming back with further questions or comments, he demonstrates how he processes information himself, allowing the client to learn these skills analogically. He may also consciously stimulate a client's information processing by asking questions which direct the client to examine his own perception, thinking, or translation of information into action. Thus a worker may ask what a client felt, what he noticed about a given situation, how he decided on a course of action, and the like. In so doing he suggests both that people have reasons for their actions and that the client is capable of figuring out his own.

Eliciting information for any purpose must be guided by the worker's assessment of a client's functioning. Since information implicit in his questions can be troubling to a client, a worker should weigh his need for assessment data against the client's possible distress in response to his questions. Thus a worker may not ask about other problems if a client seems overwhelmed by one he already has. Before giving information by means of questions, the worker should assess the client's likely ability to benefit from the information or help with information processing to be offered. If his questions will suggest to a client that he might be envious of a friend, the worker should believe that this information will be more accurate and constructive than some other that the client has, such as the idea that he must be crazy to feel negatively about his friend's good fortune. When he asks a client what made him act as he did, the worker must believe his answer will give the client more accurate information about himself, will help him process information differently to enhance his functioning, or at the very least will not do any harm.

As a second type of content-level intervention, social workers give *evaluative feedback* to clients on information they already possess or on their information processing. Techniques used here are always in response to client communication. Feedback intended to be positive includes such behaviors as nodding, looking pleased, saying, "I agree," or "That's true." These range from almost neutral acceptance of what a client has said or done, to strong affirmation that the information he possesses is accurate and useful or that he is perceiving, thinking, or acting appropriately. Another technique, intended negative feedback, rejects the client's content information or information processing with verbal expressions such as, "I don't think that's accurate," or nonverbally, perhaps by a frown. Again the strength of the rejection represents a range. This begins with mild questioning, as in, "Does it work that way?" Stronger is the expression of doubt, such as, "I'm not sure it works that way." Or the worker can imply certainty: "It doesn't work that way." While social workers can respond neutrally to client communication at times—for example, saying "Mmmmm" or simply listening—clients may interpret especially long periods of neutrality as indicating indifference.

A worker can also give evaluative feedback via selective response. Here he picks up part of the client's information or information processing for affirmation and provides neutral or negative feedback on the rest. If a client says he will either spank his child or talk to him, the worker comments that talking to him sounds like a good idea. A worker can accept part of a client's information processing, as when he says, "I think it's progress that you recognized you were getting mad and tried to control yourself, even if you couldn't fully manage it this time." He can respond positively to a client's information but negatively to the way he has processed it, particularly if expressed in inappropriate behavior. Thus a worker might say, "Your husband shouldn't have lied to you, but hurting Johnny doesn't sound like a very good way to get back at him."

All of these types of feedback help a client sort through his own information and examine his information processing to decide where he may have greater confidence in what he knows, what he may wish to discard, or how to put together the whole more effectively. When clients seek help, they often do not know which of their existing information is insufficient, inaccurate, or otherwise problematic and which can be used as is. Following appropriate assessment, the social worker can share his opinions on these matters. When a client thinks he is weak for wanting help, the worker who has heard him out may selectively accept his feelings of discomfort, reject his inaccurate interpretation of these feelings, and validate more strongly his ability to discuss them. The worker remains neutral when he has too little understanding of a client's information or information processing to know where these are constructive, and perhaps when he feels a client can evaluate his own information to reach accurate conclusions. However, the client who can gain confidence in an actually valid piece of information, such as his good understanding of happenings at his job, can often use this more effectively. Finding out that some of his information or information processing may be problematic can move a client to examine it and possibly to reject or replace it. In fact, a worker's offering varied evaluative feedback implies that the client has strengths, as well as limitations which can be changed. If the client begins to see how the worker evaluates the difference, he has also picked up this information processing skill. A related benefit is that clients can learn from a worker about people's possible range of responses to others' communication content. The worker's use of such interventions also suggest an operating rule, that he can comment evaluatively about what a client does.

A third type of content intervention consists of social workers' efforts to convey *new information* to clients, including new ideas about information processing which clients might find useful. Most such efforts involve verbal discussion, though social workers sometimes consciously use analogic communication to convey new content—demonstrating through role play, for instance, how a client or someone else might act. In either instance data offered may be substantive, as in the statement, "Lots of kids are afraid to go to camp." Or it may be inferential, as in, "You might be afraid to go to camp." Such interventions can carry content about the world at large, the worker's setting and how service is given there, the interpersonal environment bearing on the client, or the client himself, including his basic needs, information stored in memory, or information processing. The worker's giving of information about the worker-client encounter is a verbal expression of relationship information to be considered below.

A large proportion of social workers' content level interventions are essentially information giving. Workers in almost any type of practice tell their clients about community resources. They are certainly obligated to convey what services their own settings can and cannot provide. There is probably no content area in which workers have more expertise than that of people's interpersonal functioning. For example, a worker may tell a parent how other parents have found it useful to deal with their handicapped children. He may offer a client insight into why people in his family, peer group, or work setting treat him as they do. A community worker may advise a client how to calm fears of others in a social action group. To help a client deal with his own needs more effectively, a worker may also give him information directly applicable to himself. He may tell a client how other people often feel in circumstances similar to those of the client. Or a worker may offer interpretations of possible reasons for a client's behavior. To give a client new information about how to process information, a worker may suggest that the client think about what he is feeling before taking action. What a client in any circumstance sometimes needs most is time and space to talk about his problems and figure out answers for himself. This a worker can give too, serving mainly as a sounding board.

Parenthetically, a worker can usefully combine the intervention of information giving with elicitation or evaluative feedback. Concerned that a client will not understand information implied by his asking certain perhaps threatening questions, a worker can explain why he is asking them. To prevent a client's misunderstanding his neutrality, a worker can say why he is waiting to comment about what the client has said or done, perhaps because he needs a fuller picture of what is going on. When a worker believes he must reject client communication, he can give the reason which would presumably make the client want to reject it as well. The statement, "I don't agree with you, since it seems to me that threats just make your landlord more stubborn," rejects the client's plan of action but at least gives a reason for rejecting it. All such explanations work best if the reasons the worker gives seem valid to the client as well. But even if a client believes that the worker sees his reasons as valid, the client should have less difficulty accepting what the worker says. The worker's explanation also suggests an operating rule: that worker and client may metacommunicate about, or discuss reasons for, their behavior in interviews.

Any social worker's efforts to convey new content information are based on his assessment of clients' already available information and information processing. When a client has insufficient or inaccurate information for problem solving, the worker may offer new data to make up the deficiency. The client who does not know how to get public aid is told how. If a client's information on hand is conflicting, a worker may suggest that he evaluate the conflict against all else that he knows and may provide additional information during the process. Thus when a client wants something which will get him into trouble, the worker could tell him that weighing the pros and cons might be wise; later, if needed, he could suggest a compromise. The client overwhelmed with information may first need assurance that the social worker will help to limit it. For example, a mother with several small children and few environmental supports may need to know that the worker can send some of her children to camp. A worker can often convey new information that will help a client process information differently. A young adolescent might be helped to recognize his burgeoning sense of unrest as normal sexuality, so that he can begin to deal with it. In all these instances, by offering content information the worker proposes an operating rule that this content should be allowable as a part of worker-client communication.

A fourth type of intervention occurs when a social worker tries to *change environmental information* available to a client by intervening either in his external circumstances or in the context in which worker and client meet. Interventions into clients' external circumstances include contact with public welfare, hospitals, and other community resources to enable as constructive a flow of information as possible from these to clients. Interventions with family members, employers, teachers, doctors, and so on may also help clients receive needed information from these sources. The environmental intervention of working with a small system to which a client belongs, especially the family, can affect the client's information processing by changing system operating rules. A worker bases all interventions into a client's environment on his assessment that the client is receiving overwhelming, conflicting, inaccurate, or insufficient information there and that he cannot easily deal with these deficiencies without the worker's active help. For example, where a child receives insufficient love from his family, a social worker will usually try to help the family provide more love. Of course, collaterals can become clients and in any case may respond to the same type of worker interventions we have begun to outline here. Whenever a worker intervenes environmentally on a client's behalf, he proposes an operating rule that he may not only talk but also take action for the client involved.

Another sort of environmental intervention is a worker's modifying of the context in which he and a client meet. The worker who sees a client individually encourages him to participate in a treatment or social action group, perhaps to obtain more information than the worker can give about how to get along with peers or to change his community. Or he recommends that family treatment sessions be held. Workers can also change the context of worker-client interaction by the use of play, activities such as games or going for a walk together, or by meeting in a client's home rather than in an office. All such interventions may be carried out for assessment purposes: to elicit different types of information from a client or to see how he processes information in a variety of situations. They can convey new content, hopefully in line with what a client needs and can use, such as that he does not have to solve family problems alone. Besides their possible impact on operating rules within small systems to which clients belong, such interventions can affect a client's information processing in other ways. For example, a child's realizing that he has beaten the social worker at a game can help him perceive more clearly his real competence at dealing with others.

Having considered content level interventions of eliciting information, offering evaluative feedback, giving new information, and changing environmental information available to clients, let us look at how workers can use these together to give clients information over a period of time.

Using Interventions to Give Content Information

People are most likely to accept new information slightly but not greatly different from their own.[1] If, in using interventions, a worker does not give new information incrementally enough, clients can reject it, misunderstand it, or become overwhelmed with it. For example, a client is unlikely to agree with a worker's gross assertion that his reasons for feeling guilty are invalid. But he may reach this conclusion if each reason is explored and considered separately. New information can be given too slowly, too, in which case a client's boredom or restlessness may be obvious.

To see how a social worker can intervene to give content information incrementally, let us analyze one aspect of a case example over time. Bill, a fifteen-year-old boy seen in a public school setting, has academic difficulties after his parents have separated. The worker is a middle-aged woman. The case eventually involves the worker and Bill looking at his circumstances, deciding to meet, clarifying his feelings about the separation, and discussing his peer relationships; the worker's intervening environmentally to obtain tutoring; and, of course, ongoing worker-client relationship communication. We will consider interview process in just one content area, that of Bill's feelings about the separation, to see how worker interventions in this area gave helpful information over a period of seven sessions. The pair's content operating rules also change over time, and the worker gears her interventions to ongoing assessment of the client's functioning.

> While gathering information during the first interview, I asked Bill about his family, and learned that his parents were recently separated. When I wondered how that was for him, he looked embarrassed and said, "Not too bad." Later I commented that when someone had been doing well in school, as he had, and then changed, there were usually reasons for it. I doubted if he had suddenly got "lazy" (his explanation). He might be reacting to his home situation, as many people would, or to something else we didn't know about yet. When he didn't comment, I asked if he would like to return and talk about it more. After some further discussion, he agreed.

In this excerpt of process recording from the first interview, the worker elicits Bill's feelings about his parents' separation partly for assessment purposes. She knows from experience that his feelings may constitute overwhelming or conflicting information for Bill, and that he may be having trouble processing them. Further, Bill may hold the inaccurate information that he is bad or crazy to have the feelings he does. The worker does not yet share these insights with the client. She is not sure exactly what he is feeling and whether it is problematic, not sure he would understand her ideas nor whether he would find this new information constructive or more overwhelming still.

However, even in her brief comments, the worker has given Bill a small amount of very constructive new information about any feelings he may have. When she open-endedly wonders how the separation "was for him," she implies that it would be all right if he did have any feelings and that he could discuss these with her. Her opening up the topic suggests a possible operating rule that content about the separation and his responses to it are allowable. To Bill's initial mainly negative response, the worker remains neutral rather than trying to give more information at this time. Later, she asks Bill to accept only the new information that he has "reasons" for his behavior, that he may be "reacting to his situation . . . or to something else." The idea of his possibly having feelings remains implicit between them. She hedges her request with other information: she attempts to give positive feedback on his capacity to function academically, negative feedback on his feelings constituting laziness, and new content via the comment that many people would react in a situation like his. She then proposes a modified operating rule, that she and Bill talk about his "reactions" further. In sum, she has tried to change slightly Bill's probable information that his feelings are dangerous, crazy, or bad. Her idea is that such feelings are not quite so formidable and may be talked about in a veiled way.

> The following week, Bill revealed how far behind he was in his school work and how little he had been able to get himself to do about it. He felt like he was "just going through the motions" in school, and also with his family and friends. "This wasn't like him," and he wanted suggestions as to what to do about it. When I commented that he might need to talk more about changes in his life since last year, even if this was painful, Bill said maybe I was right. He didn't know where to start, but agreed to think about this before the next session.

Bill begins the second session by accepting some of the worker's information proposed in the first. He reveals a feeling, that he is "going through the motions," although he does not connect this with the separation. He implicitly accepts that he may have reasons for his behavior other than laziness by saying that this new behavior was not like him. When he asks for suggestions as to what to do, he implies hope for a less frightening solution than talking, but also some willingness to hear what the worker has to say. The worker responds by reiterating her already suggested content operating rule, that they will need to talk. In fact, the inference that talk must be about the separation ("changes in his life") is now a little clearer. Finally, the worker adds a small amount of new content, that such discussion might be painful. Her voice tone and other nonverbal communications here presumably convey that she does not find such content unacceptable or frightening.

> In the third session, Bill indicated with a great deal of hesitation that he was confused about his parents' separation. His father had indicated it was for the benefits of all of them, but his mother didn't seem to think

so. During discussion, I said again that most people have feelings in this situation and don't quite know what to think. It might be helpful just to lay out what he was thinking and feeling without knowing yet what sense we could make out of it. Bill spoke at some length about what had been happening at home, and admitted at one point he was "upset."

Again Bill begins the session by accepting what the worker had earlier proposed, that he could talk about painful feelings with her. The worker repeats information ("most people have feelings...") given earlier, showing her acceptance of Bill's content in this way and probably also nonverbally. She adds new information which accepts his confusion ("most people ...don't quite know what to think") and suggests an operating rule for work together ("it might be helpful..."). Bill can take from this a possible way of processing his feelings away from the session as well.

In the fourth and fifth sessions, Bill discussed his concern about his school work and the difficulty in catching up. Since he now felt more like working, we made concrete plans about this. Bill also said his friends did not seem to care that he had withdrawn from them. In the sixth session, we talked further about his friends. He seemed extremely hurt by their not overly neglectful behavior toward him, and at one point I asked if he might feel this about either of his parents. He informed me quite angrily that I had parents on the brain and changed the subject.

For these three sessions, Bill and the worker are focused mainly on other content areas. However, assessment based on her experience with other adolescents in this situation and on Bill's overconcern with whether his friends care about him, again lead the worker to ask about his parents. Bill rejects the implied information that he might be hurt by them, and the worker does not push the matter.

For the seventh session, Bill was about ten minutes late without offering any reason. I wondered if he might still be upset by what I had said last week. He didn't know what I meant. I referred to the question about his parents. At this point he went into a controlled tirade about how I didn't really care about how he felt, why didn't I remember that he had only been confused briefly by the separation, and the like. I said that I was glad he was telling me all this, that I did care about him but could not always know what help he needed from me unless he told me. I added that he was sure feeling that a lot of people didn't care about him lately.

At this he got a little teary and said he didn't know what his friends thought of him, what I did, and what his parents did. Nobody cared enough to tell him what was going on. I said I just did but maybe he was so full of his own feelings he didn't hear. He sobered a little and said he had. I then asked more about his parents and he revealed a welter of anger, hurt, embarrassment, and confusion because his parents can't seem to talk to him about the separation. He seemed to feel better having got some of this out. We began to speak about whether he could initiate talking with his parents about his feelings. (In one of the three additional interviews held, the worker offers to meet with Bill's parents if they can't talk with him about the separation even when he asks.)

In this session, the worker assesses Bill's lateness as possibly related to their unresolved content operating rule, and introduces the idea that they can discuss their differences. When Bill expresses negative feelings about the worker's ostensibly noncaring behavior, she carefully gives accepting feedback before volunteering new information to correct Bill's, which was inaccurate in that he believed she did not care, and insufficient in that he thought people could know what he needed without being told. The worker then seeks to elicit information about his parents (" . . . a lot of people . . . ") rather indirectly, in case Bill still cannot accept the implied information that he has such feelings. After some further discussion, he can accept it. We learn also that the worker later offers an environmental intervention, to see Bill's parents, if he cannot clarify their ambiguous communication to him. The interviews with each of his parents are analyzed later in this chapter to demonstrate worker-client relationship communication.

In view of the fairly small amount of information this worker gives Bill about his feelings, we note, first, that information given to any client should be based on assessment, and this worker deals with Bill's feelings only when she thinks they may be impeding his movement toward the service goal of improved academic performance. Second, clients often do not need a great deal of information to function better, but rather a small amount of information which they can accept. They most readily accept new information when it is given incrementally, unless it is obviously of a nonthreatening sort.

Even when clients are told about community resources, a worker does well
to proceed step-by-step, making sure they understand and can deal with
information offered. Third, content operating rules between workers and
clients tend to change gradually over time. Bill's social worker first proposes
discussing his feelings directly, has to back off from this, and then finds Bill
gradually accepting discussion of more difficult feelings over a period of
time. Finally, a worker's gradual efforts to have a client accept new information or operating rules may impact on the client's information processing. Bill may have learned from his experience with the social worker
how to handle more adaptively not only his feelings about his parents' separation but also other feelings.

Worker Relationship Communication with Individuals

Each of the social work interventions just discussed has relationship implications, depending partly on how it is used. Additional process factors,
such as whether a worker and client laugh together, also carry relationship
messages. In all their communication, workers and clients negotiate
mutual relationship operating rules. Some clients can accept relationship
flexibility if the worker proposes it. Some must begin by controlling interaction, with the worker relatively one-down. Still others will take help only
from a worker who acts more like an authority figure, or usually one-up. To
begin where clients are and to give them new relationship information incrementally, a worker must know what relationship messages his words and
actions convey.

Basic social work interventions and other worker communication can be
used differently to propose different worker relationship stances. The link to
assessment is that a worker proposes relationship flexibility, or his own
more one-down or one-up stances, depending on what a particular client will
be able to accept.[2] A worker's benignness when one-up also influences any
client's willingness to take a reciprocal one-down stance, and will therefore
be analyzed as a part of his relationship communication here. We note that
not all worker words and actions convey symmetry or complementarity in

pure form. Some suggest elements of each or are even mixed—benignly, one hopes, as when a worker uses humor in giving a client advice.

When a social worker elicits information from most clients, he can do so flexibly in a variably one-up, one-down, or symmetrical way. Workers who let clients tell their stories in their own fashion are agreeing to a one-down relationship position at the time. A worker's comments restating what a client has said or encouraging him to continue talking imply greater symmetry. If a client has begun talking about a particular content area, the worker who asks further questions about it is one-down in that he has followed the client's lead, but one-up in directing discussion momentarily. Workers who shift discussion from a client's content to some other are one-up for the moment, less so as the shift flows logically from what the client has already said. A worker's directed questions imply both his one-up position as expert who knows what to ask about, and his more symmetrical respect for the client's competence as an informant on the content in question. The more the worker asks questions that are intended to give information, the more his relationship stance moves toward being clearly one-up, though quite possibly benign. Only when he asks too many or too intrusive questions, when he seems to be testing whether the client knows something, or when his elicitations with the intent of giving information frustrate the client's wish to know what he means, is a worker's one-up stance in eliciting more likely to be perceived negatively.

A worker can convey symmetry by explaining why he is eliciting given information, implying that the client can know reasons for his behavior and that the worker is trying to help rather than pull rank. Since more symmetrical relationship partners behave similarly, a worker's stance in eliciting is also less likely to connote his being one-up overall when the client enjoys a similar prerogative. The client who is given answers when he asks for information about the service, the worker, or the worker's thinking about his problem has been allowed more symmetry than the client who is not. When the worker refuses to answer, he may again soften his one-up stance by giving his reasons for not answering. Thus a worker who declines to answer a personal question may explain that these often spring from a client's underlying concerns about using service, concerns which the client is more than welcome to voice. For a client especially sensitive about the worker's possible one-up stance in eliciting, the worker can avoid obviously directing the discussion or can pose questions in a more one-down fashion than usual, perhaps by asking if a client minds telling him about whatever he wants to know.

The content intervention of giving clients evaluative feedback can imply rather different relationship stances, depending on several factors: where on the acceptance-rejection continuum the content lies, how much the worker's contribution adds to and how much it simply reflects the client's own thinking, and how forcefully the comment is expressed. Responses that reject clients' information or actions are always and increasingly one-up as they are more categorically offered, unless the client has rejected his own information and the worker is simply agreeing with him. Neutrality is fairly symmetrical. Acceptance of the client's information or actions usually suggest the worker's symmetrical or even one-down relationship stance, since he is going along with what the client has said or done. For example, a woman has expressed feeling adequate as a mother, and the worker agrees. However, when the worker gives acceptance in such an explicit manner as to imply that it is news to a client, his relationship stance is benign one-up. If the woman speaks anxiously about her functioning as a mother and the worker says she is doing pretty well, he is one-up to her at the time. Telling someone fairly definitively that he is right or wrong, that his thinking or actions are constructive or problematic, suggests evaluation by one individual who knows more than another. Selective response can be symmetrical or more one-up, depending on whether it includes forceful or mild acceptance, on the one hand, or neutrality or negative feedback, on the other. A worker's one-up relationship stance as he offers negative evaluative feedback is softened by an explanation of why he is offering it. The worker-client relationship is more symmetrical when clients can also reject a worker's comments or can tell the worker when he is being helpful to them.

Although a social worker uses evaluative feedback for its benefits to the client at the content level, he must also consider how the implied relationship stance fits a particular client's needs. With the client ready to accept relationship flexibility, a worker can use feedback implying different stances at different times. When a client needs or prefers the worker's taking a one-up stance, the worker may give strong positive feedback, some negative feedback, or both. Thus, with a child, who appropriately should not be symmetrical with him, a worker is likely to give more praise and set more limits to behavior than with an adult. For some adult clients who take a one-down stance, positive feedback may finally strengthen their functioning so that they can become more symmetrical. With the client threatened by being anything but one-up, the worker may acquiesce by giving little negative feedback and taking care that positive feedback is not so strong that the client feels patronized. He then will be (metacomplementarily) one-down by remaining neutral or offering mild positive feedback much of the time.

The intervention of giving content information to a client almost always conveys the curious relationship stance of worker being complementary one-up, with implied eventual movement toward symmetry, since he is transferring to the client that information which now makes him more knowledgeable. Wording and voice tone significantly affect the degree to which the worker is one-up. The worker who states his opinions as facts has taken a more one-up position than one who suggests their inferential nature. For example, saying "Your hesitance means you're afraid" is more one-up than "Your hesitance may mean . . ." or "I think your hesitance means . . ." As before, in a more symmetrical relationship, the worker's giving information to help the client will be mirrored by the client's giving of some information to help the worker. A worker may welcome new information the client offers about such matters as the community, the client's area of vocational expertise, world events, the worker's use of interventions, and so on.

Often, in giving information, a worker cannot help but take a one-up relationship stance. However, clients come to him for the very reason that he has expert knowledge to give. Workers need not fear using this intervention where clients agree to an operating rule of relationship flexibility, for such individuals can reciprocate in other ways. When a client wants or welcomes whatever information is given, and even when he cannot use the information but sees the worker's positive intention in giving it, such intervention is perceived as benign. More problematic are a worker's telling clients what they already know, giving information in a voice tone which implies clients should have known this already, or continuing to give clients information they have consistently rejected. Clients who propose complementary relationship definitions may ask the worker for a great deal of information if they propose being one-down, or may have difficulty in accepting any if they propose being one-up. The worker can accommodate to

these positions by giving more or less information, or information in more or
less categorically stated forms.

The social worker's efforts to change environmental information available
to a client may again reflect different worker relationship stances in different
circumstances. The provision of concrete services, even when the client has
asked for them, usually suggests a worker's benign one-up position. Someone's asking for something when he is needy and unsure of a response
implies his momentary one-downness, although the worker may attempt to
mitigate this by noting such a client's contribution to the community or his
citizen's entitlement to resources. The worker's willingness to intervene on
the client's behalf benignly suggests that he values the client enough to put
extra effort and resources into helping him. His contacts with others in the
client's life may also place the social worker one-up, if he has initiated these
to gain information the client ostensibly cannot give or to help the client
when he cannot manage himself. The worker's position is more symmetrical
with the client if he conveys that collaterals may need his help as the client
does, or at the very least if he asks the client's permission. When a client
suggests that the worker include other family or group members as clients
with him, the worker who agrees forms a symmetrical coalition with this
client at the time. The worker's initiating the use of activities or other change
in the environment in which he and the client meet places the worker one-up
if he effects these changes unilaterally, less so if he asks the client's opinion,
and still less so if the client has suggested the move. The new context,
however, may be less threatening to the client, such as his home, or an area
in which he has shown greater mastery than in verbalization, such as play
with children or card games with a bright schizophrenic client. By initiating
change, the worker may have metacomplementarily moved the relationship
to a context in which greater symmetry is possible.

A social worker usually intervenes in a client's external circumstances to
change information available to him there, not to propose a relationship
definition. To demonstrate his benign intent, he does sometimes provide
concrete services to a client who has often been mistreated by one-up
figures. In environmental intervention generally, the worker must again note
relationship implications and how these fit with client need. A worker may
have to forego efforts to change a client's environment if the client cannot

accept the change because of his implicit one-down stance in benefiting from it, and if the worker cannot convince him otherwise. It should be noted that a worker often intervenes in the context in which he and a client meet, for the express purpose of proposing a different relationship definition. Because the worker appears less an authority figure in the client's home than in the office, for example, home visits may help a one-down client achieve greater symmetry. Ironically, similar interventions may persuade the one-up client, who feels he must put down the worker, to be more symmetrical as well.

In all the above content interventions, there is one topic of discussion with special relationship significance: that of the relationship itself. If the worker asks how the client wishes to use the relationship, he implies symmetrically that the client's views are important here. A question like "Is this okay with you?" requests a client's more passive acquiescence, whereas "What do you think?" suggests that the client define matters equally with the worker. But both questions imply more symmetry than not asking at all. Then, the worker can give evaluative feedback on client relationship stances as well as on other matters. If he conveys pleasure when the client expresses an opinion, he offers positive feedback to a more symmetrical stance at that moment. A client may read a frown in similar circumstances as a negative response to symmetry as well as to the content conveyed, unless the worker makes it clear that he is not so responding. A worker's giving new information has special relationship implications if the information pertains to the relationship itself. Telling a client that he will not be allowed to strike the social worker conveys the worker's one-up stance in this regard, while a worker's suggesting that the client should decide whether he wishes future appointments or a longer session conveys symmetry.

A social worker must also keep in mind that relationship stances are implied in the context to any interview: who has asked for the contact, who has set up a meeting, and what has happened before in relationship terms. An interview begins in symmetry if both worker and client arrive on time. If one arrives late, he is temporarily one-up because he has controlled when interaction will begin. He who starts speaking, thus setting discussion content, is one-up unless the other has waited and more or less forced him to begin. Relationship messages are contained in such interactional matters as whether worker and client laugh together, whether they use the same form of address with each other, and whether they initiate discussion topics or interrupt each other with relative equality. Significant in relationship terms is who ends the session. Every social worker is familiar with the client who takes this prerogative upon himself—either in one-up fashion, ending before the worker is ready, or symmetrically sharing responsibility with the worker for watching the time. Finally, a worker's verbal content that does not strictly speaking constitute intervention, such as his chatting with clients about the weather or vacations, carries relationship implications. The worker who steps out of his professional role, perhaps at the beginning or at the end of interviews, becomes more symmetrical with the client.

Using Worker Communication to Give Relationship Information

The skilled worker bases his use of relationship communication, as his use of content information, on his assessment of client functioning. Generally, when adult clients are willing to negotiate flexible relationship definitions, the worker must be sure that his communication suggests or confirms this norm. The Ferlugi interview presented in chapter 3 exemplifies such interchange. It is appropriate for workers to be more complementary one-up with children than with other clients, and to show greater symmetry with adolescents. The group interview with children presented earlier and the individual interview with Bill demonstrate nonproblematic worker-client relationship stances. However, some clients of any age reject a worker's proffered relationship flexibility and propose instead that they or the worker be complementary one-up. Let us examine case material to see how a worker still tries to negotiate a more flexible relationship by proposing gradual movement toward it.

Bill's social worker, whom we met earlier, has the following contacts with Bill's parents to determine whether they can talk with him about their recent separation. Excerpts from two interviews with the mother and one with the father show each parent's movement from a more complementary to a more flexible, and ultimately more constructive, relationship stance with the social worker. Content information implicit in the worker's interventions is naturally important, but will not be considered here except to note different worker-client relationship stances in different content areas. Also of interest are incremental changes in worker-client relationship operating rules, and the worker's gearing of relationship information offered to her assessment of what each parent can accept.

> Mrs. Smith came in after I had called to explain that it might help Bill if she and I could talk. She immediately said she was glad to come. She had been so worried about Bill, hadn't known what to do, and felt relieved now that I was helping him. I told her I appreciated her coming. I knew from Bill that she was concerned about his grades, as he was, and that she had supported his getting help with this problem. We talked about the fact that Bill was doing a little better academically but still seemed unhappy. I then said that Bill had mentioned his parents' separation and I imagined this was a rather hard time for her too. She said that it was. With some difficulty, and mainly in response to questions, Mrs. Smith revealed that she has not talked to Bill about the separation and feels unable to do so. She wondered whether I could help. It turned out she meant that I could explain her inability to Bill. I said that this was one possible solution, but I would rather talk with her further. We set up a second appointment for this.

Although the worker calls to propose a rather symmetrical relationship definition between herself and Mrs. Smith by saying that both can help Bill, the context of this first interview tends to place the worker one-up. Mrs. Smith conveys a one-down relationship position when she seems to give the worker all the responsibility for helping him. Still, this could be based on her inaccurate assumption that the worker wishes to be complementary one-up. The worker tries again to suggest symmetry by appreciating Mrs. Smith's having come in, her concern about Bill, and her support of his getting help. Indeed worker-client discussion about how Bill is doing seems to have been fairly symmetrical. Once the worker goes one-up to introduce content about the separation, however, Mrs. Smith moves one-down and stays there. She cannot talk to Bill about this matter, can talk to the worker only in response to questions, and even wishes the worker to take over for her in explaining her inability to Bill. Now the worker probably assesses Mrs. Smith's difficulty being symmetrical in this content area as based on more than her lack of information about what the worker expects. The worker thus does not fully reject the one-up stance accorded her, but asks for time for further negotiation. In terms of relationship operating rules, the pair has so far agreed to be symmetrical in discussing Bill, while the worker will be benign one-up in helping Mrs. Smith to consider what to do about Bill and the separation. Who will actually talk to Bill remains unresolved, but at least the worker has avoided an escalation by not refusing Mrs. Smith's relationship proposal outright.

> In her second session, Mrs. Smith waited for me to begin. I asked her how things were going ("the same") and whether she had thought about our conversation. She then said grudgingly that she probably ought to talk to Bill. He has been hinting about it and is probably getting this from me. However, if I wanted her to do this, I would have to tell her how. I said I wasn't sure I had asked her to do this and wondered what she thought she ought to do. She talked a bit to say finally that her husband used to handle decisions about Bill. I said maybe she is not used to doing so but this does not mean she is incapable. Perhaps we could talk out together what she ought to do. Mrs. Smith said if she has to talk to Bill, she might cry. I asked if that meant that she wanted to talk to him if she could figure out how, and she said she guessed she did. She still wanted my help with what to say, and I agreed. (Two further sessions are spent discussing this.)

Mrs. Smith's waiting for the worker to begin the session is one-down, but perhaps less so than her behavior in the first, when she rushed to define herself in this role. Of course, clear throughout this and the first session is the somewhat controlling nature of her one-down stance. In the second interview, again, the worker accedes to being one-up in asking questions. Mrs. Smith then volunteers to talk to Bill about the separation but still places responsibility for the decision with the worker. The worker mildly but clearly rejects this relationship definition and proposes Mrs. Smith as in charge ("...wondered what she thought she ought to do"). When Mrs. Smith tells about relationship information from her past on which she is still operating, that her husband makes parental decisions for her, the worker questions its accuracy. But she then offers symmetry, rather than proposing that Mrs. Smith take full responsibility on herself for deciding what to do ("perhaps we could talk out together..."). When Mrs. Smith conveys that she would like to talk to Bill, the worker willingly agrees to help her decide what to say. Thus, by the end of the second session the two have agreed on symmetry in regard to an important content area. Mrs. Smith must be one-up in making final decisions about it, while the worker will be one-up in eliciting information, giving evaluative feedback, and offering new information to help in decision-making.

The one session with Bill's father also illustrates the worker's incremental giving of relationship information to achieve greater symmetry, except that Mr. Smith initially proposes himself one-up. Indeed, when the worker calls to ask for his help, Mr. Smith challenges the contextual implication of her one-up stance by saying he hopes the matter is important since he will have to take off from work. The worker responds that she thinks it is.

When I began by saying that Mr. Smith did not look too happy about being here, he asked me if this is what I had called him away from work to talk about. I said not, but that I did appreciate his coming in. He looked impatient, and I asked whether he was willing to hear what I had to say about Bill. He said Bill has been getting very lazy since the separation, Mrs. Smith is egging him on and he didn't see what any outsider could do about it. I commented that he obviously had ideas about what was happening with Bill and that I would like to hear these. He then angrily told me that Bill does not listen to him, seems to shut him out, will not study, and has been nothing but trouble since the separation. He and Bill had a reasonably good relationship before and now his ex-wife must be setting Bill against him. He went on for a good twenty minutes this way. Finally I said I too was concerned about what was happening to Bill. Obviously I didn't know everything about the situation, but I might have some ideas which he could accept or not as he chose. He asked what they were. I asked if it was true he was confused about what was going on between himself and Bill. He said no, he was just telling me all this to pass the time of day. I suggested that if he could be confused, why couldn't Bill? Had he talked to Bill about any of these things? He said that if Bill trusted him, they shouldn't have to talk. I said I could be wrong, but I was not sure whether he trusted Bill. Mr. Smith thought this was a silly observation, and without resolution we terminated the session. However, I learned later from Bill that his father did ask what was going on with him, with some tolerance for hearing the response.

Since Mr. Smith has conveyed on the telephone his reluctance to be one-down, the worker is probably unwise to begin the session by offering herself as a one-up, albeit benign, interpreter of his feelings. After Mr. Smith's rejection of this stance, she backs down to propose symmetry. ("I did appreciate..." and "I asked whether..."), but still implicitly defines herself as expert about Bill's needs. When she realizes that Mr. Smith wants to share his perceptions of the situation, the worker goes one-down to suggest her willingness to hear him out. At a later point, when she must move to new content she thinks Mr. Smith needs, she does so in the least one-up fashion possible. Thus, after trying to establish a benign sort of symmetry (she too is concerned about Bill), the worker hedges her new content offerings with denials of a one-up relationship intent. She "didn't know everything..., might have some ideas, which he could accept or not as he chose." Only when Mr. Smith accepts this somewhat more symmetrical relationship definition by asking her about her ideas does she proceed, still trying to offer him new content via questions rather than more one-up declarative statements, and hedging her only one of these with "I could be wrong." The fact that the session ends without resolution does not mean that Mr. Smith cannot be one-down enough to accept the worker's content when he does not have to do so face-to-face, as she later learns.

We may conclude the following from the worker's relationship communication with Mr. and Mrs. Smith. First, as with content interventions, the "right" worker relationship communication is that which helps clients move toward service goals. Again the conveying of a small amount of new relationship information may lead to positive change. Second, relationship information conveyed in the service of achieving productive worker-client flexibility may also teach the client something about possible ways to function elsewhere. Mrs. Smith may learn, not only from content discussion but also from the worker's modeling of benign one-up and symmetrical stances with her, how to take these same stances with Bill. If Mr. Smith remained one-up in all content areas while he visited a social worker over time, he might learn greater flexibility from the worker's willingness to be one-down.

One further comment may serve to reinforce the notion that a worker's awareness of his own and clients' relationship messages is important. People gather information from other people, and in this broad sense social workers enhance client learning just as any human interaction does. Social work content interventions are heavily verbal, although evaluative feedback does allow the client's trial-and-error learning on a verbal level, and the worker's use of content interventions analogically models his information processing. While verbal discussions may further client learning about relationship stances possible in human interaction, it is doubtful whether clients ever learn new stances from social workers who do not practice what they preach. Relationship learning, like relationship communication, is likely to occur much more by analogic modeling and by trial-and-error experiences with new stances.

The present chapter has considered content level social work interventions with individual clients, and relationship information conveyed in the worker's use of these as well as in other of his verbal or nonverbal communication. We have noted that the worker's assessment of what information might be useful and acceptable to clients at a given time influences what content and relationship information he will attempt to convey. But what is conveyed, however carefully, is not always what is accepted by a client. Potential worker-client communication blocks are a phenomenon which the skilled worker must learn to understand and handle constructively, as we will now demonstrate.

Six

Worker-Client Communication Blocks

So far our communications framework for practice has implied a relatively straightforward route from social work assessment and intervention to client problem-solving: social workers provide information clients need, and clients use it to enhance their functioning. Every practitioner knows better. No matter how carefully a worker listens and observes, he can miss important data for assessment. Information he offers a client can be off-target or ill-timed. The client may reject it or respond ambiguously, leaving the worker unaware that his message has not been received. Moreover, clients can reject or simply fail to receive what should be constructive information for them. They may reject the implication of a worker's questions, that certain content would be useful to talk about, by declining to answer and thus to permit such talk. They may ignore evaluative feedback or new information a worker gives, including offers of relationship flexibility. Of course, people reject or fail to receive each other's content and relationship messages in any conversation. When do such actions lead to worker-client communication blocks?

Technically, worker-client communication blocks involve both participants. First, one party fails to accept content or relationship information put forth by the other. He may reject it outright or miss the point, in either instance sometimes responding ambiguously. To complete the block, the other party rejects or does not receive this communication by the first. For example, when a worker is silent because he has not understood a client's content, the client thinks he has and moves on. Or when a client rejects a worker's advice and one-up relationship stance in giving it, the worker offers the same again. To resolve a block, one party must receive and accept the other's original communication, his negative response, or some compromise. The alternative is impasse, perhaps with symmetrical escalations or worker and client feeling disconfirmed, outcomes that must surely impede progress toward service goals. The present chapter examines what practitioners can do about worker-client communication blocks.

Preventing and Recognizing Communication Blocks

To prevent some worker-client communication blocks, a social worker takes certain precautions with every client he sees. To recognize others before they are fully formed, he notices particular client responses to his content and relationship messages. He must also be able to recognize blocks in which he has already become involved.

The first step toward a block is taken when one party rejects or does not receive information offered by another. A social worker often prevents this happening through precautions that are a routine part of his practice. He attends carefully to client communication, trying not to miss important parts of it. He offers neutral or accepting feedback to a client more often than rejection, since the latter can lead to blocks. On the basis of his assessment, the worker tries to prevent a client's missing or rejecting his communication by using language he thinks the client can understand, by building bridges between what he thinks the client already knows and what the worker intends to convey, and by giving information incrementally. Any worker who examines his own judgments during interview process will find numerous examples of how he gave a client part rather than all of a fact or inference, or gave the fact or inference in a series of steps, rather than offering something so different from what the client knew that he would not be able to accept it. In relationship communication a worker may gradually ask the submissive client to assume some control, or the overbearing client to relinquish it, as we saw earlier with Mr. and Mrs. Smith.

Even with these precautions a worker will sometimes convey more or different information than a client can assimilate. Whenever a worker and client meet, their stores of information must vary. There will be disagreements about whose content is valid. Each party's relationship messages only propose what should exist between them, requiring further negotiation. Some mixed messages and misunderstandings are inevitable. A worker can avoid completing blocks only when he realizes they are imminent. Sometimes the first step toward a block is obvious: the worker knows he has rejected a client's content or relationship stance, or that the client has rejected his, in which case he can consciously consider what follows. More often, workers are unaware that they have ignored a client message or communicated something a client will not accept. If the client then responds ambiguously and the worker misses the ambiguity, the worker is involved in a de facto, hidden, and therefore especially dangerous communication block.

As one way to recognize potential blocks, the worker can introduce a highly important operating rule with every client he sees. It can be made clear that the client should tell the worker when he disagrees with him, has questions, or does not feel understood. In all communication, feedback is the corrective that says, "Yes, there is agreement, continue" or, "No, I cannot accept, I do not understand, give me different information." The client's clear negative feedback is in fact invaluable. Hearing it, a worker can often accept it and readjust his content information or relationship stances to meet client need. Differences which are not reconciled can at least be catalogued. Many clients will give appropriate negative feedback if the social worker specifically suggests this possibility rather than waiting and leaving the matter up in the air. Unfortunately, however, some will not. These clients can perceive any rejection of what the worker puts forth as a challenge to authority or an admission of their own failure to use help. Sometimes they are not themselves aware that they have missed or held back from accepting worker messages. As a result, many potential blocks in worker-client communication are shown indirectly, analogically, and ambiguously in spite of the worker's having asked the client to be more direct.

Another way for the worker to recognize potential blocking is to take special responsibility for noticing these ambiguous client responses to the worker's content and relationship messages. Clues may be in nonverbal communication which often accompanies buried negative feedback, such as a client's unusually rapid or hesitating speech, frown, lowered voice, or avoidance of eye contact when certain subjects are discussed. A client may decline to answer questions by changing the subject, giving tangential information, giving a selective response such as intellectualization, or arriving at an appointment too late to give needed data. In so doing he rejects the idea that review of these data would be safe or helpful to him, as well as the worker's one-up relationship stance in eliciting them. A client may not openly disagree with a worker's evaluative feedback or new content information. But he may still worry about issues on which he has received reassurance. He may continue to believe ideas the worker has discredited. Or he may keep doing something in spite of the worker's having offered apparently compelling facts or insights intended to help him stop. Rejection of a worker's content information again implies rejection of his one-up stance as information giver.

Clients can reject relationship stances proposed by the worker without seeming to reject any specific content. One individual may deny the worker's presumed one-up stance by seizing his prerogatives: perhaps eliciting information about his personal life or sitting in his chair. Another may refuse a symmetrical relationship with the worker by not smiling at his use of humor, or may decline one-up responsibility for directing the conversation when the worker has waited for him to speak. On a broader basis, some clients reject a worker's offers of relationship flexibility when they clearly or tacitly attempt to control process. They may place themselves one-up by trying to monopolize the discussion, disputing the usefulness of any content the worker offers, appearing for appointments whenever they wish, or the like. Clients can more subtly attempt to control interaction by placing themselves constantly one-down, perhaps disconfirming the worker by overtly accepting all his content information but in fact never acting on it. The client with symptoms can sometimes control process unknowingly by simply being unable to change.

Any client can also give ambiguous negative feedback to reject worker-proposed content or relationship operating rules. A worker and client begin to negotiate rules governing their interaction when they first meet. Both propose rules and then come to an accommodation, with each party's negative feedback a necessary part of the process. Subsequently, unless service is brief, worker-client operating rules must change. Relationships which have been more complementary should become more flexible, as the client gains knowledge and competence. Content operating rules should allow discussions of greater breadth and depth. A client can subtly reject these changes as he can any other of the worker's content or relationship messages, thereby beginning a potential communication block. For example, a client continues to complain about other people although he has supposedly agreed to consider what he can do to help himself. Such negative feedback is homeostatic. That is, it tends to maintain operating rules as they are rather than allowing second-order change in the worker-client system itself.

A worker's failure to notice when clients have not accepted some of his messages leads to completed worker-client communication blocks. So can his rejecting client rejections of his content or relationship information, as when a client doubts an interpretation and the worker keeps repeating it. Some completed blocks are, of course, inevitable. A worker must often examine clients' behavior over time to realize they are not accepting certain of his communication. For instance, their repeated avoidance of certain content areas or relationship stances may finally become clear. Often the worker's own feelings of frustration effectively signal an established block. If a worker finds himself having symmetrical escalations with a client about any matter, if he feels annoyed or helpless at particular times, or if he and the client seem to proceed smoothly without getting anywhere, both participants are probably involved in blocking. Blocks usually need to be removed, but practitioners must recognize the difficulty of removing them. Most social work practice skills involve sophisticated use of normal problem-solving processes: the eliciting and assessment of information, provision of feedback and new information, even the encouragement of shared responsibility for work together. The handling of blocked communication does not. His own failure to understand a client may be painful for the worker to recognize. When a client refuses to answer questions or to accept information offered, the worker's natural responses are either to give up or to fight for control; or he may even ignore the problem and thereby disconfirm the client in turn. Blocks in which both worker and client feel comfortable but which prevent them from getting anywhere are very difficult to discern. Only with self-awareness can a worker use his professional knowledge to deal with blocks in different and more constructive ways.

Evaluating and
Withholding Participation
in Blocks

After recognizing potential or established worker-client communication blocks, a worker should examine the reasons for them. Blocks can result from misunderstandings; from a worker's putting forth constructive information discordant with the client's information, with his rules for information processing, or with his small system operating rules; and from a worker's conveying information that is not constructive for the client at the time it is offered. These blocks can overlap, and each may be more or less severe. During an evaluation process a worker can withhold his participation in possible blocks by remaining neutral about them. Or, when information he offered may not have been fully constructive, a worker can accept client negative feedback or selectively accept part of this to offer compromise.

The blocks that occur when worker, client, or both fail to receive each other's messages through simple misunderstandings may reflect their different cultural or social class backgrounds. Misunderstandings can also result from failure—on the part of either worker or client—to give information clearly. They can be due to either party's insufficient knowledge about how to process information of a particular sort. The worker unaware of how medication affects people can misinterpret a schizophrenic client's lethargy. Some combination of these factors may at times lead to misunderstandings. The working-class client with psychosomatic complaints may not accept the worker's idea that stress brings them on because he is not sure what the worker means by "stress." Even if he understands the term, he may not understand the connection between stress in the environment and his physical response. Or he does not know how to discern how much stress he is under because he is not used to thinking about his environment or perceiving his responses to it in this way. Perhaps, too, the worker could have presented his ideas about stress more clearly. Still, the ability of a worker and client amicably to sort out communication problems suggests that neither is conflicted about accepting the other's information offered. A client may react strongly when what he has (mistakenly) understood the worker to mean conflicts with his information on hand. Thus someone may angrily decline to answer questions about feelings because he thinks the questions imply that he is emotionally disturbed.

It is not always easy to discriminate between the two other types of blocking: that which occurs when worker information conflicts with client information, client information processing, or small system operating rules, and that which occurs when worker information is not constructive or timely for the client. Sometimes a worker quickly realizes, when his communication is rejected, that it was probably not as useful as it could have been. For example, he suggests something a client might do, and the client rejects it and immediately comes up with a better suggestion. Sometimes a worker is not quite sure that what he is saying is constructive and is willing to wait and see. He may be saying something he thinks is valid, but which could be overwhelming to a client or somewhat off base. Sometimes a worker feels sure, on the basis of assessment, that what he is trying to get across should be constructive for a client. Perhaps he is trying to convince an obviously capable woman that she is wrong in believing herself inadequate. But there is a fine point for discrimination here. Clients can have many conflicts about accepting particular new information, as we have suggested in chapter 4. The worker may be offering apparently constructive information that really is not, for the very reason that he is not helping a client overcome blocks to processing it. When a man cannot be anything but one-up with others, for example, and the worker argues with him about it and thereby gets into a symmetrical escalation, the worker is behaving much as others in the client's environment have done. His comments may be true but they are not constructive for the client, who is unable to use them. In such instances, a worker must first withhold his participation in blocking and then proceed with more active interventions to be described below.

To withhold his participation in potentially blocked communication during an observation period, a worker can remain neutral in regard to the client's negative feedback given. That is, he can decline to make any active intervention at all. On the content level, the worker's withholding either challenge or confirmation of a client's communication can be ambiguous, but probably implies that he is waiting to see. On the relationship level, a worker's neutrality implies acquiescence to the control that the client has by definition taken in rejecting the content or relationship information offered.

Although his behavior in choosing neutrality may be the same as when he remains silent and one-down out of helplessness, the worker whose neutrality is deliberate is in a metacomplementary relationship position.

A worker's neutrality can be appropriate when he really needs more information to understand what is going on. He may gain clues about why a client rejects the idea of acting more assertively, for example, by waiting to notice that he does so when he is discussing his home situation or that he shifts to content about punishment after being asked about assertiveness. A worker may also need more information to see how a client's tendency to reject certain content or relationship stances fits into the overall picture of his strengths, problem areas, pressures from his small social systems, and so on. Greater understanding of a client's concrete situation may reveal reasons that he cannot attempt specific behavior change. Or more complete assessment of a client's perception, thinking, and actions can suggest that his fears of engaging in impulsive behavior are appropriate. Finally, if the worker suspects he has gotten into an established block with a client, his neutrality may be one way to pause and see what is happening before trying to set more constructive interaction in motion.

A worker concluding that his rejected information was probably not constructive for the client when offered can accept the client's negative feedback, thereby resolving a block before it is fully formed. For example, when a client has a better idea than the worker about what to discuss, the worker agrees that the new subject is more important. Or the client simply changes the subject, and the worker willingly follows the new line of thought. Where a client's conception of his boss sounds more accurate than the conception the worker has suggested, the worker may respond by saying the client is probably right. A worker sometimes needs to accept a client's immediate inability to deal with some new information he has offered. When a client, responding to a worker's symmetrical invitation to talk, states that he does not know what to say, the worker may have to go one-up by asking a question. This is more likely to occur early in a relationship. Any client will reject a social worker's content or relationship information when it comes too fast for him, when he does not see its relevance, or when he is unsure of the worker's intentions. If the worker thinks the client will eventually work out how to deal with the new information on his own, or that links between the new information and the client's problem solving will become clear over time, he can accept the delay rather than immediately pressing discussion of the matter.

Neutrality toward, and acceptance of, a client's negative feedback have another purpose: to let the client know that the worker welcomes such feedback and the client's temporarily one-up relationship stance it represents. The client's ability to give clear negative feedback is helpful to the worker, as we have noted, and should be encouraged where appropriate. Worker acceptance of being one-down may be reassuring to any client afraid that the worker will control him, force him to accept given content information, or otherwise place him one-down when he feels a need to be one-up in their interaction. In accepting a one-down relationship stance, the worker also demonstrates to an overbearing client that this stance can be taken without fear. Or, reacting positively to a timid client's being in control, he lets the client test himself in the one-up position—an important trial-and-error learning process for a timid person.

When a worker believes that his original communication to a client was at least partly constructive, and that the client may be able to accept part of it, he can selectively accept an aspect of the client's negative feedback and thereby suggest compromise. The worker who thinks a client is almost but not quite ready to handle information offered can indicate that he will accept negative feedback, but only temporarily. He may say in response to a subject change, "Okay, but let's get back to this later." Or he can respond to a client's rejection of content by asking the client to reconsider part of that content. To a psychiatric patient who has expressed unwillingness to leave the hospital, the social worker might say, "Maybe discharge is too much for you right now. How would you feel about trying a weekend pass?" Another tactic is to ask a client to take a step toward assuming a relationship stance he has rejected. Let us assume a social worker has tried to reduce a client's dependence on him. When this client in continued one-down fashion asks for advice, the worker may give him several pieces of advice from which to choose. In all these instances of responding selectively, the worker's relationship message may seem either symmetrical or mixed to clients. It proposes the worker's one-down willingness to compromise, but also his wish to retain some control.

We will now consider how a worker can intervene more actively when he discovers a potential or established worker-client communication block.

Intervening by
Metacommunication

A highly useful intervention is to accept the client's negative feedback in response to information the worker has offered, but to take the initiative in suggesting metacommunication. That is, the worker begins by agreeing tacitly or explicitly that the client can reject the content or relationship stance over which their communication began to block. He then proposes lifting discussion up a level to communicate about the block itself. Once the worker establishes that metacommunication can occur, he may elicit information or give new information at this level. We will shortly explicate some common forms such discussion takes. The reader must first understand why, even if a client has rejected content rather than relationship information, the worker's relationship stances in using metacommunication are crucial.

When a client ignores or rejects worker communication because he does not know how to process it, he may feel that he is dumb or that he has let the worker down. The client who rejects particular content information because it conflicts with his own thinking can have the same feelings and more, since content the worker offered seems wrong or frightening. In either instance, a client may take the one-up stance of giving negative feedback with some trepidation and an anxious wish to move on. Even the individual who declines being one-down or one-up when the worker proposes such relationship stances may do so out of fear about his vulnerability in the rejected stance. As they give negative feedback, most clients are unsure that the worker will allow them this temporary relationship control. If the worker keeps trying to push his own point of view, a client may respond with further negative feedback until a symmetrical escalation results. Pushed far enough, a client may terminate service or retreat into use of a symptom to regain control. He may say that he is too inadequate to do as the worker wishes, or he may begin to hallucinate. Metacommunication can prevent impasse only if the worker first accepts a client's momentary control of communication between them. No matter what else he does, he must believe and convey analogically that a client has the right to reject a given content or relationship stance. He may even give positive verbal reinforcement to this notion, for instance by saying that the client must have had reasons for reacting as he did. The worker communicates that he will not challenge the client who at that moment needs to be in control. The client may then be able to allow the worker to take some control in initiating metacommunication.

As the worker suggests that he and a client communicate about what has happened, he asks for the client to be neutral about the original content or relationship stance while they discuss his reasons for rejecting it. The client is assured that he may continue to reject it if he chooses. The worker, though one-up in suggesting metacommunication, also offers greater symmetry as he credits the client as a reliable informant on reasons for his behavior, as he gives accepting feedback on a client's ability to acknowledge or analyze those reasons, and as he shares his expert information about how people's communication may block. Even in confrontation, the worker does not engage in symmetrical escalations with the client about whether the client may reject information given. Rather, the confronting worker metacommunicates by accepting the client's one-up right to give negative feedback but himself takes a one-up stance to assert his understanding of what is going on. He may do so more strongly as in the statement, "You're afraid of what will happen if you say it," or less strongly, as in, "I think you may be afraid . . ." Confronting as a form of metacommunication implies the worker's strong conviction and, occasionally, the threat of serious consequences if the client does not try to move past the block. A worker who had tried other tactics to handle blocking might finally say to a client, "I know you feel ashamed to talk about your drinking. But unless we manage to talk about it, I won't be able to help you with it. We just have to find a way to overcome this obstacle."

To initiate most forms of metacommunication, a worker can elicit information about what the client thinks might be happening between them, can ask the client if anything is troubling him, or can look inquisitive. Such elicitation is usually more successful when the worker explains it first. He may say that knowing reasons for the client's hesitation will be helpful, or that people do have difficulty proceeding smoothly at times. He may note that certain behavioral signs, such as a client's lateness or frowning, can indicate something amiss in worker-client communication. He may even add that he is not mad at what happened but, rather, interested that they both learn what the client did not understand or what he was questioning when he behaved as he did. With such explanations, the worker tries to prevent the client's misunderstanding the idea of metacommunication itself because he thinks it implies he did something wrong. The worker who gives reasons for his inquiries puts forth a more symmetrical relationship message than if he simply asked about what the client thought or felt. In initiating metacommunication about an established block, a worker may symmetrically note that both he and the client are somehow having trouble dealing with the particular matter. Sometimes he can go one-down to say he has probably not been too helpful to the client in this respect. Of course, when a worker and client have already established collaboration in looking at possible blocks, the worker can simply draw attention to a client's rejection of content or relationship information to elicit his thinking about why.

If eliciting fails to stimulate metacommunication, a worker can suggest to a client what may be going on. The worker who has noticed patterns in a client's rejection of given content or relationship information, or who has inferred possible reasons for a rejection, may share these insights when a client seems ready to assimilate them. His idea can be based on practice experience as well as his assessment of the particular client's functioning. If a client seems embarrassed to talk about something, the worker can ask whether he is worried about what the worker may think of him. If a religious client refuses to discuss problems in the local parochial school, the worker can ask whether he feels it is wrong to talk since this could lead to criticizing the church. To the woman who expresses doubts about the worker's real concern for her and then suddenly recalls her father's early death, the worker may suggest that fear of another desertion could be holding her back from full trust. The worker may sometimes forestall a client's fear of talking about something or taking some relationship stance, by offering corrective information in advance. A client who is having an affair may not talk about it for fear of what the worker will think. Sensing the reason for the client's hesitation, the worker may say he is not there to make moral judgments about people. A client who receives such information may be able to move on productively, or may be able to reveal more about his fears.

All these metacommunicative endeavors are aimed at exposing misunderstandings between worker and client, their different ways of processing information, or their conflicts about information. The worker who does not understand a client's culture can be helped to do so. The client who does not see how the worker's questions are connected with his problem can be shown the worker's line of thought. The client who does not perceive his own feelings or his wife's moods can be taught these information processing skills. A worker and client who hold conflicting information about something may learn that, in fact, the client has more accurate information than the worker. For example, a client may know more than the worker does about an agency to which the worker is trying to refer him. When clients reject worker content because of environmental pressure, discussion may clarify just what the difficulty is. The adolescent who cannot accept that wanting to have friends is natural may reveal that his father discourages this, unless even revealing such a discrepancy breaks a family operating rule.

At other times, either quickly or in a series of revelations, metacommunication may help a client discover what inaccurate information of his own has prevented his accepting the worker's content or relationship messages. A client unable to accept praise from the worker may discover during a fairly extensive exploratory process that he has never believed authority figures who say positive things about him, that his parents seem never to have said positive things about him, and finally that he himself never believed he was anything but bad. A client often rejects worker information on false assumptions about its action implications: "If I admit how mad I am, I might hit her." Clients may falsely assume that there will be no way to deal with potentially negative results of behavior: "If my husband reacted by saying he'd leave me, I don't know what I'd do," or "What if I start crying when I tell you about it?" A worker cannot offer reassurance about other people's behavior, but when a client puts his own thinking into words, he is often able to question its catastrophic implications. The worker who uses metacommunication to unravel misunderstandings and conflicts of information with clients has taught them a skill valuable in their other interpersonal relationships.

Metacommunication can sometimes be used to deal with a client's difficulties in taking a one-up or one-down relationship position the worker has proposed. The worker may comment that a client seems to avoid ever disagreeing with him and may talk productively about why. Or he may note that the client seems upset whenever he makes any suggestion, and may propose possible reasons for this reaction. By initiating metacommunication, however, the worker is himself taking a one-up stance. Clients who have difficulty taking one-up positions may hear his comments as those of an authority figure who is putting them one-down. Clients who refuse ever to be one-down cannot accept the worker as one-up authority person who is giving them new, albeit metacommunicative, information. Clients with symptoms, who may also thereby reject the worker's proposals that he can influence them, often cannot productively discuss this aspect of the worker-client relationship. What they do is by definition beyond their control.

Metacommunication works best with blocks due to a client's conflicts about accepting information at the content level. It may not be effective when a client cannot accept the worker's proposals of relationship flexibility, and may then be supplemented by the use of paradox.

Intervening by the Use of Paradox

Persistently one-up clients may dominate discussion or reject almost everything a social worker says. Overtly one-down clients leave a worker drained, because they seem unable to do anything for themselves. The client with well-established symptoms may remain a frustrating puzzle. Some clients who take either an extreme one-up or one-down—therefore controlling—position within interviews, or who continue to complain of symptoms, do use information given by the worker to enhance their functioning. We saw this pattern earlier with Bill's father, Mr. Smith, who insisted on being one-up. In such instances, a client may have implicitly allowed a worker some control, and the worker should not insist on overt acknowledgment of this. Their blocked communication was more apparent than real. But when clients cannot even implicitly allow the worker to influence them, the worker may intervene by paradoxical use of his relationship messages.

With a one-up client, a worker can perpetuate a form of paradox by clearly accepting the client's one-up stance. For example, the worker lets the client set appointment time and duration, lets him direct conversation, and perhaps even commends him for being willing to take on these responsibilities. The worker's analogic communication as well as his verbal comments must convey his acceptance of the client's dominant role. The worker can also deliberately place himself one-down in the way he uses any interventions. Instead of eliciting given information, he can ask the client whether he thinks they should talk about the topic in question. In giving evaluative feedback or new information, he can express doubts about the usefulness of his knowledge. He can indicate that the client may or may not want to consider information offered. He can ask the client about community problems or about how he could be a more helpful social worker. Any such questions or comments must be genuine, but the worker can present them in a more one-down way than he would normally choose.

The worker's affirming a client's one-up stance or his own one-down stance can disarm an individual who is struggling to define the worker-client relationship precisely in this way. If the worker is already letting him be one-up, the client whose own stored information indicates he must keep himself one-up has no further need to struggle. If his efforts to be one-up no longer stimulate symmetrical escalations with the worker, as they tend to do with others, worker-client communication patterns do not support the client's accelerating one-up stands. The client who has taken a one-up stance and been confirmed in it has also accepted responsibility for the worker-client interaction. For his own self-esteem or to retain a one-up position, he should demonstrate competent management, which implies some progress toward service goals. The client may be impressed by the social worker's willingness to be one-down, and may learn this stance analogically or begin to question his own persistent need to be one-up. That is, if the use of paradox intrinsically interrupts a client's usual means of maintaining control in relationships by making it unnecessary, it can stimulate behavior change.

The client who insists on defining himself as one-down can be more difficult. He subverts all the social worker's efforts to help by remaining passive, waiting, or simply not being helped. Here again, a worker can try to impose paradox by placing the client in control. Most important, he must neither step into the role of taking care of the client nor exhort him to act differently. Such one-up moves by the worker confirm the client's inadequacy and serve as another reason for his acting one-down. They are also likely to duplicate the client's interaction patterns with others in his environment. Instead, the worker allows the client to act one-down *if he wishes*—a paradox, since the client is allowed to take over the responsibility for his own functioning that he has always in fact had. Then, the worker can himself act as one-down as possible and can fit in willingly when the client does anything more symmetrical or one-up. He may wait for the client to direct conversation, or ask the client to determine the duration of interviews (unless the client would then stay indefinitely). He may help the client to understand the real limits of the worker's knowledge or ability to help. If the client keeps asking the worker to do things for him, the worker can suggest he will do them at the client's direction, to show the client that the worker's taking over this responsibility will not help. Of course, if the client does begin to try some more symmetrical or one-up stances, the worker must be careful not to confirm whatever negative information the client had stored in memory about the dangers of doing so. The client's more assertive functioning fosters its own rewards, unless it is discouraged by social systems to which he belongs.

Where controlling behavior is based on symptoms or deeply ingrained character traits, it may not change in response to the maneuvers just outlined. Certain individuals are locked into repetitive means of controlling others unintentionally, often at great cost to themselves. The worker may then use paradox both by putting the client explicitly in charge of worker-client interaction, and by condoning that very symptom or behavior by which he has always controlled others. Using psychoanalytically oriented techniques with appropriate clients, the worker may ask a client to speak about whatever he wishes and may "expect" resistances.[1] The worker will usually show permissive interest in symptoms, perhaps by warning the client that symptoms will not disappear quickly or by suggesting that the client note and report what is happening when symptoms occur. Role playing can invite repetition of problematic behavior for the worker to observe. A worker may virtually prescribe symptoms by predicting them. For example, when an angry client who gets headaches has declined to express negative feelings, the worker may tell him that he will probably get a headache soon.

The idea of using paradox raises ethical issues. Helping the one-down client take responsibility for himself, and sometimes acceding to the one-up client's control of interaction, may be palatable if a worker sees these tactics as enhancing client self-determination. As paradoxical means to gain relationship control, the same tactics may seem underhanded. A worker's permissiveness toward symptoms may be laudable as a way of starting where the client is, but it can be criticized when seen as a way of maneuvering the client into behavior changes. Some early research has suggested that paradox can work when consciously imposed by someone trained to use it, at least to remove symptoms or to change behavior with which clients have requested help.[2] Still, those without such training should not take paradox too far.

To complicate the matter further, communication theorists are not sure why paradox works as a therapeutic technique. Some say it is because paradox prevents a client from using his symptoms to control a helping professional, as earlier elaborated. Others say it is because the professional declines, unlike others in the client's environment, to join the client in communication patterning that will support his dysfunctional behavior.[3] By not demanding that the disturbed client give up his symptoms, not engaging in symmetrical escalations with the one-up client, and not agreeing to take care of the one-down client, the worker surprises each of them and perhaps stimulates different behaviors. Acting the same is hard when others act differently. Professional use of paradox may also free clients who try to start or stop behavior that is by definition involuntary. For example, a client keeps telling himself to relax, when relaxing must be spontaneous.[4] The social worker who accepts such a client's nervousness as something to work on together, or who permissively asks him to notice when he gets nervous, may have freed him from his own problematic solution to a problem that originally was not so serious. Paradox, by suggesting that a client actively engage in behavior everyone has been telling him to avoid, may introduce temporary uncertainty and therefore allow different functioning in response.[5] Once having changed, a client may feel more mastery, or may find that change was not as frightening as it had seemed earlier. We assume here, of course, that others in a client's social systems can respond positively to such change. If not, environmental intervention rather than paradox may be appropriate.

Intervening by
Environmental Work

As we have noted in chapter 5, a social worker may try to change environ-mental information available to any client by modifying the circumstances in which he and the client meet, by work with collaterals who may or may not become clients, or by intervention into the client's larger environment. The first type of intervention can be useful to deal with blocks due to some kinds of misunderstandings or to client conflicts about accepting some kinds of content or relationship information. The others, not unexpectedly, can help clients who are receiving from their social workers different information from that which they receive from others in their environment.

Modifications of the environment in which worker and client meet include such contextual changes as moving from office to home visits, using ac-tivities instead of talk, and changing from individual to family or group sessions, or vice versa. All these convey content in terms of what the worker thinks would be helpful for the client, often through nonverbal means. They also convey relationship messages, with less formal settings or activities usually allowing greater worker-client symmetry; and the idea of changing to individual or multiple-client sessions suggesting the worker's coalition with the client or clients who preferred the new arrangement. Blocks that occur when clients misunderstand and reject a worker's verbal message can some-times be resolved when the message is clarified analogically. The opposite sequence may also occur. The client who cannot believe that the worker wishes to be symmetrical with him may come closer to believing it when the worker agrees to come to his home. The child who thinks a worker's playing games with him means their contact is not for serious purposes may learn otherwise if the worker explains why they are meeting. The client who thinks that the worker believes him to be causing other family members' problems can correct this misunderstanding if the worker decides to see and help everyone together.

When possible blocks are due to conflicts between information the worker is offering and what the client already believes, modification of the worker-client environment can be helpful in several ways. For one thing, if the worker's information was not really as constructive as it could have been for this client at this time, worker-initiated changes in context can accept the client's negative feedback. A timid client implies he does not feel comfortable in the worker's office, and the worker suggests meeting in the client's home; or a paranoid client becomes fearful about coming in weekly, and the worker proposes to meet twice a month. Allowing an adolescent to be in group treatment if he feels he can learn more from his peers than from seeing the worker alone may resolve a block. In a subtle way, the worker's shifting to a less verbally oriented context can also serve as a selective response when a client rejects the idea of being one-up or one-down in a formal interview. The worker does not press his point verbally but asks the client to try being symmetrical—which is one step toward the stance the client fears—in his home or in activities where the worker's authority position is less clear. Activities in which the worker demonstrates his own lack of fear at being one-up, or his pleasure at a client's assertiveness, may reeducate the timid client exactly as he first learned about these matters: analogically and by trial and error. For the aggressive client, the worker may similarly demonstrate that he is not afraid of being one-down.

Changes in context in which the worker and client meet can be used along with metacommunication and in the service of paradox. The combination with metacommunication works well especially to evoke information which a client had learned earlier, perhaps analogically or by trial and error. Consider the situation in which a school-age child cannot believe that his assertion and accompanying one-up relationship stance would be acceptable to the worker, because at an earlier time his parents rejected these. If the conflict were in consciousness, he might be able to metacommunicate about it. Metacommunication about feelings and fears within the worker-client relationship might also make him aware of underlying information on which he was operating. However, many clients, particularly children, have neither the conscious awareness nor the immediate verbal facility to articulate such matters. Playing games sometimes evokes problematic information, as when this child expresses the idea that the worker may not like him because he has won. Metacommunication can then follow. For an adult, use of context to deal with possible worker-client communication blocks can include role playing combined with metacommunication. An adult harboring a conflict about dependency, but unable to articulate it, may role play with the worker asking his wife to be closer to him and thus discover fears which he can discuss verbally. To use change of context as a form of paradox, a worker may place a number of insistently one-down clients together in a group. Here at least some clients must be less one-down than others and therefore more one-up. The paradox exists in that the worker does not ask them to change, and may even explicitly permit them to continue acting as they do by saying that the group is for people who have trouble asserting themselves. When some clients are more helpful or capable than others, they may learn and even model for others the fact that someone with their difficulties can survive being one-up.[6]

Clients who reject workers' content or relationship information because it conflicts with information or operating rules within their social systems may require other forms of environmental intervention. One of these is to work with one or more members of a family or other natural group as collaterals. The worker can also see those with significant control of a client's other social systems—perhaps the schoolteacher, the employer, or the landlord. A worker may intervene with a physician in his own setting or with another social worker who is helping a client elsewhere. It may be that a client cannot accept what one professional is telling him because another is conveying a different message. We note, as an indirect environmental intervention on a client's behalf, that any worker encountering serious communication blocks with a client should seek supervisory or consultative help. A worker may also need to intervene directly in a client's larger environment, as by trying to change resources available to him within an agency, community, or social welfare system. The lack of these can quite naturally cause clients to reject worker communication. A hungry man may be unable to accept and use a social worker's content or relationship stances suggesting what he should do about other problems. Of course, a worker will often intervene environmentally without waiting for his and a client's communication to block.

This chapter has considered the very important matters of how to prevent, recognize, evaluate, and intervene in potential or established worker-client communication blocks. Intervention possibilities include the worker's use of metacommunication, paradox, and attempts to change the client's environment or the context in which he and the client meet. When family or group sessions are indicated, especially when blocks cannot be resolved at the individual level, a worker must be prepared for small system practice. We will discuss social work interventions with families and groups in the following chapter. Interventions with blocked worker-client communication in small system practice are examined in chapter 8.

Seven

Interventions with Families and Groups

A social worker can have major impact on clients in small system practice as he helps them change together or pool their resources to change their environment. He will use interventions somewhat differently than with individuals, occasionally to help system members unblock communication among themselves. In trying to offer useful content, relationship stances, and mutual operating rules, a worker always assesses clients' functioning. When he sees more than one person at a time, he must think about what information everyone needs for problem solving and how clients will exchange information to influence each other. He is especially concerned about their existing or proposed operating rules. Sometimes he sees a family or other natural group because its rules are dysfunctional. Sometimes he takes responsibility to form a group, and will try to influence the nature of rules negotiated there. He must bear in mind that his interventions convey information and affect operating rules differently with families and groups than with clients seen individually.

Content Level Interventions with Families and Groups

A social worker uses the content-level interventions already identified when he sees more than one client at a time. An intervention may be directed to a whole family or group, to a subsystem, or to an individual; yet each intervention offers information to everyone. The link to assessment must again be clear.

A worker can *elicit information* from one person, several, or everyone present in a session. To elicit from a given individual or subgroup, he is likely to use names, designate common characteristics as in, "What do the girls think?'' or turn and look at the person or persons involved. When he addresses the family or group as a whole, and especially when he would like self-selected members to initiate discussion, the worker may try to manage eye contact by looking at each in turn. Of course, any client may also give information when the worker has asked or looked toward someone else.

In practice with small systems, as with individuals, the worker may elicit both to gather information and to give information to clients. But his eliciting gives more clients information in more ways. As before, he reveals his own ideas, information processing, and preferences for operating rules. When he asks members of an alcoholics' group about their job experiences, he suggests that he thinks this matter important and wishes such discussion to be allowable. Each person's answer will reveal relevant information he has on hand and something about his information processing, such as whether he can remember these experiences. Members' interaction around answering suggests whether system operating rules indeed permit them to discuss this content and, if so, from what relationship positions. Not only the worker but also the group members are exposed to all this information.

Indeed, social workers often use elicitation in family and group practice especially to expose members to each other's information, their information processing, and their possible openness to new content operating rules. In formed groups, members usually have much to teach each other about how each person comes across, how to get along with others, how to accomplish social action, or the like. The group member who describes how he reached a certain conclusion may be a less formidable model of information processing than is the social worker. In natural groups, members can learn useful things they had not known about each other. It may become evident in a family session, for example, that a wife is really very hurt by her husband's unemotionality. System members, after observing a worker, may acquire new skills at eliciting mutual information. Family members especially may learn to ask about each other's feelings and perceptions and to listen more effectively. The worker who probes family or group operating rules by eliciting information in a new content area often hopes that some members' answers will help swing others toward greater openness. If a worker can get one family or group member to admit that he has feelings about termination, for example, others may follow suit.

To ensure that information revealed in his elicitation or in response to it will not be harmful, the worker needs to take greater precautions with multiple clients than with individuals. He might avoid asking a small system member whether he was envious of a friend, if he thought that others might condemn that member for having such an emotion. Workers may wait to propose discussing certain content until they think that no system member will be overwhelmed by it. Presumably, however, a worker would not be seeing clients together unless he felt they could correct each other's insufficient, inaccurate, or otherwise problematic information or information processing in at least some content areas. The worker's eliciting can then seek to further such information exchange.

A worker's *evaluative feedback* with families and groups again gives information to all. When a worker praises one client's efforts to help himself, others can expect that he would appreciate similar behavior from them. When a worker selectively accepts one family member's good intentions although his actions are problematic, others can understand this member and perhaps also themselves differently. When a worker rejects one family or group member's information, thinking, or behavior in a given instance, others may be dissuaded from their similar ideas. The worker who gives evaluative feedback models an important communication skill. By giving feedback to one system member, however, a worker sometimes unknowingly implies his opinion of someone else. Especially if family or group members are differentially punctuating a series of events—one saying, for example, that he is picked on and others pointing out that he invites it—a worker's agreement with either side can seem to reject the opposite point of view. He may instead choose to give a selective response to everyone, making it clear that all the points of view are true, but that they are limited because everyone participates in maintaining the pattern. By focusing negative attention on the scapegoating pattern, the worker also offers negative feedback on the implied operating rule that members must support it.

Directing evaluative feedback to a subsystem or to a whole family or group can convey more than the obvious content. Feedback directed to a subgrouping suggests the worker's perception of the members of that subgrouping as alike, and as different from members of other subgroupings present. Such comments tend to mark boundaries. Within a family, a worker may affirm parents' disciplining their children, thus giving positive feedback to their shared right to do so and their difference from the children in this regard. Positive feedback directed to everyone, such as a worker's saying that family or group members seem to care about each other, suggests their shared strengths and thereby furthers unity and trust. A worker's selective acceptance of something in which all system members take part may similarly inform them about shared positives as well as indicating where all might consider change. When a worker offers negative feedback to a family or group as a whole, he disarms blame by implying that everyone is involved, perhaps even including himself. A statement such as, "We have to stop discussing alternatives and start trying to solve the problem," exemplifies such all-inclusive use of the intervention.

Evaluative feedback should benefit at least some system members and harm none. In a family session the worker might not condemn a child's actions if the child could use the feedback but a guilt-ridden parent might be upset by it. A worker also considers how system members may respond to the idea of their differences or similarities implicit in his directing feedback to one member, to a subsystem, or to the whole family or group. Directing feedback toward an individual affirms or proposes an operating rule allowing diversity. This may be ill advised at first in systems showing so much diversity they threaten to fly apart, as in a family or group where competitiveness is predominant. Giving feedback to a subgrouping can propose greater subsystem boundaries, often between children and parents. In some families this is useful, but in others there is too much separation between them already. The worker's directing feedback toward a whole family or group can be planned consciously to support unity or to move the system toward allowing appropriate interdependence.

To convey *new content information* to small system clients, a worker may tell any family or group about outside forces that he thinks are affecting members, about services he can offer them, about how he perceives system operating rules, about individual difficulties that may or may not be impeding system functioning, and so on. If directed toward an individual or subsystem, the information can still be received and used by all. Sometimes a worker sees clients together to give information that everyone may need. He might see a family in crisis to suggest how they could cope with it, an adolescent group to explain birth control methods, or a community group to posit effective strategies for neighborhood change. We have noted that most group and family members can be mutually helpful and informative if the worker can get them talking to each other about content important to them. As in practice with individuals, the link between a worker's assessment of what information is needed by system members and his provision or stimulation of this information should be clear, again with the proviso that information given not be detrimental to anyone.

Information on family or group members' operating rules is especially relevant to small system practice. The worker may want to make clients aware of rules so that they can decide whether they wish to continue them. A worker may comment that parents and one child seem cut off from each other, and may wonder if this distance is something they want. We note here the detrimental effect of addressing clients about operating rules as if only some are responsible. If the worker said that the parents were cutting off one child, he would very likely stimulate their defensiveness. With a community group, a worker may state that members seem loath to consider handling their problems in any way except by staging a protest demonstration. He thus makes explicit for group members' consideration their operating rule restricting discussion about what to do. If family or group members have insufficient or inaccurate information about potential operating rules, a worker can intervene to correct the deficiency. Seeing parents of a young adolescent, a worker may tell them how others have managed to deal with the inconsistent demands for independence that adolescents make.

A social worker gives important information in small system practice when he teaches clients how to metacommunicate about their differences in order to unblock communication, perhaps allowing second-order system change. Consider the situation in which a marital couple engages in escalations, rejecting each other's content while becoming increasingly angry and hurt. The worker can ask them to stop and reveal the misunderstood or conflicting information which makes them hold on so tenaciously to their own points of view. If he succeeds, the pair may be surprised to learn that each thought the other did not love him, each thought he was right because that's how things were done in his family of origin, each thought the other had no reasons for his behavior except stubbornness, or each thought happily married couples never disagree. In group practice, a worker may also teach that misunderstandings and conflicts can be resolved if people look at information on which they are operating. He may need to be specific about metacommunication skills, explaining the proper relationship stances of neutrality, and even the possible discussion steps involved. It is particularly necessary to point out that in most situations, people have different information without one of them being "right." Whether or not clients use metacommunication to change other family or group operating rules, their learning how to resolve conflicts differently introduces a new operating rule about conflict resolution itself.

A worker may intervene to change *environmental information* available to small system members when he provides concrete services to some or all. He makes an environmental intervention as far as the system is concerned when he sees members outside a family or group session, or sees collaterals, such as schoolteachers, who can influence clients. A worker may encourage system members to change environmental influences on others or on the system as a whole. He can suggest that a parent confer with his child's teacher or that a group consider taking community action. The worker can also modify the environment in which he and clients meet, whether by adding or removing a system member, meeting in a different place such as a client's home or a restaurant, or shifting from verbal discussion to activities.

A worker's decision to provide concrete services or to see collaterals implies, as in individual work, that clients' problems do not lie fully or at all within the clients themselves, and that the worker is willing to take action on their behalf. Environmental interventions are usually undertaken when system members face deficiencies of information available to them which cannot be remedied in family or group interviews alone. Such interventions may even help clients unblock communication between themselves and some aspects of their environment, or may change system operating rules, as when a teacher says that a child needs help with homework and a parent becomes willing to provide the help. Whenever the worker singles out one individual for a special appointment with him, all system members may assume, unless they are told otherwise, that this person is more of a problem or more important in problem solving. A worker may see one client separately when he needs information for assessment that this person will not give with others present, or when he thinks the client needs information that others cannot constructively use.

Of all changes of the context in which workers and clients meet, the most important is to add or remove a system member. This action must affect what content information is exchanged in the newly constituted system, as well as the agreed-upon operating rules. Shifting a family or group meeting to a different physical environment may stimulate different memories, seating arrangements, and degrees of comfort and hence influence the members' exchanges of content information and agreements about operating rules. The use of activities necessarily gets system members interacting with each other and with the worker in different ways than verbal discussion does. Role playing, family members' placing each other in live "sculptures" to illustrate each member's ideas about the family,[1] and the use of other activities are more frequent in small system work than with individuals. The worker who uses any such intervention will first have assessed its potential for correcting problems with system members' information, information processing, or operating rules. A worker might remove a group member who was overwhelming others with bizarre information, or might add a grandmother to a family session so that others could benefit from her wisdom there. He might use activities to allow group members to demonstrate nonverbal behavior such as physical skills, which others might copy to enhance their functioning.

Using Interventions to
Give Content Information

By analyzing excerpts from meetings of a tenants' group, we will illustrate some ways in which social workers may offer content information and operating rules to clients in small system practice. Here, as in work with individuals, it can be important to offer only gradually ideas that are different from clients' own. We will concentrate on content aspects of worker communication but mention relationship messages when these are salient. A family case to be presented later in this chapter will focus on worker relationship communication as influencing clients.

The following excerpts summarize contacts between a group of tenants

and young male social worker attached to a neighborhood association, over
the first two months of their meetings.

> After receiving a call from Mrs. Johnson, I met with her and three other
> tenants in her apartment on December 14th. As she had warned me on
> the phone, the building was cold, the hallways smelly, and the front-door
> latch broken. All the ladies present, led by Mrs. Johnson, were eager
> to tell me their tale of woe about building violations. The heat had
> hardly been on since the cold weather began. There are rats. With the
> door latch broken anyone can get in, and so on. They're worried for
> their children and themselves. In fact it was hard to get them off this. I
> did learn they have talked to the man responsible for maintenance when
> they can find him, and have called the city but feel they are getting the
> run-around. I told them I was willing to call too, but in my experience
> the best way to have clout was to try to get a lot of tenants together. We
> decided to see what happened when I called the city and, if necessary, to
> consider getting other tenants involved.

In this first meeting of a few tenants, the worker is mainly concerned with
eliciting information for assessment purposes but manages to give some as
well. First, he learns about the problem, which could be regarded as one of
blocked communication between tenants and their landlord: the tenants
have rejected the landlord's actions, or his inaction, and he has disconfirmed
them by ignoring them. The worker's willingness to come to the building,
ask questions, and listen to the tenants suggests his acceptance of the idea
that they have something valid to say. His later attempt to introduce a new
content operating rule, that he and they need to discuss solutions as well as
problems, appeared reasonable enough to be accepted by the women after a
time. The worker finally gives a small amount of new information—that he is
willing to make an environmental intervention by calling the city and that
getting tenants together might be a way to have clout. So far, the worker has
used the group to elicit and give information more efficiently than if he had
met with each tenant alone. Moreover, the women may have learned from
each other more than they knew before about the extent of violations and
the strength of everyone's feelings about them.

> On December 16th, I called Mrs. Johnson, telling her the city had told
> me that they were "working on the problem" and that this landlord has

violations in several buildings. I suggested a strategy meeting, at which three of the prior four ladies and one new one were present. After I had repeated my message to them, the women were discouraged and wondered what to do next. I asked if they were still concerned about the problems. They were, and the new lady complained about the same things the other ones had at the first meeting. After a little of this, I told her she was saying what a lot of the building's tenants probably felt. I repeated my idea of a tenants' group. When the woman wondered if anything would be accomplished, I shared some of my past experiences with them. Essentially, I said there are a lot of strategies, such as pressure on the city or the landlord, court, etc., but they mostly depend on numbers. I said I would be willing to help. They finally decided to try to get more people involved, and we talked about how.

This session illustrates more giving of information by the social worker, some important worker-client relationship messages, and also the worker's seeking to affect small system content operating rules based on client goals and his assessment of client functioning. In this second meeting of the still small group, the worker conveys what he has found out from the city, his impression that many tenants probably feel as these do, possible courses of action based on his experience, and his willingness to help. He may confirm Mrs. Johnson in a group leadership role by first calling her rather than one of the other tenants, and he suggests the new participant's unity with the others by noting what she has in common with them. In symmetrical fashion, he leaves it to the group to decide what to do. However, he has also proposed content operating rules based on clients' chosen goal to get something done about the building, and on an assessment of their apparent ability to act. Thus the worker does not suggest talking more about the tenants' feelings of discouragement, nor does he encourage the new tenant's extensive repetition of complaints similar to those given at the meeting before. Instead, he focuses discussion on immediate steps to do something about the problem at hand.

In the following week, I talked with Mrs. Johnson once by phone, and visited two of the other women to find out how their efforts to recruit more tenants were going. Then the furnace got fixed, and I was off a week for the holidays. In early January the women said they had found others who still wanted to meet, and we did so on the 13th with about fifteen people present. As we had arranged, Mrs. Johnson explained that our purpose was to see if people wanted to get together to try to do something about the building's problems. She also briefly explained my role. Again there was an outpouring of complaints, and I suggested listing these. When we had done some of this, one of the two men present asked what a tenants' group could do. Mrs. Johnson said maybe some of them talking up more was what got the furnace fixed. After some general discussion, there was consensus that there were still plenty of violations and a need to have something done. But what could they do? I warned that it would take hard work and maybe some time, but there were options, of which I mentioned a few. At my suggestion they elected some officers. We decided to meet the following week to plan definite action.

In this series of occurrences, the social worker consults with the women who are trying to get other tenants involved, and apparently advises them on how to run a larger meeting. At this meeting, he gives more information in the form of suggestions to list complaints and to elect officers, as well as repeating what options are available for action. The new group's content operating rules move from discussing complaints to considering possible solutions, as they have done in each earlier session, but now with more people involved and with an important new relationship rule—that the tenants are more symmetrical with the worker or sometimes one-up to him in conducting the proceedings themselves.

The meeting January 20th was a productive one. Eighteen people were present, including most from the week before. Mrs. Johnson read the list of complaints and one or two more were added. Someone asked how many of these were actually legal violations, and we decided on about five. They asked me how they should proceed, and one man asked if they could withhold their rents. I said this was possible but was a pretty severe strategy which might get them into legal trouble, especially if many in the building were not involved. Someone else suggested going to the city again with a united front. After some further discussion they decided to send a letter, which I would help them draft, to both the landlord and the city, stating the violations and how long these had been going on. I congratulated them on their efforts, and four people agreed to meet with me to do a letter.

This meeting sees a real shift of content operating rules, with the group more solution-oriented. In relationship terms there is also continuing symmetry, with members asking the worker about strategies but also suggesting some themselves. To one client's input the worker gives a selective response ("this was possible but . . ."). He also gives positive feedback to the group's efforts as a whole, very possibly to further their sense of unity. In this session, the worker's role as consultant emerges more fully. He does have expert information on strategies, but the tenants must decide what strategies they finally wish to try.

On January 24th, I met with four tenants to draft the letter. It was relatively easy to agree on facts to be given, but several difficulties arose. One was whether there should be an "or else" clause to support our plea that something should be done, which we finally resolved by saying, " . . . or else we will have to consider what other options are open to us." The other was how the letter should be signed. We thought the officers would sign for the now formed tenants' association, but several were afraid of being evicted if their names appeared. I was able to reach a lawyer, who verified that such eviction would be absolutely illegal but could occur and would then have to be fought in court. His agency would probably be able to help with this. After much soul searching and promises of support from the rest of those present, the president and vice-president agreed to sign. We also added a clause to the letter stating that I had been working with them on this.

Again the worker serves as expert information giver here and as someone able to tap an environmental resource, the lawyer, more easily than clients could. The new content operating rule introduced in this ad hoc session also implies worker-client symmetry: the association officers will have to take some reality risks to stand up for their principles, and the worker will commit himself on paper as well.

We called a meeting on February 3rd to review where we had gotten, which was unfortunately not very far. The city had acknowledged our letter and again said they were working on the problem. The landlord had not responded. About twelve people attended the meeting, and they were split between some who were discouraged and others who wanted to go on. I said I was sorry the letter hadn't worked yet, and it was their choice as to what to do. Mrs. Johnson made a rather rousing speech, saying she and Mr. Olney, the vice-president, had put themselves on the line by signing the letter, and where had their support gone? They all knew it wouldn't be easy, and she was not one for giving up. The group then discussed what could be done, and I volunteered to ask a lawyer to speak with them about possibilities through the court. Ten people definitely agreed to attend this meeting, assuming it could be at our regular time, and each promised to ask other potential new members whether they would like to join in.

In this final excerpt of meetings given here, the worker stays in the background, letting tenants run their own group in accord with a symmetrical relationship operating rule. However, he does offer acceptance of a subgroup's feelings of discouragement, perhaps helping all tenants present to accept these feelings in others and possibly in themselves but then to move on. Finally, when it seems that the tenants wish to continue to fight, the worker again volunteers an environmental intervention—to bring a lawyer in. We note that this worker, bit by bit, has been teaching clients to deal with blocked tenant-landlord communication by using strategies from his own intervention repertoire. That is, their letter to the landlord has suggested metacommunication about tenant-landlord differences, with some threat of confrontation since softer attempts have already failed. Further, the worker has helped tenants toward intervening in their and the landlord's environment through a significant external system—the city housing bureau. Other external systems, including the courts and the press, may also be available for work. In certain circumstances the tenants might even be able to use paradox with the landlord, as by sitting passively at his business office if they could locate it. The paradox would be in their taking on an obvious waiting, supplicant role rather than condemning the landlord, but placing with him clear one-up responsibility for instituting any change.

Worker Relationship Communication with Families and Groups

The relationship messages that a social worker puts forth in small system practice are more complex than in individual work. First, any of a worker's communication, depending on how it is directed, proposes his immediate symmetry or complementarity with the whole family or group, with a sub-system, or with one member. The worker who asks, "What would you like to do next?" suggests his symmetry with the person or persons he looks at as he asks. Intervention directed toward individuals or subsystems tend to define a worker as temporarily in coalition with them. To keep family or group members from feeling left out, the worker should try to form coalitions fairly equally with everyone.[2] Worker-client relationship communication in small system practice also affects relationship positioning among all members. The client who has taken a new stance with the social worker, or who has witnessed others doing so, may learn to behave differently within the system[3] and perhaps elsewhere as well. A worker either reinforces or seeks to modify small system members' proposed relationship operating rules.

Some clients show age-appropriate relationship flexibility toward the worker and each other, vary their coalition partners, and clearly maintain any generational boundaries. With them, a worker should make sure his relationship messages do the same. Other clients relate to the worker and each other less ideally, but well enough to achieve service goals. Here, a worker may go along with existing rules, as when he forms a symmetrical coalition with the rather authoritarian leader of a social action group. Where dysfunctional relationship operating rules are a major reason for a small system's needing help—for example, where parents remain too com-plementary one-up with a boy who is becoming painfully withdrawn—a worker will almost certainly have to offer new relationship information to affect existing operating rules. In the example given, he may try relating somewhat flexibly to the son, hoping the parents will do the same. A worker must always know what relationship messages of symmetry or complemen-tarity, and what coalitions, his basic interventions and other words and actions convey.

By the way he elicits information with families and groups, a worker proposes symmetry or complementarity between himself and an individual, a subgrouping, or everyone. If he asks everyone about a new content area, he has momentarily proposed himself one-up to them. If he asks a few people about content already under consideration, he is symmetrical with these individuals and, when listening attentively, even one-down. Any elicitation implies that those asked are capable informants on the matter at hand. Where eliciting from one system member is clearly intended to inform others, it may further suggest that this person is more knowledgeable than others or one-up to them in the particular content area. The worker who elicits any information from an individual or a subgrouping forms a coalition with the person or persons involved, except when others have actually encouraged the elicitation. The worker who concentrates on asking one family member about himself may be doing so because this person is an "identified patient,"[4] whom others want to define as the only one needing help.

The relationship positions a worker takes in eliciting propose operating rules in that they suggest what stances he proposes to take with whom. By listening attentively to a child, he shows he is willing to be one-down to the child and in coalition with him for a time. By asking everyone about some new content, he shows he is willing sometimes to be one-up to all. Because the worker is such a powerful ally within the family or group, his relationship positions in eliciting can also affect the stances clients allow among themselves. Eliciting certain information from every member of a group suggests a worker's willingness to be symmetrical with all. These clients are less likely thereafter to agree to a rigidly hierarchical pecking order among themselves. The worker who usually elicits from a one-up member of the client system, thus forming a coalition with him, may reinforce existing system operating rules. In the opposite circumstances, he may either change such rules or stimulate homeostatic reactions from system members. The latter reaction commonly occurs when the worker allies with a scapegoated child, perhaps asking him concerned questions while ignoring the parents, and succeeds only in stimulating the parents' greater efforts to keep both worker and child one-down.

For assessment purposes, a worker may have to take a one-up stance in pursuing given content. He may also direct his questions to everyone together, to see who answers, or may encourage contributions from a usually silent system member, to probe everyone's tolerance for greater relationship flexibility. Once the worker begins to have some sense of system members' relationship operating rules, he must decide whether he wants his eliciting to support or to counter these rules. Most workers in small system practice propose as much relationship flexibility as they think system members will tolerate at a given time. They do so by using forms of eliciting that imply varied age-appropriate stances with each individual, by directing elicitation such that they form coalitions with different members consecutively, and by sometimes eliciting from the family or group as a whole.

The form and direction of a worker's evaluative feedback also have relationship implications. By giving strong positive or negative feedback to an individual, a subsystem, or a whole family or group, the worker places himself complementary one-up to any one of these. Mild positive feedback implies a worker's symmetrical or one-down stance to recipients, as do neutrality and sometimes selective response. When a worker directs positive feedback to an individual or subsystem, he implies a coalition with the recipients. When he similarly directs negative feedback, he may be perceived as in coalition with system members who also disagreed with the information or actions in question. Nevertheless, the worker maintains a relationship with recipients of negative feedback; he does not with clients to whom he offers disconfirmation. It is especially important that a worker not disconfirm a family or group member—by ignoring him, for example—for more than a short time.

The worker who frequently gives strong feedback to whole systems or to all members equally suggests an operating rule that he can be perennially one-up. Such frequent one-up stances are generally to be avoided, although they may be necessary with young children or a severely disturbed family or group. The relationship operating rule proposed by a worker's mild, intermittent positive feedback is that he can form symmetrical coalitions with system members involved. With families and groups able to tolerate his temporary coalitions and age-appropriate relationship flexibility with all, a social worker can give varied evaluative feedback. The worker who wishes to violate existing relationship operating rules in offering feedback must assess whether change is feasible for the particular client system at the time. If he uses positive feedback to form a coalition with a one-down spouse, for example, the couple may simply engage in an unpleasant symmetrical escalation until the worker's coalition partner gives in.

A worker who offers new content information to clients proposes himself one-up to a greater or lesser degree. In giving content information to one individual or subgrouping, he also defines his one-up coalition with these.

But when information given seems to be for the individual or subgroup to use in dealing with others present, the coalition is close to a symmetrical one. A social worker who tells parents how they can discipline their children is in a fairly symmetrical coalition with them, implying both his and their complementarity to the children. A worker's suggesting that some system members give information to others defines the former members as one-up to the latter, while his suggesting that everyone exchange information posits symmetry.

All such worker information giving may affect worker-client system relationship operating rules. A worker will often propose relationship flexibility among system members by suggesting that they exchange content information, and by giving information to the system as a whole. He may also form coalitions at different times with everyone present by giving information to individuals or subsystems equally. In other situations, he may wish to confirm appropriate complementarity within a system by sharing more information with parents or group leaders. The worker must also take care that his information giving does not confirm dysfunctional system operating rules. He would not, for example, want to suggest to one sibling how to handle another, who was an identified patient, but would rather try to give similar information to both.

Worker interventions which change environmental information available to family or group members almost always carry one-up relationship messages, though less so as clients ask for any changes made. The worker who performs concrete services or sees collaterals on behalf of everyone is one-up, presumably benignly, to all. Whenever a worker intervenes environmentally on behalf of an individual or sees an individual or a subgroup alone, a coalition results. When he makes an environmental intervention at some system members' specific request, he enters into a fairly symmetrical coalition with them. The worker who calls a child's teacher at a parent's request is fairly symmetrical with or even one-down to the parent involved.

Changing the context in which he and clients meet makes a worker complementary one-up to everyone, but less so with those who asked for the change. When a worker adds a system member or removes one, members of the newly constituted system must renegotiate any preexisting relationship operating rules. If the worker suggests a new meeting place, clients may end up changing existing relationship operating rules to fit this context. For example, the mother who is cowed by the worker's authority in his office, and accepts a one-down stance to her husband and children there, might act differently toward all during a home visit. A worker-initiated change from verbal discussion to activities can also have considerable impact on system members' relationship operating rules, as when use of games in a children's group allows especially athletic or bright members to assume new leadership roles.

Finally, worker communication that does not readily qualify as intervention carries proposed relationship definitions and operating rules in small system as in individual practice. Such worker activities as thanking system members, apologizing to them for something he has done, and acquiescing to whatever control they take of process, define the worker at the time as one-down. A worker's willingness to laugh with system members, to use the same forms of address toward them that they do toward him, and to reveal personal matters such as his own feelings, all propose symmetry. Failing to perform small courtesies, not laughing, interrupting clients more than clients interrupt the worker, and generally controlling process are all complementary one-up (if sometimes justified) moves. When a worker behaves differently toward some clients within a family or group than toward others in such matters, coalitions are formed. Sometimes these are appropriate, as when a worker calls children by their first names and parents by their last, or shares his personal feelings to a greater extent with parents. Sometimes they are not, as when the worker calls a man who is diagnosed as schizophrenic by his first name and his wife by her last.

Using Worker Relationship Communication in Small System Practice

Although a social worker may value clients' age-appropriate relationship flexibility both with him and among themselves, he must gear his relationship messages to what he thinks will help them achieve service goals. In our earlier practice example of a tenants' group, the worker achieved symmetry with members in general but also, when indicated, defined coalitions with the group's benign natural leaders. Here, we consider uses of a worker's own relationship communication to affect incremental change in a family's relationship operating rules.

The family consists of a middle-aged alcoholic man employed as an insurance salesman; his wife, who works part-time as a bookkeeper; and their two children, a girl of thirteen and a boy of ten. The family was self-referred to a community mental health center, the husband having called for an appointment. Excerpts from their first interview with an older male social worker highlight the worker's relationship communication with family members as a crucial beginning element in effecting change.

> After introducing myself to Mr. and Mrs. Stanhope, Sheila and Mike in the waiting room, I guided them to the office and said there were a few things I wanted to share with them before we got started. First, Mr. Stanhope had told me on the phone that he had a drinking problem and wanted to do something about it. I was the one who had asked the whole family to come in, and they were probably a little nervous and wondering why. But I did appreciate everyone getting here. Did they have any questions so far? Mike asked if I was a doctor. His mother shushed him but I said it was okay, and explained my role as helping people talk so they could get along better or help each other more, whatever they wanted. I added that I would like to hear what everyone thought about being here.

Besides introducing content operating rules—that Mr. Stanhope's drinking, the worker's motives for bringing the family in, and the family's reaction to this are fit subjects for discussion in the interview—this worker sends several interesting relationship messages in just a few minutes. His using the parents' last names, the children's first, and presumably his own surname in introducing himself, defines an age-appropriate symmetry of the adult generation. The worker thereafter takes a one-up prerogative to begin the interview, and assumes responsibility for having invited the family in. However, his content in general is geared toward defining symmetry between himself and everyone. First, he wants the whole family to know what he knows about them, or rather about Mr. Stanhope, who has made the intake call. Then, he accepts everyone's probable nervousness and their questions, as he twice elicits information from all. Finally, he takes a one-down stance toward eveyone by appreciating their "getting here," a word usage subtly suggesting that each family member took some active responsibility for coming in. These maneuvers avoid defining Mr. Stanhope in the one-down, identified patient role. The worker even responds symmetrically to ten-year-old Mike's question, politely rejecting the mother's reminder that the child should stay one-down and again defining his own role as a helper, not specifically to Mr. Stanhope but to everyone. All of the worker's relationship messages so far test the family's beginning response to his proposed flexible relationship operating rule.

> Mrs. Stanhope began that she was not quite sure what they were all doing here. Her husband had had a drinking problem for years and she was glad he wanted to work on it, if he really did this time, but what did it have to do with them? I said, if she didn't mind, I would like to hear everyone's ideas about this, and after a pause I looked to Mr. Stanhope. He said as I knew from the telephone conversation, he had been drinking and causing everyone heartache for years. Now he wants to change, but he's not sure why everyone has to be here with him either. I nodded and turned to Sheila, asking what she thought about them all being here. She said it was okay. I looked at Mike who said, "no comment" with a shy smile. I smiled back and said that didn't count, and we would get back to him. I then said that in a general way, I thought families usually had some unhappiness if one family member did. We could all decide later whether the family should come in together, but meanwhile I would like to know a little more about all of them. Could each tell me something about himself, where he worked or went to school, or whatever he wanted to say? After looking at his wife, Mr. Stanhope started, telling mostly about his drinking problem. Mrs. Stanhope added information and corrected him at times.

Here the worker attempts to involve all family members in giving information to him, eliciting first in a more one-up and later in a more open-ended, symmetrical fashion. He shows his one-down deference to Mrs. Stanhope in asking if she would mind, before moving away from talking to her. This move conforms with existing family relationship operating rules, where Mrs. Stanhope apparently takes a one-up role. His asking something of each family member then allows the worker sequentially to form coali-

tions with everyone. His efforts draw forth relationship information as well
as content; Mrs. Stanhope thus far is the dominant one, with Mr. Stanhope
and Sheila following her lead and forming one-down coalitions with her.
Mike's position is ambiguous. The worker will now make more planned
relationship interventions based on his assessment so far.

> After Mr. and Mrs. Stanhope had spent about twenty minutes telling me
> about his drinking problem, I said I would like to interrupt. While I was
> interested in this information, I had some other questions to ask. I then
> asked if everyone was pretty well aware that Mr. Stanhope had had a
> drinking problem and everyone thought it would be a good idea if that
> could change. All agreed except Mike, who looked troubled. With some
> prodding he said he guessed so, but his Dad seemed happier sometimes
> when he had been drinking. Before the others could comment on this, I
> said Mike might have a point; would anyone mind if we amended that
> statement to say that Dad should be happy sometimes even if he doesn't
> drink? Mr. and Mrs. Stanhope looked embarrassed but did not object. I
> said now I had a hard one for them. Everyone knew how to act with the
> Mr. Stanhope who had a drinking problem, but probably no one was
> quite sure how to act with a Mr. Stanhope who wanted to change. Mrs.
> Stanhope said her attitude was one of wait and see. I said I could under-
> stand that; did she mean she would pretty much keep treating him the
> same until she could see he had changed? She said she guessed so. I
> asked Sheila, who said she would trust him more if he really stopped
> drinking. Mike's comment was that he didn't know.

In this section of the interview, the worker first takes a one-down stance of
listening to Mr. and Mrs. Stanhope tell what they perceive as the problem,
both to gain content information for assessment and to examine existing
family relationship operating rules. When he sees that the family will so far
identify no difficulties except for Mr. Stanhope's drinking, he develops a
strategy for still trying to involve everyone together in change. First, the
worker interrupts with a selective response, not putting down Mr. and Mrs.
Stanhope's information giving but announcing that he will for the time being
take one-up responsibility for interview process. He then involves everyone
in agreeing on the problem and goals for change, again trying to define a
symmetrical stance toward all. When Mike breaks rank to suggest a different

view, which in fact implies family difficulties and an underlying father-son coalition, the worker seeks to incorporate it with a supportive comment rather than probing, because he does not wish to push Mike further, perhaps into a symmetrical escalation with one or both parents about whether such difficulties exist. Again, the worker accedes to existing patterns. His next comments, directed to the subgrouping of family members which does not see itself as needing help, moves toward defining these as indeed needing help to support Mr. Stanhope's efforts to change. The relationship message implied is that the worker may accept Mr. Stanhope as one-down problem bearer, but all must bear equal, or symmetrical, responsibility for a solution. In the next portion of the interview, this communication will become clearer.

> Mr. Stanhope added that he didn't blame everyone for being unsure about him. He has tried to go on the wagon before. I asked if he could do it alone, and he said he didn't know, but he wasn't sure he deserved any help after what he's put the family through. Mrs. Stanhope said of course they wanted to help him whatever way they could. I told them I wanted to stop a minute to see what we all meant by help. Mrs. Stanhope wondered what I thought they should do. I said, usually when someone has been drinking, that represents one way the person has of handling all kinds of different stresses, usually without even knowing it. Everyone in the family gets used to their own ways of handling stresses too. It's pretty hard for one person to think about handling things differently, for some reason, unless others in his family do. But that means a lot of thinking, discussion, and sometimes going into some uncomfortable things for everyone. There was a silence, and Mike said he would like to help his father be happier. I said that was nice of him, but it depended on the others too.

Here we see a series of shifts in relationship communication between the worker and family members, although the family's existing relationship operating rules have not yet begun to change. First, Mr. Stanhope accepts the one-down relationship stance that may well be consistently accorded him in family interaction, except when his symptom of drinking allows him greater control. The worker addresses him fairly symmetrically: he asks Mr. Stanhope's opinion on what should be done, but also tries to involve him in a symmetrical family-wide coalition for change. When Mrs. Stanhope volun-

teers to help, she is responding in part to the worker's content, but in part to
her husband's one-down message implicitly asking for a benign one-up figure
to take over for him. Again the social worker gently interrupts this pattern
with a request for everyone's participation, here in defining what all mean by
"help." Interestingly, Mrs. Stanhope goes one-down to the worker to ask
what they should do. But her question implies an intended coalition between
two relatively one-up figures: she and the worker will decide what they can
do to help Mr. Stanhope change. The worker accepts the new one-up role of
information giver, but defines the coalition as not with Mrs. Stanhope alone
but symmetrically with everyone. He does so by conveying important
content—that to solve this problem, they will all have to change. His message also carefully disarms blame. At the end of it, he in effect leaves them in
a fully symmetrical position with each other and with him, to decide whether
they all want help on these terms. Again he gently discourages Mike's
breaking rank, as he wishes to settle for no less than the involvement of
everyone.

> I turned to Mrs. Stanhope and said she and her husband might have to
> work especially hard on this, unfair as it might seem, and I wondered
> how she felt about it. She asked if I was saying her husband had been
> drinking because of her. I said no. Rather that I suspected she had been
> trying to help him for some years, and he had been trying to stop, and
> what they did hadn't worked for whatever reason. Now I was asking
> them both to work on it in a different way, which might mean changes
> for the children too. Mr. Stanhope said he didn't want his wife blamed,
> and Sheila added, "Daddy, he didn't say that." I asked where they all
> stood. Mrs. Stanhope said she was ready to try anything; it's true what
> they had done before hadn't worked. I looked at Mr. Stanhope, and after
> some further discussion he and the children agreed.

Having given family members his idea for symmetrical work on their
problem, the worker defers once more to Mrs. Stanhope's position in the
hierarchy. Although "she and her husband might have to work especially
hard," it is her response he seeks first. The worker now accepts the role of
benign one-up figure Mrs. Stanhope earlier accorded him, and promises to
treat her well in the interaction if she will indeed let him have some control.
His answer to her question about blame further clarifies his intent. He does

not ask her to accept blame for not having helped her husband in the past, but only to share equally now in the burden of change. When Mr. Stanhope moves in to question the worker on his wife's behalf, his content is redundant but his relationship stance is also benign one-up to his wife, perhaps even slightly competitively with the worker. Sheila puts him down, taking over the mother's one-up role. But she is also won over to the worker's promise of help in which family members can be symmetrical as well as sometimes complementary with each other. The stage is very tentatively set for later interviews, where change can be brought about in the family's relationship operating rules. Eventually, the worker's relationship messages may even have an impact on clients' communication blocks. As long as Mr. and Mrs. Stanhope maintain a complementary relationship definition, each is likely to ignore or reject some of the other's valid needs: his for assertiveness, hers for dependency. If the worker helps them become more symmetrical at times, and flexible overall, the possibilities for better marital communication should grow.

Change, however, does not always take place easily in practice with families and groups. Worker-client communication here, as in work with individuals, can threaten to block, especially when small system operating rules have dysfunctionally rigidified. The following chapter takes up intervention possibilities in such instances.

Eight

Worker-Client Communication Blocks in Small System Practice

Communication not only between clients but also between the worker and one, several, or all members of a client system can block. A worker can easily miss one client's communication during a lively family or group interview. He is quite likely to convey content or relationship information that someone will find unacceptable. If a client then hides his negative responses, blocking will almost surely occur. These processes can also occur between the worker and several or all members of a client system. A worker may persist in offering information with which any number of clients disagree. All family or group members' participation in blocking often suggests worker-client differences about operating rules. If a worker keeps trying to get parents to talk about their relationship, for example, and finds everyone involved in diversionary tactics, he has probably triggered homeostatic mechanisms against second-order system change. The worker who prevents some blocks and intervenes to resolve others constructively has not only enhanced worker-client interaction but has often demonstrated important interpersonal problem solving skills for clients to pick up and use.

Preventing and Recognizing Worker-Client Communication Blocks

As with an individual client, the worker can prevent some blocks by attending carefully to what system members communicate, offering neutral or positive evaluative feedback more often than rejecting client communication, using language he thinks clients will understand, building bridges between what clients know and what he is suggesting to them, and offering new information incrementally. In small system practice, however, the worker must try not to miss nuances of more people's behavior. His positive evaluative feedback to one or a few individuals may be rejected by others; yet the worker can hardly be neutral all the time. While some small system members are close to one another in the language they understand and the knowledge they have on hand, allowing the worker to gear his interventions accordingly, others are not. Those in formed groups are especially likely to vary in what they understand or already know.

The worker in small system practice must find ways to deal with these difficulties. To miss as little client communication as possible, he can begin to see the inherent patterning within it. We know that people together tend to repeat content and relationship messages, to signal their differences via homeostatic mechanisms, and thereby to demonstrate existing or nascent system operating rules. The worker aware of such matters is less overwhelmed by the totality of client communication and more able to hear idiosyncratic nuances within it. To avoid the block created by some clients' rejecting the positive evaluative feedback that has been offered to others, the worker can direct such feedback toward the whole family or group rather than toward an individual. He may say, for example, that he appreciates everyone's wish to change. He can accept contributions of several clients in quick succession. When giving positive feedback to an individual or a subgrouping, he can add in an accepting fashion that others may feel differently. Such content messages propose an operating rule that the worker will support all clients equally. A worker can sometimes prevent certain clients' rejection of his content and relationship information by asking others to help the potential rejecters understand what he is trying to get across. A client whose store of information is somewhere between the worker's and that of another client can often help the latter make connections between the worker's newly offered ideas and his own. The group member who does understand the worker's point about why people get depressed may be able to explain it to a client who does not. A worker can also avoid some blocks by giving information about system operating rules themselves rather than about the content and relationship matters that the rules govern. For example, he may comment on a marital pair's efforts to decide who is right about some content, rather than himself entering the fray.

To enlist clients' help in preventing blocks, the worker asks system members to tell him when he seems to have missed their messages, when they do not understand his, or when they cannot accept what he has suggested to them. Persuading clients to clarify their differences with the worker is not always difficult. Some family or group members, like some individual clients, are perfectly willing to do so, once the worker has sanctioned such an operating rule. Some even gain status by disagreeing with the social worker, as when adolescents respect the group member who challenges authority. Small system clients then learn from experience whether the worker really wants them to surface negatives. If he shows that he does, and that he can move to resolve the potential blocks discovered, the worker has taught system members a valuable communication skill.

Some family or group members may not surface any difficulties with worker communication, but may misunderstand or disregard it silently. They may deny differences with the worker of which they seem to be well aware, or may seem not to know themselves what is the difficulty. If one or two system members do ask the worker for clarification, point out his lapses in understanding, or question what he offers them, others present may look disapprovingly at the questioner or isolate him as being bad, crazy, or the worker's pet. Such responses are particularly common when system members do not allow open discussion of missed or rejected communication among themselves. A family in which children are not allowed to question parents is unlikely to sanction their questioning the social worker.

When clients reject the idea of differing with the worker openly, the worker must know how to recognize potential hidden blocks. Clients may show their uncertainties about his content or relationship stances through symbolic verbal communication. A family, for example, talks about the dangers someone they know ran into doing something similar to what the worker has proposed. Nonverbal responses suggesting hidden blocks include one or more clients' frowning, looking away, changing the subject, or maintaining behavior after apparently having accepted information which implies changing it. Clients express rejection of the worker's flexible relationship stances sometimes by passivity, sometimes by taking over an interview. The rejection of a worker's ever being one-up is implied when system members ask for help and still do not change because one individual's symptoms are supported by family or group communication patterns. In any instance, small system members' ambiguous responses to worker content or relationship messages may also signal their disagreement with his proposed operating rules. Thus members of an alcoholics' group digress in talking about their job experiences when they really do not think the subject of working should be taken up.

The small system client who does not want to reveal his negative responses to worker communication can hide these in ways not available to clients seen individually. In family and group sessions, client feedback is transmitted less often through words. The worker must rely heavily on catching individuals' nonverbal messages. Although everyone is continually communicating in this way, such data are ambiguous, and the worker may have little chance to clarify a particular response verbally. Then, multiple clients can more easily remain neutral, leaving the worker's content or relationship information hanging, with no one taking responsibility to comment on it definitively. Small system members can also readily deny negative feedback toward worker communication by directing it to each other instead. The worker who finds one client attacking another without adequate cause should wonder whether he himself has just said something the angry client did not like. Quite commonly in small system practice, one client habitually is the scapegoat to whom others direct negative feedback when they really cannot accept worker messages. Even in families and groups where some members are allowed openly to reject worker communication, the individual demonstrating negative feedback may be doing so at the subtle instigation of others whose own negative responses remain hidden. A social worker can sometimes infer total family or group response to given information when no one challenges an individual's rejection of this. In other circumstances, system members can band together against the worker instead of surfacing in group antagonisms. Here their negative feedback is not really in response to the worker at all. When clients' negative messages are directed toward anyone, including the worker, who does not seem to have stimulated them, the worker must ask himself who did.

Inevitably, the small system worker will become involved in some established blocking of which he is unaware. As with individuals, he may become frustrated by family or group members' stubbornness, and may then stubbornly repeat interventions which had not been useful before. He may find himself in symmetrical escalations with any number of individuals, or disconfirming them by sullen silence or by giving up. A worker sometimes believes clients have heeded his new content or relationship information, only to find them reverting to their old patterns. As in individual practice, the worker's best clue to his own involvement in blocking may be his sense of impasse when clients seem not to change. If he can identify which of his communications have been missed or rejected, the worker can consider how to handle the potential blocks.

**Evaluating and
Withholding Participation
in Blocks**

A worker who senses potential blocks between himself and multiple clients can evaluate possible reasons for these. He can withhold his participation in blocks by remaining neutral or by accepting or selectively accepting clients' negative feedback. Each of these worker responses gives more clients more information in small system practice than in work with individuals.

Where blocks are caused by misunderstandings, it may be that the worker or the client was unclear in his original communication, that the worker and some number of clients missed each other's messages entirely, that one or more clients heard something the worker did not really say or misread his nonverbal communication, or that the worker misheard or misread clients' messages. When several clients together misunderstand a worker's communication which was presented clearly, the worker can consider whether they all lack understanding about how to process the information involved. Thus all members of a family, or a group with social class factors in common, might misunderstand worker information about certain feelings if none really knew how to perceive and evaluate these. Where misunderstandings can be clarified with relative ease, conflicts about information offered are unlikely to be present.

A worker's apparently constructive content or relationship information offered, however, can sometimes conflict with that already held by any number of family or group members. The worker who suggests to an adolescent group that masturbation will not cause insanity may encounter differing beliefs from one member, from several, or from everyone. New ideas offered by a social worker may conflict with one or more individuals' rules for information processing, as when a worker suggests talk before action and certain clients are opposed to such a stricture. Worker information may conflict with operating rules within the client system itself, or with rules affecting clients from other systems significant to them. In a family interview, a worker might try to address someone other than the family spokesperson and meet opposition from everyone. In a group session, the worker might touch a client and receive horrified looks from others, because, for them, touching has implications that it does not have for the worker. Conflicts between worker information and clients' external system operating rules can occur in family practice when clients are influenced by operating rules of their extended family, peers, work group, or community group. Formed group members are especially likely to be bound by what their nuclear families, peer groups, and other social systems allow and forbid. As in individual practice, the small system worker must be prepared to evaluate impinging system or other environmental influences by picking up clues about these from clients, by asking clients or collaterals, or by face-to-face observation of significant outside systems in which clients are involved.

Multiple clients can also block in accepting worker ideas that are not really constructive for them. The worker within a treatment group can be so afraid of dissent that he stifles members' differences or their efforts to introduce more open content operating rules. Or a worker can give nonconstructive information in unknowing conformity with existing family or group operating rules. The child's hyperactivity, which distracts his parents from arguing during a family session, may lead the social worker to attend to and make his interventions with the child as well. The child, unable to change until the family patterns do, will then ignore what the worker tries to accomplish with him. Finally, a worker can contribute to blocks when he keeps offering apparently constructive information to clients even though clients persist in rejecting it. By focusing repeatedly on the parents' arguing in the example just cited, the worker finds their discomfort as well as the child's hyperactivity intensified. The information the worker offers may be nonconstructive just because he fails to help family or group members to deal with it differently.

While assessing potential or established worker-client blocks, the small system worker may remain neutral for a time. Or, if he realizes information he was offering was not constructive or only partially so, he can accept—perhaps selectively—clients' negative feedback.

First, when one, several, or all family or group members reject worker information, the worker can decline to respond conclusively, whether by silence, by not commenting on clients' rejection of his content, or by not challenging their refusal to accept his proposed relationship stances. If his information has been rejected by all clients, his neutral response suggests his willingness to be one-down to all. This response reassures clients afraid of being overcontrolled and may lessen clients' hesitation about sometimes being one-down in turn. If the worker declines clear response to an individual rejection, everyone present can perceive his neutrality regarding this information and his willingness to be one-down to this individual. Being somewhat ambiguous, however, worker neutrality does not convey a definite coalition as many other interventions do. A worker often remains neutral simply because he needs more information before taking a stand. He may wish to observe consistencies in what is rejected and in who rejects what. His neutrality with natural groups such as families can be a beginning way not to side with someone as relatives and friends may have done. It can also serve as a retreat when a worker fears he and clients have entered into an established communication block. Although neutrality will not help clients unable to understand, or conflicted about, worker information, at least it will not do any harm during any observation period.

When potential worker-client communication blocks occur, it may be right for a worker to accept clients' negative feedback. He may have conveyed something inaccurate, or not useful to one or more clients at the particular time. He wants to confirm that clients can tell him when they do not understand, when they are not sure how proposed content fits in, when they have heard something different before, or whatever. Clients should also be able to reject a worker's proposed relationship definitions, particularly when they feel capable of leadership and he has proposed himself one-up. The worker who accepts such feedback again conveys his support for an operating rule of relationship flexibility, assuming that at other times he is willing to be one-up. A worker's accepting negative feedback from one or a few clients can be problematic because of the coalition implied, unless he also accepts other clients' negative feedback in other circumstances. Of course, a worker may not wish to close off further discussion by accepting negative feedback if he thinks what he has suggested should have been constructive for these clients at the time.

Selective acceptance of clients' negative feedback can also forestall some blocks. The worker can accept their rejection in full but only for a limited time. He might say that he hears parents telling him they have trouble talking about themselves as husband and wife, but at some point they will have to get to this. He can accept part of a rejection: when he has asked members of a community group each to call up several potential new members, and they have refused to call up more than two, he may say two is enough. A worker can accede to clients' rejection of his content but not of his relationship messages, or the opposite. After a group of hospital patients has refused to voice valid complaints to their doctors, the worker may ask them to do something else for themselves. His selective response would accept their refusal of his content but not the idea that they could be more symmetrical with him. Or he might accept only the clients' rejection of symmetry, by volunteering to speak to the doctors himself. In using selective response, a worker conveys a mixed rather than a pure one-up or down relationship position, and any coalitions are ambiguous. Selective acceptance resolves communication blocks when clients are willing not to reject a worker's communication if he will meet them half-way.

Intervening by Metacommunication

The worker can metacommunicate with clients about mutual communication blocks in order to achieve discussion in which some resolution occurs. The impact on clients varies, depending on whether possible blocking is between the worker and one individual, several, or everyone.

When one or a few system members reject his content or relationship information, the worker may metacommunicate by accepting any client's one-up stance in having given negative feedback, but himself going one-up to suggest consideration of the block. In the ensuing discussion he will sometimes learn that one or more clients misunderstood what he said, or that his ideas about their situation were less accurate than what they already knew. Some members of a mother's group, for example, may have rejected his suggestion about how to handle their physically handicapped children because they had tried something similar but without success. Clients may respond to metacommunication by revealing conflicts between information they hold and information the worker is offering—conflicts which can be resolved. In discussing why he had rejected a worker's constructive suggestion about dealing with his adolescent son, a father may realize that his information on hand was learned from his own parents and was insufficient at best. Whenever one or a few clients engage in metacommunication with him, a worker can comment on the usefulness of examining reasons for people's behavior, can give positive feedback for someone expressing what he thought would happen if he accepted the worker's information, and so on.

If the worker and some clients resolve blocking by metacommunication, others present can analogically learn this problem-solving skill. Practice in metacommunication can even help clients learn how to resolve their own future blocking. A worker may see family or group members begin to emulate his way of holding a neutral position while getting differences into the open. Moreover, when a worker and one or a few clients explore their differences, others can sometimes correct their own misinformation. If a client reveals during metacommunication that he thought needing help was a weakness, the worker's corrective information may reassure everyone. One client often gives a worker negative feedback designed to enforce family or group operating rules. The adolescent who rejects the worker's invitation to stand up for himself in a family interview may be showing the one-down deference toward adults his parents insist upon. If such rules are not rigidified, the worker's successful metacommunication with an individual may then lead to second-order system change. In the example just cited, the adolescent's saying that his parents expect obedience may make them aware that he is getting too old for such a totally one-down role.

One difficulty in metacommunicating with specific individuals is that the worker forms a temporary coalition with these. If such coalitions consistently involve the same client, others may object. Another problem arises if metacommunication with one or several individuals often fails. Everyone may assume that these clients' information is accurate, even if it is not, or that people's differences cannot be successfully surfaced and resolved. Such failures are more likely when those who reject worker messages are defending everyone's rigidly held system operating rules. For example, when the worker asks one family or group member about a very personal matter, this individual may decline to answer him. Engaging this client in metacommunication, the worker might learn that he thought that revealing himself would lead to his being attacked as weak. If all clients present had tacitly agreed that they should not reveal themselves, they might indeed verbally attack the individual who broke this rule when he revealed his fears to the social worker.

If a worker suspects that one or more clients' negative feedback serves to protect an existing operating rule, he may wish to direct metacommunication to the family or group as a whole. He can ask family or group members to consider that they are avoiding a certain subject area, and may wonder benignly whether they could discuss what is unattractive or frightening about it. For the marital pair whose mutual protectiveness is inhibiting examination of their feelings, the worker can suggest that they rethink with him whether such protectiveness is necessary. When a group is balking at work on a task, the worker can question what might be repelling them, rather than pushing for greater efforts. As in all metacommunication, his nonverbal behaviors should generally convey his acceptance of system members' right to determine what they will finally do, but also his wish to encourage examination of information on which they are operating. Even in confrontation, the worker's concern for clients and willingness to discuss reasons for his and their behavior should be in evidence. In directing metacommunication to the entire family or group, the worker avoids singling out an individual who may have been enforcing operating rules, and conveys symmetry with everyone by taking first the one-down, then the one-up relationship stance. His metacommunication with all system members suggests that everyone is involved in and must work together toward resolving blocks.

The appeal to everyone present is especially appropriate when worker-client communication threatens to block on the very subject of blocking between clients, this blocking often supported by system operating rules. Consider the very common client problem of continued symmetrical escalations between spouses, between parents and an adolescent, or between group members competing for power. In each of these circumstances, the implied operating rule is that no one involved may take anything but a one-up relationship stance. Each thus rejects the proposed one-up stances of others and by definition perpetuates mutual communication blocks. Worker-client blocks can begin when the worker suggests possibilities for different behavior, and clients do not act on the suggestions. Then, with whom should the worker seek to metacommunicate? If he approaches any of the clients individually, or even a subsystem such as the adolescents' parents, he implies that only these clients should be one-down in accepting information from him and that only these should change. His asking one client, ''Can we talk about why it seems so important for you to be right?'' rather than asking all involved, would most likely invoke the defective operating rule rather than helping everyone move up to the metacommunicative level to observe and comment upon it. Even when client relationship stances are not at issue, as when group members perpetually misunderstand the worker and each other, a worker who fails to direct metacommunication to all clients suggests that some need not be responsible for affecting change. There is a difference between his saying to one family or group member, ''You seem to miss other people's messages,'' or to all, ''What people are saying seems to get lost between us here.''

As a general rule, blocks which involve only one or a few clients with the worker in misunderstandings or in conflicts about information or information processing can often be handled between the people concerned, or even with other clients' impartial help. When blocking seems to reflect widespread misunderstandings between worker and clients, or their conflicts about operating rules, metacommunication should be addressed to everyone. Crucial in both instances is that the worker establish an atmosphere in which metacommunication can readily take place. Everyone should be able, without fear, to stop and look at information on which he is operating. Even if the worker points out client operating rules, he must do so in the spirit of inquiry and discussion rather than condemnation. Metacommunication in this atmosphere sometimes makes it clear that system members have rejected information in response to information or operating rules from impinging external systems, and stimulates discussion of what to do about this. The worker may learn from talking with a group of psychiatrically disabled veterans that they are afraid of losing their pensions if they should try going to work.

In some instances, metacommunication simply does not work to resolve worker-client blocks. Sometimes family or group members are not sufficiently comfortable with looking at themselves to use this form of discussion productively. Sometimes their individual needs to maintain relationship control or their rigidified system operating rules do not allow the worker to influence them in this direct fashion. Metacommunication that brings out conflicts between the worker's information and that which clients are receiving from their environments may point to the need for environmental intervention. Thus social workers may also consider using paradox, and must sometimes intervene environmentally, to resolve blocking. The worker's choice of intervention depends on which will best help clients move toward service goals.

Intervening by the Use of Paradox

When clients block in accepting worker communication in the broad sense that they seem unable to let the worker influence them, he may use his own relationship stances to put one, a few, or all clients present in paradox. That is, the worker deliberately places himself one-down and particular clients one-up, or in control of interaction between themselves and the worker, at the very time that clients are already explicitly or implicitly exerting such control. The paradox is that if clients keep trying to be in complete control, they are complying with the worker's wishes and thus letting him influence them. If they do not, they have changed their behavior, which was his original intent. The worker may use paradox to resolve blocks with persistently one-up or one-down family or group members almost exactly as he would with an individual client, with some similar and some different results. He may also use it to deal with all clients' rejection of his efforts toward change implied in their continued compliance with dysfunctionally rigidified family or group operating rules.

At times some number of family or group members insist on being perpetually one-up to the social worker, clearly controlling interaction within the interview and thereby rejecting the worker's proposals of relationship flexibility. Their negative feedback constitutes the first step toward a worker-client communication block. To impose paradox, the worker suggests that the client or clients in question be one-up, or agrees without rancor that they already are. As in individual practice, this tactic can disarm clients who have prepared themselves for a protracted battle for control. Thus, after a domineering parent has indicated that he is perfectly capable of running his family without suggestions from the social worker, the worker may concur and ask his advice about what should be talked about. He may further offer this parent credit for carrying the burden of making everyone's decisions, perhaps inducing him to question whether he really wishes to do so. Within a group session with adolescents, a worker can ask members who have controlled discussion with disruptive outbursts to take leadership positions, often persuading them to be benignly rather than destructively one-up. Or when all group members have been talking incessantly, the worker may disarm them by confiding that he does not have anything important to say.

There are more dangers to this use of paradox in small system practice than in individual work. The worker who affirms one or a few individuals' control of process inevitably forms a coalition with these. He thereby risks alienating others unhappy with, for example, the domineering parent or the disruptive adolescent group members. When the worker affirms a whole family or group's control over worker-client interaction, system members afraid of carrying this may behave more disruptively to get the worker to take over, as in the adolescent group. Or system members unhappy with the status quo can become discouraged, thinking that things are hopeless for them. The worker often cannot afford to take these risks.

Small system clients who define themselves as one-down to the social worker, who are perhaps even unable to take care of themselves because of symptoms beyond their control, may thus, without conscious volition, control the worker. Through helplessness, passivity, or symptomatic behavior, they start blocks by rejecting his suggestions that they take greater responsibility for themselves. The worker may respond to such clients' underlying control by validating it, as by noting that he cannot change them although they may wish to try to change themselves. The worker's conveying acceptance of these clients' behavior through voice tone and other nonverbal indicators as well as through words is, as before, imperative. The paradox exists in that the worker has either acceded to one or more clients' unacknowledged control or has actively encouraged it, again taking a metacomplementary relationship position no matter what the clients subsequently do.

But problems can arise here too. For example, the social worker may try to counter a mother's remaining helpless in a family session by saying that, as she is the mother, he cannot presume to tell her what to do. Or he might plead ignorance as to how to handle the children within sessions since he is not a father himself. By these tactics, he hopes that the mother will make some reasonably effectual one-up move, which he can encourage further. But the worker's attempt to be one-down to the mother, and thereby persuade her to be one-up, will fail if a child who acts the role of a parent in the family immediately takes charge. If a total family or group waits helplessly for the worker to take over, and he does not do so, one client may be forced into a leadership role. Since this client in a natural or established formed group has probably taken this role before, the worker's attempted use of paradox has achieved no particular change. In a formed group where clients are all expert at being one-down, such as a group of passive, clinging individuals, the worker's paradoxically forcing some clients to take over may achieve success by showing others that they are capable of leadership too.

Small system clients who adhere to rigidified operating rules, thereby rejecting a worker's possible influence on them, exert control unknowingly. Here, the worker may most effectively use two interrelated forms of paradox, the first really a mixture of paradox and information giving. One is reframing clients' behavior, or defining it differently from the way they usually see it, without asking them to change. The other is more actively suggesting that clients continue to behave as before.

Reframing is close to the technique of worker information giving, but with a paradoxical twist. Consider the situation in which a worker tells a married couple who argue a lot that they must love each other since they stay together nonetheless. The worker has given them new content information, tangentially related to their arguing as a relationship operating rule. However, if the worker tells the couple that their arguing shows they love each other since they are trying to reach out to each other through it, he has not only given information but also imposed a paradox. While arguing, each spouse most likely thought of himself as justifiably angry at the other and therefore forced to seek redress. By upholding the mutual operating rule that such argument is a part of their interaction, the couple also unknowingly controls the social worker by rejecting his attempts toward change. With his reframing comment, the worker paradoxically encourages them to argue, and thereby takes control of the situation. He also gives them information which should have the effect of reducing their arguing, since two people mad at each other do not wish to do something defined as reaching out. Even more intolerably, their arguing now smacks of weakness, need, or being one-down at the very time when their operating rule suggests that they must try to be one-up.[1]

All reframing combines the worker's seeing clients' behavior as meaning something different, usually more positive, than they thought, and also his clear implication that they may continue to behave this way if they wish. Thus in family practice the worker may define a mother's dominance as her having a strong sense of responsibility, and a father's passivity as patient forebearance. The operating rule of mother's being defined as one-up may be more difficult to follow, once each parent thinks of himself as having chosen his role for positive reasons rather than because the other forced him into it. Within a treatment group, the worker can define some clients' exposure of feelings as a courageous act, one which others might have to put down until they are more ready to join in. Here the worker gives new information and allows—but obviously makes it more difficult for clients to follow—a group operating rule that those who expose feelings are to be attacked.

Paradox in which a worker suggests that clients behave as they have been behaving, at least for a time, is in a sense implied in his permissive acceptance of clients' actions, his eliciting information by asking clients to tell about their problematic behavior, his giving information that such behavior will not immediately change in work together, and even his metacommunication when the worker accepts clients' right to continue giving negative feedback if they wish. However, once a worker is aware of dysfunctional operating rules in a particular family or group, and has found that his efforts to change them stimulate blocks, he may wish to use prescriptions of clients' behavior more consciously. Perhaps under the guise of learning more about these processes, a worker can ask a married couple to argue once more just as they usually do. A worker who notices that a family member's symptoms occur during a particular sequence of events—everyone becoming anxious about some content, for example—may ask this member to let him know about everyone's anxiety by producing the symptom at will. In milder form, a worker may suggest to a wife who is frigid that she plan not to enjoy sex for a while. In group practice, workers may intuitively prescribe interaction by such measures as predicting that one member will now take up the gauntlet dropped by another and begin an argument as he always does.

In family and group practice as with individuals, a worker may wonder about the ethics of using reframing and other forms of paradox to deal with worker-client communication blocks. Part of the issue, again, is that no one really knows how such interventions work: whether it is a matter of clients' changing behavior that no longer serves to control the worker, whether paradox, or at least reframing, makes clients uncertain about how to behave and thus leads to change; whether the worker, by condoning clients' behavior rather than asking for change, differs from outside parties, such as in-laws who have helped perpetuate clients' problematic functioning before; or whether the dynamic is something as yet unknown. Many social workers are willing to use interventions which invite clients to change their behavior, but not to see some of their interventions as conscious attempts to force change. For example, a worker may see reframing as ethical so long as he intends it to give information in a permissive way, rather than to disrupt clients' compliance with dysfunctional operating rules. Most workers are cautious in their use of paradox. While some clinicians argue that paradox is ethically justified because it helps clients,[2] social workers rightly hold back from its more radical uses unless they have had special instruction in these.

Intervening by
Environmental Work

To deal with blocked worker-client communication in small system practice, a worker may need to intervene into the context in which he and clients meet or into clients' larger environments. The first type of intervention often resolves blocks when clients can take in new information more readily through analogic or trial-and-error learning than in verbal form. The second is appropriate, as always, when the larger environment in which families or groups function keeps them from being able to change.

When clients reject his ideas because of their adherence to rigidified system operating rules, a worker may wish to make changes in the environment in which he and clients meet along with or instead of using metacommunication and paradox. Besides the more common strategies of using activities, meeting elsewhere than in an office, or requesting that people sit differently, the worker can take some system members out to observe others through a one-way mirror, videotape sessions and play them back for clients, suggest family sculpting, or suggest tasks for clients to try. More radical strategies are to bring in a second professional or consultant to meet with clients; or, temporarily or permanently, to change some of the participants of the group seen. Let us briefly examine two cases in which interventions into context deal with blocking due to worker-client conflicts about operating rules when other interventions alone do not.

A common problem in family practice is a mother's overinvolvement with a young son. The son is likely to function adequately except for some noticeable symptom or other, while a passive father looks on. If a social worker suggests that the parents pay more attention to each other, they may ignore this idea and thereby begin a communication block. The worker could then try metacommunication, perhaps eliciting the parents' fears about getting involved with each other. He might impose a paradox, suggesting that the mother hold on to her son as long as she feels uncertain that both she and her husband wish to be mutually involved. Finally, the worker might try to deal with the blocking implied by the family's continued adherence to a rigidified operating rule—that mother and son must be overinvolved and father peripheral—by changing the context in which he and these clients meet. If the father and son were mechanically minded, the worker might suggest using a session to put together a model. He might propose a tour of the factory in which the father worked, with or without the worker and the mother present. Operating rules always depend to some degree on the context in which they occur, and the father's one-down role in the family might change slightly in situations where he could show mastery. If father and son did begin to move together, the problem would not necessarily be resolved, but the worker might then have greater leverage for metacommunication about how and why system operating rules should change.

In this same case, the worker might meet similar goals by using alternative contextual interventions. He might ask the boy and his father to sit and talk together in the session or to accomplish a task together away from it.[3] Such interventions as family sculpting, videotaping and playback, or clients' observing each other through a one-way screen could also be tried to interrupt system members' operating rules by having them observe themselves. If both parents loved their son, they might be startled into changing family operating rules if, for example, the boy created a sculpture in which his mother was holding him very close while his father had his back turned. Family members who observe a videotape or look through one-way mirrors may be horrified to see themselves playing out a pattern they now realize is very destructive. The worker saying that the mother has trouble letting her husband and son be together may not be half so compelling as the mother's recognition of herself preventing this on videotape.

Adding a co-therapist or consultant to a small system interview will have an impact on extant operating rules simply because another person is present. To continue our case example, a consultant who engaged in activities with the son might leave the parents little chance but to begin talking with each other and the original social worker. This is in addition to whatever the consultant might say. Changing the constitution of the group, at least temporarily, might achieve similar results. The worker could simply ask the boy's parents to come in without him. Such an intervention can be highly useful at times, in defining appropriate subsystem boundaries. It can also create anxiety about who is involved with change, both for those singled out to come in and for those excluded, unless the worker explains his reasons and plans.

Let us turn to a more limited practice example: a group in which adolescent members have hinted about sexual concerns but seem unable to bring these up openly, even when the worker tries to help them do so. The worker may attempt metacommunication about their fears, or paradox as by suggesting that they hint about the matter when they are ready to talk about it. An intervention into the context in which worker and clients meet may be called for, however. The worker may propose the use of films; suggest meeting in a more relaxed atmosphere, such as on a camping trip; suggest tasks in which each adolescent could find out certain factual information; ask if he should bring in a doctor as a consultant; or consider splitting into same-sex subgroups to discuss the matter. In all these instances, the worker is getting around the operating rule that forbids any member to start formal verbal discussion of sexual concerns. He dodges the rule by proposing other means to open the subject.

By the kind of environmental interventions we have been describing, the worker resolves blocking by giving information in a different form from that tried earlier, frequently allowing clients to learn through analogic means or trial and error. The worker who says that a father and son should be more involved with each other and the one who proposes that they play a game has given about the same content and relationship information in both instances, but the clients may receive information better in the second form. The worker's verbal suggestion that father and son increase their involvement may seem like a major sort of change, frightening partly because what would happen is unknown. If the worker persuades the two to play a game together, they may find out without taking much risk that they enjoy each other's company, perhaps overcoming a fear about which they could not have metacommunicated. When workers help clients simply to behave differently, the information on which their subsequent actions are based may change through normal feedback mechanisms.

As a final possibility, a worker may intervene in small system members' larger environments in order to resolve a worker-client block. If a child has been involved in dysfunctional communication with his teacher and classmates, he may have trouble carrying out in school the behavior he has learned in family sessions. The mother who learns with the social worker to parent her children effectively may resume her former inappropriate symmetry with them when her own infantilizing mother is present. Members of treatment groups have families, peers, and work situations which may impel their rejection of a social worker's ideas. A social action group may fail to carry out its mission if an older community leader, who has been left out of decision-making, disapproves. Family or group members can be subject to poor agency service, prejudice, and poverty, over which they have little or no control. A responsible social worker must always stand by to intervene in clients' environments, in ways that we have already described in chapters 5, 6, and 7, when clients need such help to achieve valid service goals.

The past four chapters have elaborated many possibilities for social work intervention generally with individuals, families, and groups. Another, highly important form of practice in which social workers need to be competent is interprofessional work, our last major area of discussion here.

Nine

Interprofessional Practice

A social worker must know how to work with other professionals, whether these belong to his own or to allied disciplines, if he is to help clients effectively. Within or between professional settings he may collaborate on a single case with a fellow social worker, a physician, a psychologist, a nurse, a teacher, or someone from still another discipline. Usually within a setting he may participate in co-therapy, team efforts on behalf of many clients, or consultation in which he gives or receives case-oriented help. All such practice forms are important because of their sure influence on service delivery. Professionals who work well together tend to learn from and support each other, enhancing what each has to give clients he sees. Clients suffer when professionals involved with them do not get along.

Not always with conscious intent, social workers assess the functioning of professional colleagues, as well as of clients. They also exchange information with colleagues so as to affect their functioning, and in this sense may be said to intervene. While communication between professionals can block, social workers may try to prevent such blocks and may intervene to resolve them.

Assessment in Interprofessional Practice

To engage in competent practice with other professionals, a social worker must be able to assess their functioning. What he assesses, of course, depends on how much and why he and any colleagues meet, and on the worker's sources of information about a colleague at a given time. In most instances, a worker will first notice another professional's apparent ability and willingness to help clients in ways that the worker thinks he should. The colleague's proposals about relationship definition between himself and the worker are an additional concern. If there are problems, or if he will be working with a colleague extensively, a worker may then think about why this colleague behaves as he does. To put together his data for assessment, he can consider relevant content and relationship information on which another professional may be operating, and his ability to process new information offered him. Finally, to understand another influence on his own and colleagues' functioning, a worker can analyze operating rules within small systems constituted by himself and those involved with him in regular collaboration, co-therapy, team functioning, or consultation.

A one-time contact about a particular client may require assessment of another professional's functioning geared only to the task at hand. A worker who calls a physician to learn about a mutual client's medical condition will be less concerned with the doctor's willingness to relate to him symmetrically than if he were to work with him on a regular basis. With staff of a worker's own agency, hospital, school, or other host setting, more thorough assessment is desirable. Sometimes a worker must know how to serve as consultant for others and is thus interested in what they know and what they still wish to learn. Or, if a colleague is to offer consultation to him, a worker may wonder what he has to teach. When a social worker and a colleague are to collaborate on certain cases, still more awareness of each other's professional functioning is appropriate. The most intimate collegial relationships are probably those among members of an interdisciplinary team, or between two professionals engaged in co-therapy. Team members or co-therapists must understand each other especially well to work together effectively.

Most often a worker will gather information about colleagues informally, hearing what clients and others tell him but relying especially on what he sees and hears firsthand. Observing colleagues with clients or other professionals, he notices how they interact. The teacher unable to say how he loses control of a child may demonstrate loss of control during an actual class session. The physical therapist who is quiet with co-workers may speak warmly to a disabled man. Through his own interaction with colleagues, the worker will learn what they think about clients and how they act

with respect to other professional matters such as giving or receiving consultation. Noticing colleagues' behavior with him, a worker will also see how
these individuals propose to relate. When he needs information from a new
head nurse, a worker is interested in whether the nurse wishes the worker to
relate as a greater authority in the situation, as a peer, or as a supplicant. In
general, when he or others offer new information, a worker can watch how
colleagues process it and respond. Should he wish to consider small system
operating rules, he can begin to search for regularities in his own and other
professionals' reciprocal content and relationship messages. A worker
should be aware of colleagues' significant personal circumstances which
they have chosen to reveal; professional identifications; and the agency,
community, and societal contexts within which professional colleagues
interact, since all of these must influence their functioning. Having gathered
information in these various ways, the worker is ready for assessment itself.

   A social worker's underlying assumption with colleagues, as with clients,
should be that their functioning makes sense in relation to their total information on hand. The worker who makes a referral assumes, until shown
otherwise, that the professional in another setting will put together what he
knows about the client's needs, his own agency services, and the good will
of the referring social worker and will behave appropriately. If not, there
may be other information on which this individual is operating. For example,
he may have had bad experiences with similar clients before. The worker
uses several perspectives for assessing colleagues' functioning as he does
with clients. On the one hand, he assesses information on which colleagues
may be operating to try to understand their behavior. He may ask them
about this information or may infer it from what he knows about their professional role and other of their circumstances. Then he looks at their behavior and infers from this their possible information on hand. Consider the
situation in which a night nurse seems to have neglected a patient who
repeatedly buzzed for her. Before forming any conclusion, the worker
should know more about information available to the nurse at the time—
whether she heard the patient buzzing her, whether she was dealing with a
more pressing emergency, or whatever. If the nurse's behavior has been
neglectful in other circumstances, the worker might infer that she was

operating on different information, such as dislike of her job, personal problems, or a weak sense of professional responsibility. A worker considering information on which colleagues might be operating should not overlook these individuals' inner states. An associate angry at a client or at some happening in his personal life may bring forth this affect toward the social worker. More positively, workers who hope to understand other professionals may notice how they behave when someone enhances their self-esteem.

If a social worker and one or more of his colleagues agree about who will do what on behalf of clients, about how they will carry out their mutual responsibilities while maintaining a pleasant association, about what has resulted in a given instance and what this implies for further action, the need for assessment may fade. On the other hand, when a worker's efforts to collaborate or consult with other professionals are problematic, the difficulty can lie with insufficient, inaccurate, conflicting, or even overwhelming information that any participants have on hand. A worker must look to his own functioning in a situation to see whether his own information was inadequate. Colleagues may be struggling to understand what a client needs, or may misunderstand the role of the social worker, simply because they lack adequate information. The lawyer who talks brusquely to a mutual client may not realize how emotionally fragile this person is. The doctor who expects a social worker to be his handmaiden may not have learned differently in medical school. A further question is whether such colleagues can accept constructive new information offered by a social worker, or whether they will block in processing it.

Assuming a worker has tried to correct any of his own blocks in processing content or relationship information, he may assess similar blocks in his colleagues. A colleague may fail to process information simply because he missed it, or because of language or cultural differences, pressure, or fatigue. Different jargons, different uses of the same terms, and different models of practice between professionals often cause content-level misunderstandings. The behavioral psychologist may not follow a social worker's explanations of a client's functioning given in Freudian terms.

Colleagues, like clients, can block because of conflicts between information offered by a social worker and their own information, information processing, operating rules within the interprofessional staff, or larger environmental influences. A behavioral psychologist may understand a social worker's Freudian notions, but still refuse them as incompatible with his own professional knowledge base. A physical therapist may not be able to believe a worker's assertion that a complaining patient is really trying to help himself, because, in the therapist's family, complaining was a sign of weakness. A technicality may prevent a social worker in another setting from seeing a certain client as eligible for services, though the client clearly needs help. In spite of a genuine desire to provide good client service, professional colleagues often find their communication blocked due to relationship issues. A psychiatrist may accept a social worker's information about a client's behavior but not his opinion about what such information implies. If the conflict were about content only, the psychiatrist would be able to accept the worker's professional opinion at another time. If the psychiatrist believes the worker should not propose himself as symmetrical by giving such opinions, the conflict of information is on the relationship level and must be dealt with as such.

To understand his own and colleagues' interprofessional functioning, a worker may examine operating rules within the small social systems formed when people work together over a period of time. As he observes what happens between colleagues, the worker can infer what discussion content and behavior generally seem to be allowable. Do the professionals in question talk about clients' behavior, give opinions about assessment and intervention planning, but never say what they have actually done? Do they discuss wider professional concerns, administrative problems of the setting, or personal matters almost exclusively? Can members of a professional staff lunch together or touch each other affectionately? A worker may become more aware of such operating rules when he breaks one and sees homeostatic mechanisms instituted. The young worker who nervously continues presenting his case at a diagnostic staff, rather than laughing at a colleague's joke, may be teased for being too serious.

Colleagues, of course, also establish their own mutual relationship operating rules. Between any two professionals there may be symmetry, complementarity, or relationship flexibility overall, while in larger groupings coalitions will often form. Relationship definitions established between two or more individuals may be the same or different in different content areas. For example, where two social workers do co-therapy with a family or group, one may dominate within sessions while both share responsibility for later evaluation of results and treatment planning. Within an interdisciplinary team, colleagues who share similar points of view often form coalitions to espouse these. Generally speaking, sound professional relationships are flexible in that each participant is able sometimes to be one-up, particularly in his area of expertise, and to accept one-down and symmetrical stances at other times. Such relationships most often occur when colleagues agree on their different areas of expertise or responsibilities in a particular case situation, and when each sees the other as competent. It is undoubtedly helpful, too, for administrators, supervisors, and others to demonstrate flexible relationship positioning rather than that they and their professional staffs should be rigidly hierarchical. Some social workers believe it is part of their professional role to facilitate effective collegial relationships within and between settings. If so, they probably should use this metacomplementary stance to help other disciplines feel responsible for their own collegial relationships, much as a client must ultimately be symmetrical enough with a social worker to take charge of his own functioning.

Operating rules within a staff group can be dysfunctional when one or more professionals feel discomfort with them, or—more important—when professionals may be comfortable but clients are poorly served. A worker might notice that colleagues within his setting are comfortable with an elaborate intake procedure, but that many clients drop out. If he suggests change and other professionals give the idea serious consideration, the rules are merely dysfunctional. If the idea of change is seen as suspect or inherently bad, the rules are rigid as well. Problematic rules may also exist on the relationship level, as when one professional within a setting cannot use all of his skills because others are threatened by these. Social workers themselves can unknowingly uphold dysfunctional operating rules, sometimes the very ones to which they most strenuously object. They might object to psychiatrists' exalted status within a hospital or clinic, yet continue to turn to them for consultation rather than using available social workers.

Interventions in
Interprofessional Practice

Two or more professionals who participate in consultation, who work together, or who otherwise share responsibility for a case, must exchange
information if they wish to serve clients well. Social workers may use interventions already identified and can, where appropriate, make sure that their
communication with colleagues proposes flexible relationship positions.

In interprofessional practice, as with clients, eliciting information serves
several purposes. A worker may ask colleagues about their experiences,
opinions, or plans in regard to particular clients to supplement what he
knows and to coordinate intervention efforts. At the same time or in separate
discussions, a worker can gear his eliciting to learn a colleague's general
approach to clients, his depth of professional knowledge, his stand on administrative issues, and the like, in order to work with him more effectively.
A worker's questions, whether intentionally or not, reveal to the other professional the line the worker's thinking has taken. A worker might ask a
nurse whether she had noticed a hospitalized child's terror, mainly to draw
her attention to it. Eliciting information when several colleagues are present
can be informative for all. A worker's questions to a psychologist on an
interdisciplinary team may help him explain testing data such that other team
members also understand the client better. Sometimes other colleagues'
presence can make a worker's eliciting more difficult, as when a new worker
wants to ask about something that others already know.

When he asks for someone's opinions about a case, the worker implies
that the other professional is an expert informant and therefore one-up in this
way. His asking for facts is a more symmetrical move, especially if he might
then reciprocate by telling the other professional what he knows. A worker
may, however, seem to put the other professional one-down when his questions apparently demand a response, test whether the other professional
knows what he is doing, ask him to review his own information possibly to
revise his conclusions, give him information surreptitiously, or demand that
he take unwanted responsibility for a case. A worker can avoid such implications in the way he phrases questions or by telling why he has requested
information. For instance, he might say to a physician, ''Do you have time to

help me understand this diagnosis better?'' rather than, ''I'd like to know what this diagnosis means.'' He might explain to a worker in another agency, ''I'll be working with Mr. X and it would help me to know what happened when he saw you,'' instead of, ''Please tell me what you did with Mr. X.'' Finally, the coalition aspects of eliciting information must be considered when more than one colleague is present. As an example, nothing can exclude other professionals more than a worker's consistently asking the opinions only of one.

When a worker sees particular strengths in one or more colleagues' performances, he may foster good will by giving positive evaluative feedback. In offering consultation, a worker's use of such feedback to reinforce participants' strengths is especially in order. Careful giving of negative feedback can help colleagues too, as when a worker gently warns someone that he comes across as a know-it-all. Neutrality or selective response may be used when a worker is not sure if he can go along with colleagues' ideas but does not wish to disagree openly.

The worker who gives strong positive or negative feedback to an associate about the accuracy of information he possesses, how well his thinking processes are working, or the effectiveness of his actions has taken a one-up relationship stance that may be unacceptable if he seems to have set himself up as knowing more in what the colleague considers his own area of expertise. For one co-therapist to tell another he has done something poorly is acceptable only if their association is a complementary one, as between a supervisor and student, or if the other co-therapist can freely reciprocate. A worker must also take account of other colleagues' presence here. A hospital social worker who says that several new residents are doing a good job may be seen as inappropriately evaluating and therefore taking a one-up role with them.

Symmetrical rather than one-up, because the worker is offering mild positive feedback in an area of which any professional in the setting might be aware, is a worker's saying to a nurse, ''You have a reputation for watching the effects of medication very closely,'' or to an occupational therapist, ''I see how carefully you explain things to patients.'' Giving noncondescending positive feedback to colleagues tends to cement relationships as benignly symmetrical, as long as the worker can receive such feedback too. For a worker simply to accept another professional's ideas about what should be done with a client is an often appropriate one-down act. Selective response to a colleague's contribution can also be useful in avoiding power struggles. If a colleague mentions several equally possible alternatives for his work with clients, the worker may fairly symmetrically comment on the advantages of one for what he hopes to do. To a psychiatrist who was thinking of ordering psychological tests on a child soon or at a later time, the worker might say that sooner would be helpful to him in dealing with the parents' worries about retardation. He has thereby indicated a preference, but not suggested more than a symmetrical relationship stance. When other colleagues are present, the advantages of a worker's softening his relationship stances in giving feedback are even more apparent.

Social workers obviously offer new content information to professional associates. They may reciprocally offer both facts and opinions on given clients. They may know more than other disciplines about family practice, community resources, and how to enhance interprofessional relationships themselves. A social worker's offering new information to colleagues is a one-up move, which should be acceptable when information given is within the worker's area of expertise. A worker must sometimes struggle himself to be comfortable with the one-up role implied in information giving, for example during consultation. To forestall relationship difficulties when he uses this intervention, a worker can explain his role before offering information. He can attempt to move between his conceptions of clients' needs and that of his colleagues, rather than just presenting a conclusion, unless another professional is willing to concede him his area of responsibility and does not want to hear the details. He can explain his willingness to listen to the colleague in turn. Perhaps most important, he should convey some understanding of other professionals' viewpoints or of environmental circumstances which influence them, assuming everyone's mutual intentions to offer service competently. Relationship preferences within a group may influence the way a social worker gives information to colleagues. Thus in a consultation session, a worker might avoid singling out a staff member who particularly needed certain information, and instead offer it to all.

A worker may intervene to effect change in the larger environment which influences him, his setting, his colleagues, and clients—by engaging in social action to have laws changed, funding redistributed, and the like. His motives sometimes include a wish to ameliorate conditions under which he and colleagues work, and thus perhaps to improve their relationships. At some point, such activities form a continuum with the other type of environmental intervention, a worker's efforts to change the context in which he and colleagues directly function together. Here we include such actions as a worker asking for a meeting of two professional groups to discuss how to work together, or his suggesting that he and a colleague have lunch. As with clients, a worker's interventions to change the environment in which he and colleagues function can be one-up in that the worker is initiating action, but the final message may be one of symmetry. The worker who asks a colleague to lunch, for example, is suggesting that they relate as peers or friends.

In general, which colleague initiates any contact, who keeps whom waiting and whether a valid explanation is offered, who can use humor and who can accept it from another, in whose office meetings are held, and other minutiae of everyday interaction are additional indicators of what relationship stances each colleague proposes or accepts. A social worker will usually hope to share flexible relationships with colleagues in these ways as in others, unless assessment indicates that a colleague prefers to be one-up or one-down and the worker elects to agree. Thus a worker might meet in the office of a colleague with more seniority or with greater responsibility for client care.

Using Basic Interventions in Interprofessional Practice

Let us analyze the following interprofessional interchange, which exemplifies a worker's careful use of interventions on both the content and the relationship levels.

The setting is an acute care ward of a large hospital, the participants Miss Lee, a young female social worker, and Dr. Thorne, a young male resident. The two are working with Mrs. Wilmington, who is terminally ill.

Our meeting began when Dr. Thorne saw me coming down the hall, said we needed to talk, and guided me into a conference room. Then he blurted out that I just had to do something about Mrs. Wilmington. When I asked what he had in mind, he wanted me to stop her from making so many unreasonable demands on him. She is always asking for long explanations about everything to do with her condition. He has too many patients to see already and can't possibly spend so much time with any one. I said I was always amazed at the amount of work the residents are responsible for and manage to do each day.

So far, Dr. Thorne and Miss Lee have begun a content interchange in which the doctor suggests that they meet, that the social worker do something to ease his interaction with a patient, and that he needs this help because he has too much to do. Miss Lee elicits some of this information by direct questions and by attentiveness, which encourages him to go on. In terms of assessment, the worker already knows that Mrs. Wilmington is terminally ill, and that this can be overwhelming information for any professionals involved. She can also sense from Dr. Thorne's pressured speech that he may be feeling overwhelmed and inadequate in the circumstances. Thus, partly to certify one of his strengths, she gives positive feedback to the idea that this resident manages to carry a heavy workload.

Relationship issues are also of interest here. Dr. Thorne is contextually in a one-up position, since physicians have higher status than social workers in the hospital setting. He has also initiated contact, and his demands that Miss Lee do something tend to define him in a one-up stance. However, there are one-down elements in Dr. Thorne's communication which in fact make his relationship messages more mixed. One factor is his being a resident, and thus not very high on the medical status ladder. Another is his desperation. He really needs Miss Lee's help in this case, and almost overtly reveals how one-down he probably feels in the face of the patient's illness. Finally, the doctor's giving an explanation of why he is making his request immediately places this in a more symmetrical light. That is, by asking Miss Lee to do something for him he is not pulling rank. In view of all that Dr. Thorne conveys, Miss Lee's relationship positions are carefully balancing. She elicits information in one-down fashion, but in fact remains neutral, and therefore ambiguous in relationship terms, about whether she will finally do as the resident asks. Her admiring positive evaluative feedback about his workload suggests her one-down agreement with him, but, because the feedback implies evaluation of his performance, her stance is also somewhat one-up. Further, with this statement Miss Lee agrees that he needs help from her rather than that she will give him the type of help he asks. As their interaction continues, these two professionals' relationship negotiation will become more intense.

> To Dr. Thorne's next statement that he was amazed himself at how he did it all, I responded that I could understand, in view of this, how hard it must be to contend with the kind of emotional needs so many of our patients have. He nodded and said he knew how rough it was for most of the patients, but he just couldn't spend the time with them that they sometimes seem to want. I continued that maybe we could work together to reassure Mrs. Wilmington so that she wouldn't ask so many questions, adding that I would like to tell him what I thought was happening. However, Dr. Thorne interrupted to say that he knew what was happening. He then explained again that Mrs. Wilmington's medical condition was terminal. They have taken every kind of test, have tried different treatments, and now just do not know what to do.

This interchange consists, essentially, of the worker's trying to convey new content and relationship information and the resident showing increasingly negative responses. The two begin on a positive note, with Dr. Thorne's accepting the worker's feedback about his workload. Miss Lee's next statement subtly suggests the content information that the resident may be feeling overwhelmed, at the same time conveying her acceptance of this feeling. On the relationship level she thereby proposes symmetry or even that she can be benignly one-up by giving more positive feedback and new information to him. The doctor puts forth what is essentially a selective response. He accepts part of the worker's content, that the patients are needy. But he still implies that, because of his workload, Miss Lee will have to deal with Mrs. Wilmington's emotional demands. The relationship message again is mixed. Dr. Thorne can agree with the worker and be one-down with her in this way, but will still assert his one-up right to his opinion about what should be done. Had she assessed this relationship message accurately, Miss Lee might have given subsequent relationship information more incrementally. Instead, she overtly proposes that she and the resident handle Mrs. Wilmington symmetrically ("we could work together") and even goes

one-up to try to tell him "what . . . was happening." Dr. Thorne clearly
rejects these overt relationship stances, placing himself one-up in that he
"knew what was happening," even though, a moment before, he did not
know what further to do.

> I finally asked Dr. Thorne hesitantly if he was going to continue treating
> Mrs. Wilmington. He responded that of course he wouldn't simply let
> her die. I said I could see he was thinking a lot about this case. He said I
> didn't know the half of it. I agreed that I probably didn't but added that
> Mrs. Wilmington and her husband might need to know what was going
> on. I thought one of the reasons she was so scared of being abandoned by
> him and the hospital was that all the treatments had been stopped, and
> she thought everyone had given up.

To get across content information she thinks Dr. Thorne needs without
challenging his preferred one-up relationship stance, Miss Lee begins with a
hesitantly asked and thus presumably one-down question. This does, however, manage to convey content that the resident's continuing to treat Mrs.
Wilmington may be a matter of concern. Then, to Dr. Thorne's statement
that he will continue treatment, Miss Lee gives more positive feedback, that
he seems to have been thinking a lot about this case. The relationship message here is more mixed, in that the worker is again conveying feedback of a
mildly evaluative sort. Dr. Thorne responds with a rather mixed relationship
message himself, that the worker didn't know the half of it—on the one hand
defining himself as a busy physician one-up to her, on the other as one who
might need her support. Miss Lee now uses a reciprocal message carefully.
She first goes one-down in agreeing that she probably did not know the half
of it regarding his thoughts about this case. Then, she can add in one-up
fashion the content she has been waiting to get across: that she thinks Mrs.
Wilmington is afraid because the treatments have indeed been stopped.

> Dr. Thorne explained that he was only trying to give Mrs. Wilmington
> some respite from all those needles while they tried to figure out what to
> do. I said I thought that was very sensitive of him, but wondered if he
> had told her his reasons. After sheepishly admitting that he hadn't, Dr.
> Thorne asked if I felt he should have. I said I thought what was impor-
> tant now was for the Wilmingtons to know some treatment would be given
> again. That might reassure them and make the barrage of questions stop.

Dr. Thorne said he was willing to explain to Mrs. Wilmington and her husband, and would do so that evening. He then added that if this didn't work, I would have to do something to help.

Here Miss Lee manages to get across more content and relationship information by continuing to give both incrementally. Having assessed Dr. Thorne's functioning so far, the worker infers that he feels overwhelmed by Mrs. Wilmington and her illness but cannot admit this openly. He also sends mixed relationship messages but will not accept being clearly one-down. However, Dr. Thorne has been willing to accept some new content as well as the one-up relationship stance on the worker's part that the content implies, as long as these are offered unobtrusively. For example, he has accepted some positive feedback and some questions that indirectly conveyed new content information. To complete their interaction, the worker uses these tested techniques again. She approves Dr. Thorne's sensitivity, but wonders if he has told Mrs. Wilmington what he is telling her. When Dr. Thorne then places himself one-down by asking if Miss Lee feels he did the wrong thing, she avoids using her one-up response to evaluate but instead gives new information, conveying what Dr. Thorne might do to solve the problem he has brought to her. When he leaves, the resident must again reassert that he is not willing to be permanently one-down to Miss Lee, although he has accepted her ideas in the present circumstance.

Let us briefly examine the content and relationship operating rules this pair seems to have accepted here. Most of their content pertained to their mutual patient and her needs. The rest was more personal, having to do with Dr. Thorne's workload, and Miss Lee did not reciprocate. The pair's relationship stances were more varied, with each sending mixed, one-up and one-down messages which on balance amounted to flexibility. The resident was in charge of Mrs. Wilmington's medical care, but the worker might have at least equal control of psychosocial matters with the patient and even at times with the resident, who clearly needed support. The worker nevertheless had to hide her one-up stances or at least not assert them openly. This last operating rule, allowing the worker covert but not overt relationship flexibility with a traditionally higher-status colleague, is prevalent in medical and psychiatric settings. It raises professional issues about self-esteem, pay differentials, and sometimes sexism which are beyond the scope of discussion here.

**Interprofessional
Communication Blocks**

Unresolved blocking between or among colleagues can lead to discomfort for those involved. More important, such blocks impede service to clients.

A social worker's efforts to prevent blocked communication with his colleagues are similar to those taken with clients. A worker tries to listen carefully and to observe colleagues' actions so as not to miss important messages. He may notice, for example, that a nurse is uncomfortable with anyone's questioning the hospital administration. He will sometimes give information incrementally or build bridges between a colleague's probable information and what the worker is now offering. Thus a worker might agree with a colleague that a mutual client is a real handful before talking about how to coordinate their intervention efforts. A worker should also offer negative feedback to his colleagues sparingly.

As with clients, the social worker tries to institute an operating rule among colleagues that each should be able to make questions or disagreements overt. The importance of this cannot be overemphasized. Nothing is more destructive than unverbalized interprofessional problems, which lead to discomfort, subtly antagonistic coalitions among staff members, backbiting—or, worse, displacements of anger onto a helpless client group. A worker should also pay close attention to his associates' lateness, hesitation, hostile voice, or whatever which may indicate unexpressed difficulties. Established blocks in which the worker participates may be apparent in repeated symmetrical escalations, continuing disconfirmation of lower-status professionals by those with higher status, or cycles in which parties leave communication unclear and then castigate each other when no one does what clients need.

Most benignly, potential blocks between or among colleagues are due to simple misunderstandings on the part of parties concerned. A nurse may not have heard a social worker who asked her to call when she had time. More serious is blocking caused by colleagues' conflicts about content information, relationship stances, information processing, or operating rules within the interprofessional group. When social workers in two settings keep disagreeing about what should be done with a child, they may be operating on different theories of human development. They may be noticing different things about the child's situation and thus using different data for assessment. They may be engaged in a continuing power struggle about who will make a final decision in the case. Or, each may be struggling with a different professional mandate from his agency or community, as when one is concerned with the child's delinquency and the other with his emotional state. Sometimes two professionals hold such different views that mutual clients are not served. Even if one is in some final sense more correct, both are acting nonconstructively.

When some of a worker's communication is rejected by a colleague, the worker can wait without comment, agree with the colleague where the other's view is valid, or perhaps give a selective response by suggesting some compromise. When more active intervention seems indicated, a worker can consider metacommunication, paradox, or environmental intervention.

Metacommunication is often effective to sort out colleagues' misunderstandings and disagreements on the content level. For example, the police officer who rejects a social worker's thinking might gladly discuss their need to find a common language. To initiate any metacommunication, a worker may symmetrically ask whether a colleague would like to discuss their differences rather than himself saying that they ought to, and should indicate willingness to consider how he arrived at his own conclusions if the colleague will do the same. He may ask if a colleague would mind sharing information on which he is operating, rather than simply inquiring as to what this information is. If he thinks he knows what a colleague's problematic information may be, a worker can sometimes gently identify it. He might say to the occupational therapist who seems embarrassed to discuss a boisterous schizophrenic man that he would not be surprised to hear that this client had done something inappropriate. Confrontation usually facilitates metacommunication only between associates who know each other well and who have agreed that strong disagreements are allowable within their operating rules. Metacommunication among a number of colleagues can often reconcile staff differences that have caused discomfort for all.

To use paradox with a colleague who insists on perpetually being one-up, a worker may agreeably follow his lead as long as clients are not harmed, may commend him for his willingness to take responsibilities upon himself, may elicit information with a tone of respect, or may make clear that he offers any information to be used as the colleague sees fit. Such a colleague is often disarmed in these circumstances. Because he is designated as more powerful, he may benignly allow the worker greater symmetry, perhaps encouraging him to take on responsibilities in what the worker already considered his own domain. A social worker should use this intervention only if he has sufficient respect for the one-up colleague that his communication, though influenced by his assessment of the situation, can be genuine. Occasionally a colleague will act inappropriately one-down to a social worker, even asking the worker to take over some of his professional functioning. Here, metacommunication or environmental intervention through a visit to the colleague's supervisor are more suitable than paradox. But a worker may successfully use paradox to startle colleagues into metacommunication when operating rules within the small social system of a professional work group have dysfunctionally rigidified. With two other professionals who often get into escalations, a worker might comment that they should keep doing so because they feel things strongly and it is good for them to let their feelings out.

A change of the context in which colleagues interact, whether to a lunch room or a consultant's office, can facilitate metacommuniation about any type of block. As a last-resort environmental intervention, a worker may have to involve co-workers, supervisors, administrators, or even the community in helping staff members resolve their differences.

Conclusion

This book has used communication theory to develop a generic practice framework for social work. The framework is a relatively simple one. It is based on the assumption that people behave understandably in response to what they know. In assessing possible reasons for clients' behavior, a social worker thus examines what the clients may know—the information available to them from their thoughts, feelings, bodily sensations, past learning, and current social and physical environments. When clients seem to have trouble using new information, a worker may evaluate blocks to their doing so, including constraints placed upon them in their families and other social groups. He may then intervene at the individual or small system levels, with clients' larger environments, or even with other professionals, to offer clients different information or to help them deal with information differently. In this process, he must also be able to resolve communication blocks between himself and clients and sometimes between himself and other professionals.

The framework presented here could be extended to such social work activities as administration, supervision, and further aspects of community work. It also has potential as a research and teaching tool.

Research on social work practice is coming into its own. Global studies of the effectiveness of social work have proved to be of limited usefulness, and investigators have become more interested in what interventions based on what assessment help what clients when. In order to examine interview process and to do research on the single case,[1] one needs operational definitions of social work procedures that can be used reliably by different judges and preferably even researchers studying different practice models. Research instruments based on communications concepts hold promise for the field. Several small studies have achieved reasonable reliability measuring symmetry and complementarity between marital partners,[2] social worker and clients,[3] and field instructors and students.[4] Social work students conducting single-subject research on a trial basis have found that communication theory helps them to specify client behavior within interviews and interventions that may affect it.[5] Researchers' use of any agreed-on operational definitions of social work techniques could make different studies more comparable. For such definitions, communications concepts have the advantage of being relatively simple and generic enough to test hypotheses generated from a number of practice models. Research based on communication theory may help determine what sorts of content and relationship information clients with particular problems are most likely to need. It can also begin to test the vast store of social work practice wisdom so far based only on experience. For example, most workers probably believe that an explicit operating rule allowing clients to question them is desirable. Using communications concepts, one could test the relationship of such a rule to clients' continuing service.

Like systems theory, a communications framework for practice can serve to organize social work knowledge for the learner and thus make it easier to assimilate. In the author's experience, students can understand clients' behavior more quickly when they think about information on which it is probably based. A mother's hostility in an initial interview seems less irrational when one realizes that she probably expects blame. The idea that interventions always carry content as well as relationship information helps explain why, for example, this mother balks at questions about the way she handles her child. The learner is relieved to find that blocked communication between himself and clients can be evaluated and dealt with in various ways. Theory about small system operating rules begins to suggest how family and group members influence each other, and makes multiple-client interviewing more manageable. The sooner a student grasps ideas such as these, the sooner he can explore other practice theories and more sophisticated communications concepts.

It is hoped that readers will try out in practice some of the ideas offered here, to affirm, reject, clarify, and add to them. If they are stimulated to do so, a major purpose of this volume will have been served.

Notes

Chapter One

1. Ruesch and Bateson 1968, pp. 3–20.

2. Material in this section, excepting applications to social work practice, is an amalgam of ideas found in Ruesch 1972, pp. 67–91, 125–37; Deutsch 1970, pp. 57–74; Bateson 1972, pp. 159–76, 279–308, 399–467; and Ruesch 1959, pp. 896–908. These sources use the term "information" as I have described it here, although they define it in more complex fashion, e.g., as "a patterned relationship between events." See Deutsch 1970, p. 62.

3. Warren W. Weaver as quoted in Ruesch and Kees 1956, p. 1.

4. Watzlawick, Beavin, and Jackson 1967, pp. 39–43, 53, 94; and Haley 1963, p. 169. Metacommunication can also refer to nonverbal communication or to contextual data which qualify verbal messages. These usages will not be employed in this volume.

5. Watzlawick, Beavin, and Jackson 1967, pp. 22, 48–49.

6. See Birdwhistell 1970; Hall 1959 and 1966; Hinde 1972; Ruesch and Kees 1956; Scheflen 1972; and Bateson 1972, pp. 411–25.

7. Watzlawick, Beavin, and Jackson 1967, pp. 60–67.

8. Bateson 1972, pp. 288–92; Ruesch and Kees 1956, pp. 13, 46, 66–75; and Watzlawick, Beavin, and Jackson 1967, p. 132.

9. Bateson 1972, pp. 279–308; and Ruesch and Bateson, 1968, p. 171.

10. Bateson 1972, pp. 159–76; Ruesch and Bateson 1968, pp. 6–9, 34–44; and Ruesch 1972, pp. 143–57.

11. Ruesch and Bateson, 1968, pp. 18, 286–89.

12. The present author has evolved the concepts of information processing blocks and communication blocks, based on her own use of communication theory in education and practice.

Chapter Two

1. Major concepts and ideas introduced in this section, excepting applications to social work practice, are from Watzlawick, Beavin, and Jackson 1967, pp. 51–54, 67–70, 107–17; and Haley 1963, pp. 6–12.

2. Various criteria for classifying dyadic communication in terms of symmetry and complementarity are suggested in Watzlawick, Beavin, and Jackson 1967, pp. 107–17 and 160–86; Carlos E. Sluzki and Janet Beavin, "Symmetry and Complementarity: An Operational Definition and a Typology

of Dyads,'' in Watzlawick and Weakland 1977, pp. 71–87; and Ericson and Rogers 1973, pp. 245–67.

3. This notion is implied in Watzlawick, Beavin, and Jackson 1967, pp. 75–78, 83–85. It has been further developed by the present author, based on her own use of communication theory in education and practice.

4. Ruesch 1972, pp. 356–60. The idea of selective response has been further developed by the present author.

5. The observations on mixed relationship messages derive from the author's dissertation research, partially summarized in Nelsen 1974, pp. 237–43.

6. Watzlawick, Beavin, and Jackson 1967, pp. 86–90.

7. Watzlawick, Beavin, and Jackson 1967, pp. 75–80.

8. Haley 1963, pp. 13–19.

9. Haley 1963, pp. 16–19, 70–85, 179–91; Watzlawick, Beavin, and Jackson 1967, pp. 230–56; and Watzlawick, Weakland, and Fisch 1974, pp. 114–57.

10. Accommodation processes in families and groups are described, although not necessarily using the terms suggested here, in Satir 1967, pp. 8–61; and Whitaker and Lieberman 1964, pp. 14–139.

11. This paragraph is an amalgam of ideas found in Deutsch 1970, pp. 57–74; Don D. Jackson, ''The Study of the Family,'' in Watzlawick and Weakland 1977, pp. 2–20; Watzlawick, Beavin, and Jackson 1967, pp. 129–48; Haley 1976, pp. 100–128; and Ruesch and Bateson 1968, pp. 5–9, 27–44, 176–91. The notion that small system operating rules influence system members' information processing has been further developed by the present author.

12. Antonio J. Ferreira, ''Family Myths,'' in Watzlawick and Weakland 1977, pp. 49–55.

13. Haley 1963, pp. 169–74; and Haley 1976, pp. 100–128. These ideas have been developed further by the present author. Haley 1976, p. 109, differentiates between coalitions and alliances, the former seen as always being formed against someone.

14. Jackson, in Watzlawick and Weakland 1977, pp. 2–20; and Haley 1976, pp. 100–128.

15. Haley 1963, pp. 16–18.

16. Watzlawick, Beavin, and Jackson 1967, pp. 54–59.

17. Watzlawick, Weakland, and Fisch 1974, pp. 10–28.

18. Deutsch 1970, pp. 57–74; and Minuchin 1974, pp. 51–52.

19. Weakland 1976, pp. 111–28; and Haley 1963, pp. 8–19, 117–78.

20. See William Fry, "The Marital Context of an Anxiety Syndrome," in Jackson 1968b, pp. 41–48.

21. See Steinglass 1976, pp. 97–124.

22. See Paul Watzlawick, "A Review of the Double Bind Theory," in Jackson 1968a, pp. 63–86.

Chapter Three

1. Case examples used throughout this volume are based on the author's experience and on process recordings from other social workers. All have been disguised.

2. In this volume, a social worker's attempts to give clients evaluative feedback are considered an intervention. We recognize that, technically, only information which actually influences behavior constitutes feedback.

3. See, for example, Haley and Hoffman 1967, pp. 97–264; and Minuchin, Rosman, and Baker 1978, pp. 92–107.

4. Minuchin 1974, pp. 123–37.

Chapter Four

1. Don D. Jackson, in Watzlawick and Weakland 1977, p. 14.

2. Minuchin 1974, pp. 56–59.

3. For a discussion of this process in group treatment see Whitaker and Lieberman 1964, pp. 116–39.

Chapter Five

1. Ruesch 1959, pp. 904–5.

2. The author bases this assertion on her clinical experience. It is also supported inferentially by her dissertation research, in which field instructor–student pairs were more likely to report relationship strain when field instructors did not accommodate to students' preferences for greater symmetry or complementarity; and by Sonya Rhodes's dissertation research, in which worker-client pairs were more likely to negotiate contracting successfully if they also achieved reciprocity on more symmetrical or more complementary relationship definitions. See Nelsen 1974, pp. 241–43; and Rhodes 1978, pp. 122–31.

Chapter Six

1. Haley 1963, pp. 68–85.

2. John H. Weakland, Richard Fisch, Paul Watzlawick, and Arthur M. Bodin, "Brief Therapy: Focused Problem Resolution," in Watzlawick and Weakland 1977, pp. 274–99.

3. Haley 1963, pp. 68–85.
4. Watzlawick, Weakland, and Fisch 1974, pp. 67, 87–88.
5. Watzlawick 1976, pp. 15–33.
6. The benefits of placing dependent and manipulative depressed clients together in a group are described in Levine and Schild 1969, pp. 46–52.

Chapter Seven

1. Simon 1972, pp. 49–57.
2. Jay Haley, "Toward a Theory of Pathological Systems," in Watzlawick and Weakland 1977, pp. 46–47; and Haley 1976, pp. 119–20, 162–63.
3. Haley 1963, pp. 138–39.
4. Satir 1967, pp. 1–2, 110.

Chapter Eight

1. Haley 1963, pp. 141–49; and Watzlawick, Weakland, and Fisch 1974, pp. 92–109.
2. For an interesting discussion of such ethical issues, see Haley 1976, pp. 195–221.
3. For these and similar contextual interventions in a similar case situation, see Haley 1976, pp. 224–37.

Conclusion

1. See, for example, Howe 1974, pp. 1–23.
2. Ericson and Rogers 1973, pp. 245–67.
3. Rhodes 1978, pp. 122–31.
4. Nelsen 1974, pp. 237–43.
5. Nelsen 1978, pp. 12–19.

Bibliography

Bateson, Gregory. 1972. *Steps to an Ecology of Mind*. New York: Chandler Publishing.

Birdwhistell, Ray. 1970. *Kinesics and Context: Essays on Body Motion Communication*. Philadelphia: University of Pennsylvania Press.

Buckley, Walter. 1967. *Sociology and Modern Systems Theory*. Englewood Cliffs, N.J.: Prentice-Hall.

Deutsch, Karl. 1952. "Communication Theory and Social Science." *American Journal of Orthopsychiatry* 22:469–83.

———. 1970. "A Simple Cybernetic Model." In *Readings on the Sociology of Small Groups*, compiled by Theodore Mills with Stan Rosenberg. Englewood Cliffs, N.J.: Prentice-Hall.

Ericson, Philip, and Rogers, L. Edna. 1973. "New Procedures for Analyzing Relational Communication." *Family Process* 12:245–67.

Haley, Jay. 1963. *Strategies of Psychotherapy*. New York: Grune and Stratton.

———. 1976. *Problem-Solving Therapy*. San Francisco: Jossey-Bass.

Haley, Jay, and Hoffman, Lynn. 1967. *Techniques of Family Therapy*. New York: Basic Books.

Hall, Edward. 1959. *The Silent Language*. New York: Doubleday.

———. 1966. *The Hidden Dimension*. New York: Doubleday.

Hinde, R. A., ed. 1972. *Nonverbal Communication*. Cambridge: Cambridge University Press.

Howe, Michael W. 1974. "Casework Self-Evaluation: A Single-Subject Approach." *Social Service Review* 48:1–23.

Jackson, Don D., ed. 1968a. *Communication, Family, and Marriage*. Human Communication 1. Palo Alto: Science and Behavior Books.

———, ed. 1968b. *Therapy, Communication, and Change*. Human Communication 2. Palo Alto: Science and Behavior Books.

Levine, Baruch, and Schild, Judith. 1969. "Group Treatment of Depression." *Social Work* 14:46–52.

Minuchin, Salvador. 1974. *Families and Family Therapy*. Cambridge, Mass.: Harvard University Press.

Minuchin, Salvador; Rosman, Bernice L.; and Baker, Lester. 1978. *Psychosomatic Families: Anorexia Nervosa in Context*. Cambridge, Mass.: Harvard University Press.

Nelsen, Judith C. 1974. "Relationship Communication in Early Fieldwork Conferences." *Social Casework* 55:237–43.

———. 1978. "Use of Communication Theory in Single-Subject Research." *Social Work Research and Abstracts* 4:12–19.

Rhodes, Sonya L. 1978. "Communication and Interaction in the Worker-Client Dyad." *Social Service Review* 52:122–31.

Ruesch, Jurgen. 1959. "General Theory of Communication in Psychiatry." In *American Handbook of Psychiatry, Volume 1*, edited by Silvano Arieti. New York: Basic Books.

———. 1972. *Semiotic Approaches to Human Relations*. The Hague: Mouton.

Ruesch, Jurgen, and Bateson, Gregory. 1968. *Communication: The Social Matrix of Psychiatry*. 2d ed. New York: W. W. Norton.

Ruesch, Jurgen, and Kees, Weldon. 1956. *Nonverbal Communication*. Berkeley: University of California Press.

Satir, Virginia. 1967. *Conjoint Family Therapy: A Guide to Theory and Technique*. Palo Alto: Science and Behavior Books.

Scheflen, Albert. 1972. *Body Language and Social Order: Communication as Behavioral Control*. Englewood Cliffs, N.J.: Prentice-Hall.

Simon, Robert M. 1972. "Sculpting the Family." *Family Process* 11:49–57.

Steinglass, Peter. 1976. "Experimenting with Family Treatment Approaches to Alcoholism, 1950–1975: A Review." *Family Process* 15:97–123.

Watzlawick, Paul. 1976. *How Real is Real? Confusion, Disinformation, Communication*. New York: Random House.

Watzlawick, Paul; Beavin, Janet; and Jackson, Don D. 1967. *Pragmatics of Human Communication: A Study of Interactional Patterns, Pathologies, and Paradoxes*. New York: W. W. Norton.

Watzlawick, Paul, and Weakland, John, eds. 1977. *The Interactional View: Studies at the Mental Research Institute, Palo Alto, 1965–74*. New York: W. W. Norton.

Watzlawick, Paul; Weakland, John; and Fisch, Richard. 1974. *Change: Principles of Problem Formation and Problem Resolution*. New York: W. W. Norton.

Weakland, John. 1976. "Communication Theory and Clinical Change." In *Family Therapy: Theory and Practice*, edited by Philip J. Guerin, Jr. New York: Gardner Press.

Whitaker, Dorothy, and Lieberman, Morton. 1964. *Psychotherapy through the Group Process*. New York: Atherton Press.

Index

Absences, clients', 48–49; influences on, 44–48, 56–57; intervention regarding, 46–48, 57

Acceptance of communication, 1–2, 22, 26–31, 34, 40, 96, 113, 115; among members of client systems, 29, 62, 81–83, 145, 150, 154; by clients, with workers, 19, 26, 29–30, 55–56, 69–70, 77–78, 89–132 passim; by small system clients, with workers, 60, 62, 85, 141, 147–48, 156, 158–60, 162–63, 165, 167–68; by other professionals, 180–82, 184–86, 188, 190. *See also* Positive evaluative feedback as intervention

Accommodation processes, 32–33, 36, 42; between workers and clients, 32–33, 57, 61–62, 84, 104–5, 116. *See also* Operating rules; Starting where clients are

Activities, use of, as intervention, 14, 27–28, 95–96, 105, 130–31; with families and groups, 139–40, 150, 173–75

Ambiguous communication, 18–20, 22, 28–29, 31. 34; among members of client systems, 81, 83, 100; between workers and clients, 29–30, 113, 115–16, 119, 159–60, 163–64; among professionals, 187, 191. *See also* Mixed messages

Analogic communication, 12–15. *See also* Nonverbal communication; Symbolic communication

Analogic learning, 16, 19, 37–39; clients' earlier, 78, 86, 131; clients', from workers, 16–17, 27–28, 90–91, 93, 111–12, 125, 127, 131; clients' in small system practice, 16–17, 59, 135, 140, 145–47, 157, 159, 163, 165–66, 173–75. *See also* Modeling

Assessment of clients, 43, 66–88, 114–20, 125, 157–66; information gathering in, 13–14, 27, 29, 36, 66–68, 72–90, 96–97, 105, 113–20, 135, 140–41, 147, 153, 157–63; as ongoing, 43, 66, 68, 89; scope of, 66–68, 72–75, 78–80, 86–88, 162; use of communication theory in, ix–x, 1–10, 12, 14–15, 27, 29, 32–33, 36, 38, 41–42, 66–72, 194; use of other theories in, ix, 5–8, 66–67; use of research in, 74

Assessment as influencing intervention, ix, 2–3, 8–10, 12, 36, 38–39, 43, 53, 66–68, 86–114, 119; with worker-client communication blocks, 120–21, 124, 126–28, 130, 132; with families and groups, 36, 38–39, 41, 134–56, 158; with worker-client system blocks, 163–64, 166–76. *See also* Choice of where to intervene

Assessment of other professionals. *See* Professionals, other: assessment of; Professionals, other: assessment as influencing intervention

Bateson, Gregory, x, 1–2
Behaviorism, ix, 6–8
Birdwhistell, Ray, x
Blocks. *See* Communication blocks; Information processing blocks

Change: behavioral theories on, 6–8; in people, 1–2, 15–19, 37–38, 40, 72; in relationship definitions, 23; in small social systems, 4, 21, 37–42; between system levels, 4, 21, 37–38
Change in social work practice: other theories on, 5, 7–8; by clients, 12, 15–17, 19, 30–31, 67, 76, 87–90, 96–101, 107–12, 120, 127–29, 132; clients' openness to, 19, 30, 71, 75–78, 116–17, 120, 128; by small system clients, 3, 16–17, 36–41, 57, 61–65, 80, 87–89, 95, 134, 138–45, 147, 150–56, 165–75; small system clients' openness to, 41, 71, 79, 82–88, 148, 157, 159, 161–62, 171–73; in worker-client system operating rules, 41, 84–86, 89, 97–101, 107–10, 116–17, 135–56 passim, 165, 168; other professionals' openness to, 180–82. *See also* Environment, clients' changing of
Choice of where to intervene, 19, 38–41, 56–57, 86–88, 95, 105–6, 130–33, 139–40, 149–50, 173–76; explaining to clients, 46–49, 57, 105–6, 139–40, 151–56, 174; implications of, for clients, 41, 45–46, 57, 87–88, 96, 105, 130–32, 139–40, 149–50, 173–75
Coalitions, 32–36; among members of client systems, 82–83, 146, 153–54; between workers and clients, 23, 41, 45–46, 57, 62–63, 105, 130, 146–55, 163–65, 169; among professionals, 181–82, 184, 191
Collaterals: in client assessment, 66, 73, 79, 162; intervention with, 95, 100, 105, 107–11, 130, 132, 139, 149
Communication, defintion of, 12–14. *See also* Content information conveyed by interventions; Nonverbal communication; Relationship information conveyed by interventions
Communication blocks, 18, 113; between clients and others, 139, 141, 145; among members of client systems, 18, 75, 134, 138–39, 156, 166–67; between workers and clients, 18, 26, 52, 75, 89, 112–33, 156–76, 194–95; interventions with, with clients, 89, 114, 117–34, 138–39, 145, 156–59, 161, 163–76, 194–95; among professionals, 177, 181, 191–93; interventions with, with professionals, 177, 191–93
Communication theory, 1–4, 9, 24, 129; compared to other

theories, 4–8; as unified theory, x, 3–4, 8; uses of, for social
work, ix–x, 1–43, 56, 66–72, 194–95
Complementary (one-up, one-down) relationships, 21–28, 31–
36, 40; between members of client systems, 45–46, 60–64,
71, 77, 82–83, 132, 146–50, 152–56, 165, 167, 169–71, 173;
between workers and clients, 25–31, 36, 45–56, 76–78, 101–11,
113, 116–17, 119–29, 131; between workers and small system
clients, 23, 46, 58–60, 63–64, 143, 146–55, 159, 163–64, 166–71;
between professionals, 179, 181–90, 192–93; research on, 195
Conflicts about information or operating rules, 18–20, 40;
clients', 19, 41, 69–72, 75–78, 85–88, 94–95, 97, 118–19, 122,
138–39; between workers and clients, 19, 52, 75–78, 85–88,
118–19, 125–26, 130–32, 161–63, 165, 167–68, 173; intervention
with, with clients, 19, 41, 86–88, 94–95, 97–101, 122–33, 138–
39, 163–76; between professionals, 180–81, 191–92; intervention with, with professionals, 192–93
Confrontation: clients' use of, 145; as intervention with
clients, 123, 166; between professionals, 192
Consultation: to clients, 144; to other professionals, 177–80,
183–85; use of, 132, 173–75, 177–80, 182–83, 193
Content information, giving of, as intervention, 13, 15, 19, 23,
33, 43–51 passim, 53–56, 69–70, 76–78, 89, 93–106, 108–111,
113, 116–17; with worker-client communication blocks, 114–
15, 122–32; with families and groups, 41, 45, 47, 49, 57–65
passim, 85–86, 137–44, 148–49, 151–57, 161; with worker-
client system blocks, 157–59, 164–75; with other professionals, 183–85, 188–93
Content information conveyed by interventions, 23, 27, 43, 45,
47–56, 89–101, 106–7, 113, 195; with worker-client communication blocks, 119, 123, 130–31; with families and
groups, 45, 47, 57–60, 62, 65, 134–45, 151–57; with worker-
client system blocks, 158, 163–64, 167, 170–71, 175; with
other professionals, 183–90
Content information held by clients. *See* Information held by
clients
Content information held by other professionals. *See* Information held by other professionals
Context, influence of, 4, 12–13, 15, 19, 32, 40, 173; on workers
and clients, 15, 43–50, 73, 95–96, 105–6, 108, 110, 130–32; on
workers and small system clients, 44–48, 57–58, 63, 139–40,
149–50, 173–75; on professionals, 179, 182, 187, 193. *See
also* Environment, influence of

Context, intervention into, 43–44, 46–50, 89, 95–96, 105–6, 130–32; with families and groups, 39, 139–40, 149–50, 172–75; with other professionals, 186, 193. *See also* Environment, intervention into

Contracting, 55–56, 97–98, 108–9; with families and groups, 57, 61, 65, 141–43, 153–56

Control within relationships, 2–3, 21, 23–26, 30–31, 34–35, 41; among members of client systems, 154; between workers and clients, 25–26, 30–31, 51, 54–55, 77, 101, 106, 109, 114, 116–17, 119–23, 126–29; between workers and small system clients, 41, 64, 150, 155, 163, 168–72; between professionals, 192–93. *See also* Metacomplementary relationships; Paradox; Symptoms

Co-therapy, 174, 177–78, 182, 184

Culture (sociocultural factors), influence of, 17, 19, 32, 38; on workers and clients, 1, 17, 44, 46, 70, 72, 76–78, 118, 125, 161; on professionals, 180

Deutsch, Karl, 1

Disconfirmation, 26, 29, 31, 34–35; of clients by others, 78, 141; among members of client systems, 29, 48, 60, 81, 83–84; between workers and clients, 29, 48–49, 56, 113–14, 116–17, 148, 160–61; among professionals, 191

Double-binding in schizophrenia, 1, 41

Dysfunctional operating rules, 24–25, 35, 40–41; in client systems, 3, 8, 36, 41, 57–58, 61, 63–65, 71–72, 83–88, 134, 146–56 passim, 166–68, 171–75; intervention into, with clients, 36, 57–58, 61, 63–65, 87–88, 146, 149, 151–56, 166–75; in professional systems, 182, 193; intervention into, with professionals, 192–93. *See also* Openness of operating rules to change; Rigidified operating rules

Ego psychology, ix, 5–8, 67

Eliciting information as intervention, 23, 28, 47–56, 73–76, 89–91, 94, 96–100, 102–3, 105–13 passim, 116–17, 125, 195; with worker-client communication blocks, 120–24, 127; with families and groups, 57–65, 79–80, 82, 85–86, 134–36, 141–42, 146–48, 151–55, 171; with worker-client system blocks, 166–67, 172–73; with other professionals, 179, 183–84, 187, 189–90, 192–93

Environment, clients' changing of, 86, 95, 134, 138–39, 141–45

Environment, influence of, 1–2, 4–7, 9–12, 15–19, 21, 32, 37–

40, 42; other theories on, 4–8; on clients, 2, 7, 10, 19, 38–39, 42, 66–79, 86–88, 118–20, 127–29, 194; on small system clients, 41, 79, 81, 83–85, 162, 167–68, 172–73, 175; on professionals, 179–81, 185, 192. *See also* Context
Environment, intervention into, 10, 12, 19, 38–39, 51–54, 68, 75, 86–89, 95–97, 100, 105–6, 194; with worker-client communication blocks, 129–32; with families and groups, 41, 62, 139–41, 144–45, 149–50; with worker-client system blocks, 168, 172–76; with other professionals, 185–86, 192–93. *See also* Context, intervention into
Evaluative feedback as intervention, 13, 23, 27–29, 31, 41, 47–56, 76–77, 89–94, 96–100, 102–3, 113, 199 (chap. 3, n. 2); with worker-client communication blocks, 114–23, 126–31; with families and groups, 41, 59–63, 65, 136–37, 141–42, 144–45, 147–48, 151–55; with worker-client system blocks, 157–59, 161, 163–66, 169–72; with other professionals, 182, 184–93

Feedback, 9–12, 16, 18–19, 90, 115; clients' giving of, to workers, 115, 158–60; clients' receipt of, 12, 90, 175; workers' giving of, to clients, 13, 16. *See also* Negative evaluative feedback as intervention; Positive evaluative feedback as intervention; Responses to communication; Trial and error learning
First-order change, 39, 41–42
Flexibility in relationship stances, 25, 34; among members of client systems, 62, 83, 146, 149–50, 156; between workers and clients, 25–29, 50–56, 77, 101–11, 113, 116–17, 126; between workers and small system clients, 58–62, 85, 140–150, 152, 156, 159, 163, 169; among professionals, 181–83, 186, 190
Freudian personality theory, ix

General systems theory, ix, 4–5, 7, 195
Goals of service: theories on, ix, 8; establishing, 26, 56, 67–68, 153; as limiting assessment, 67–68, 72; influences on progress toward, 62, 80, 113–14, 127, 146; interventions as leading toward, 65–68, 89, 100, 111, 142, 150, 168, 174, 176

Haley, Jay, x, 2
Homeostatic mechanisms, 32–33, 35, 40–42; among members of client systems, 81–84, 158; between workers and clients,

82, 117, 147, 157, 159, 162; among professionals, 181. *See also* Rejection of communication
Home visits, 95–96, 105–6, 130–31, 139, 149–50

Identified patient, 48, 63, 147, 149, 152
Information: definition of, 1, 9; influence of, ix–x, 1–21, 30–32, 36–40. *See also* Content information conveyed by interventions; Relationship information conveyed by interventions
Information held by clients: assessment of, 9–10, 27, 36, 66–79, 125, 194; influence of, 2, 15, 18–19, 27, 36, 44–46, 51–52, 66–79, 118–19, 124–25, 131, 194–95; assessment of, in small system practice, 79–86, 135, 164–66; influence of, in small system practice, 33, 45–46, 57, 61, 79–86, 88, 161–62; adding to, 10, 20, 56, 86–87, 93–94, 97–100, 114, 127, 158, 194; evaluative feedback on, 3, 52–53, 91–92, 109, 128, 136; making clients aware of, 12–13, 19, 124–26, 131–32, 139, 165–68, 173; paradox with, 127–28
Information held by other professionals: assessment of, 178–81, 183, 190, 192; influence of, 179–81, 191–92; adding to, 191; evaluative feedback on, 184; making professionals aware of, 183, 192
Information processing, 1–2, 5–6, 9–12, 15–20, 32–33, 36–40, 42; clients' 2, 6, 12, 19–20, 27, 29, 33, 36, 66–78, 87–101, 118–20, 122–25, 194; interventions as affecting clients', 2, 12, 16, 19–20, 33, 66–67, 76, 87–101, 112, 125; small system clients', 36, 79, 81–86, 135–36, 140, 161–62, 167; interventions as affecting small system clients' 36, 85, 135–36, 140, 167; other professionals', 178–81, 184, 191
Information processing blocks, 18–19, 40; clients' 19, 29, 66, 69–70, 75–78, 85–88, 119, 194; other professionals', 180
Interdisciplinary teams, 177–78, 182–83, 186–90
Interventions. *See specific interventions*

Jackson, Don D., x, 2

Learning: as explained by behavioral theories, 6–8; influence of, 15–20. *See also* Analogic learning; Information: influence of; Trial and error learning

Metacommunication, 13, 19–20, 34, 197 (chap. 1, n. 4); among members of client systems, 13, 81, 85, 138–39; clients' learn-

ing of, from workers, 85, 138–39, 145, 159, 165; between
workers and clients, 13, 33, 56, 94, 115, 158–59, 165–68

Metacommunication as intervention, 13, 19, 122–26, 131–32;
with families and groups, 41, 164–68, 171, 173–75; with other
professionals, 192–93

Metacomplementary relationships, 21, 24–25, 30–31, 35; of
workers with clients, 24–26, 30–31, 41, 51, 104–5, 120, 170;
between professionals, 182. See also Paradox

Misunderstandings: among members of client systems, 13,
138–39, 167; between workers and clients, 13, 46–47, 51, 55,
94, 96, 115, 118–19, 124–25, 130; between workers and small
system clients, 57, 159, 161, 164–65, 167; among professionals, 180, 191–92

Mixed messages, 28–29, 31, 34; among members of client systems, 71; by workers, with clients, 29–30, 102, 121, 164;
between professionals, 187–90

Modeling: by workers, 16–17, 27–28, 90–91, 93, 111–12, 121,
125, 127, 131; by workers and small system clients, 16–17,
41, 132, 135–36, 140, 145–47, 157, 159, 163, 165

Myths, family or group, 34

Negative evaluative feedback as intervention, 27–29, 48–56, 77,
91–92, 94, 98, 103–4, 106, 108–9, 113–17; with families and
groups, 41, 60, 65, 136–37, 147–48, 152, 157; with other professionals, 184, 191

Negative feedback, 11. See also Homeostatic mechanisms;
Rejection of communication

Neo-Freudian personality theories, x

Neutrality toward communication, 29; among members of
client systems, 81, 139, 165; of clients with workers, 123,
160

Neutrality toward communication as intervention, 29, 48, 52–
53, 56, 91–92, 94, 97, 103–4; with worker-client communication blocks, 114, 118–21; with families and groups, 60, 62,
148; with worker-client system blocks, 157–58, 161, 163,
165; with other professionals, 184, 187, 192

Nonverbal communication, 1–2, 5, 12–15, 21–22, 26–29, 31,
33; among members of client systems, 19, 81–83, 86, 159; by
clients, with workers, 14, 33, 80, 96, 115–16, 123, 159–60;
by other professionals, 191

Nonverbal communication, workers' use of, 14–15, 23, 27–28,

47–52, 77, 90–93, 98–99, 101, 104, 106, 112, 161; with worker-client communication blocks, 122–23, 127, 130; with families and groups, 134–35, 146–47, 150; with worker-client system blocks, 166, 170; with other professionals, 192–93

One-up, one-down relationships. *See* Complementary relationships
Openness of operating rules to change, 40; in client systems, 65, 71, 79, 84–86, 147, 165; in worker-client systems, 117, 135–36; in professional systems, 182. *See also* Rigidified operating rules
Operating rules, 3, 5, 32–42, 173; among members of client systems, 32–33, 36, 38–43, 57–58, 61–66, 69–72, 79–88, 95, 137–58, 162, 165–75, 195; between workers and clients, 32–34, 36, 42–43, 49–56, 89–90, 93–101, 104, 108–10, 115–17, 195; between workers and small system clients, 41, 57–65, 84, 134–60, 162–63, 166, 174–75; among professionals, 178–82, 190–93
Organizational theories, 7

Palo Alto theorists, x, 2–3, 8
Paradox, 26, 30–31; to change environments, 145; as intervention with clients, 30–31, 41, 126–29, 131–32, 168–74; with other professionals, 192–93
Patterns in communication, 3, 7, 21, 23–24, 31–39, 41–42; among members of client systems, 39, 63–65, 71, 80–84, 87, 136, 154–55, 158–62, 172, 174; between workers and clients, 36, 124, 127–29, 161; between professionals, 191
Pecking order, 32, 34–36; among members of client systems, 62, 82–83, 147
Play. *See* Activities, use of, as intervention
Positive evaluative feedback as intervention, 13, 23, 27–29, 31, 41, 47–56, 76–77, 90–92, 97–100, 102–10; with worker-client communication blocks, 114–15, 118, 120–23, 126–31; with families and groups, 59–63, 65, 136–37, 141–42, 144–45, 148, 151–55; with worker-client system blocks, 157–59, 161, 163–66, 169–72; with other professionals, 182, 184–93
Positive feedback, 11, 28. *See also* Acceptance of communication
Prescribing symptoms or behavior, 31, 128, 171–72
Process of communication, relationship messages in: between

workers and clients, 101, 106–7, 150; among professionals, 186

Professionals, other: in client assessment, 66, 73, 79, 183; assessment of, 177–82, 191; assessment as influencing intervention with, 184–90, 192–93; intervention with, 89, 95, 132, 164, 175, 177, 183–94

Psychoanalytic theory, 7, 128

Punctuation of events, 38, 136

Reframing as intervention, 170–72

Rejection of communication, 1, 3, 10, 22, 26–32, 34–35, 115; between clients and others, 131, 141; among members of client systems, 29, 76–77, 81, 83, 138, 156, 159–60, 166–67; by clients, with workers, 6, 19, 28–30, 48, 56, 69–70, 76–77, 96–100, 103–4, 107, 111, 113–32; by small system clients, with workers, 48, 85–86, 157–71, 173, 175; by other professionals, 181, 184, 188–90, 192. See also Negative evaluative feedback as intervention

Relationship communication. See specific types of relationships

Relationship communication as differing by content, 23–25, 32–33, 35–36; among members of client systems, 82–83; between workers and clients, 54, 56, 107–11; among professionals, 181–82, 185, 190

Relationship information conveyed by interventions, 23–31, 43–56, 77, 89, 93, 101–12, 116, 195; with worker-client communication blocks, 119–32; with families and groups, 57–65, 134, 140, 142–56, 158; with worker-client system blocks, 163–75; with other professionals, 181, 183–90, 192–93

Relationship information held: by clients, 15, 19, 27, 36, 44, 51–52, 70–71, 74, 77–78, 109, 124–28, 131; by small system clients, 33, 57, 84, 173; by other professionals, 178, 180–81

Research: in behaviorist models, 8; on paradox, 129, 172; uses of communication theory for, ix, 1, 8, 194–95; uses of, in social work, 7, 74, 194–95

Resistance, 5–6, 128

Responses to communication, 1–2, 22, 26–31, 34. See also specific responses

Rigidified operating rules: in client systems, 65, 71, 84–86, 156, 166, 168, 170, 173; in professional systems, 182, 193. See also Dysfunctional operating rules; Openness of operating rules to change

Role play as intervention, 16, 93, 128, 131–32, 140
Ruesch, Jurgen, x, 1–2
Rules for information processing, 9, 11–12, 17–19, 32, 36–37,
    39–40; clients', 12, 36, 69, 75–79, 87–88, 118, 162

Scheflen, Albert E., x
Sculpting the family as intervention, 140, 173–74
Second-order change, 37, 39–42; by clients, 89; in client sys-
    tems, 41, 57, 63, 71, 79, 84–88, 138, 157, 165; in worker-
    client systems, 41, 84, 117, 165. *See also* Openness of
    operating rules to change; Rigidified operating rules
Secrets, family or group, 34
Selective response to communication, 22, 28, 31; by clients,
    116; by other professionals, 188
Selective response as intervention, 28–29, 52–53, 55–56, 92,
    103, 108–9; with worker-client communication blocks, 118,
    121, 131; with families and groups, 60, 65, 136–37, 144, 148,
    153; with worker-client system blocks, 161, 163–64; with
    other professionals, 184–85, 192
Small group theories, ix, 7
Small social systems, 2–5, 7, 17, 21–42; clients as influenced
    by, 2–3, 9–10, 19, 36–39, 44–46, 56–57, 66–88, 95–96, 118–20,
    125, 128–29, 132, 194; small system clients as influenced by
    other, 79, 162, 167, 175. *See also* Operating rules
Sociocultural factors. *See* Culture
Starting where clients are, 7, 56, 65, 101, 129. *See also* Accom-
    modation processes, between workers and clients
Strengths: clients', 25, 52, 69–73, 93, 96, 105, 119–20; small
    system clients', 62, 65, 79, 134, 137; other professionals',
    184, 187
Symbolic communication, clients', 73–74, 78, 159
Symmetrical escalations, 25, 27, 31, 34–35; between members
    of client systems, 25, 82, 85, 138, 148, 154, 166–67; between
    workers and clients, 109, 113–14, 117, 119, 122–23, 127, 129,
    160–61; among professionals, 191, 193
Symmetrical relationships, 21–29, 31–32, 34–35; among mem-
    bers of client systems, 25, 64, 77, 80–85, 148–49, 154–56,
    166–67, 175; between workers and clients, 25–29, 45–48, 50–
    56, 76–78, 101–11, 113–14, 116–17, 119–24, 127–31, 182; be-
    tween workers and small system clients, 58–61, 142–55, 160–
    61, 164, 166; between professionals, 178–79, 181–89, 191–93;
    research on, 195. *See also* Flexibility in relationship stances

Symptoms, 30–31, 34, 40–41; clients', 23, 30–31, 77, 116, 122, 126, 128–29; small system clients', 41, 84, 154, 159, 169–70, 172–73; intervention with, 23, 30–31, 128–29, 151–56, 169–74
Systems. *See* Small social systems
Systems theory. *See* General systems theory

Tasks, use of, as intervention, 173–75
Transference, 5–6
Trial and error learning, 16, 19, 37–38; clients' earlier, 78, 131; clients', from workers, 16, 111–12, 121, 131; small system clients', 16, 146, 159, 173, 175

Videotaping, use of, as intervention, 173–74

Watzlawick, Paul, x, 2